ABOUT THE AUTHOR

Don Shaw has been a full-time writer for film, stage, radio and TV since 1968, and before that a teacher of the deaf. He won his first award in 1968 and went on to become one of the top TV writers, winning awards both at home and internationally. He was the creator of the BBC drama series *Dangerfield*, and was Visiting Professor in Drama at Derby University for many years.

Don has run marathons from the age of twenty-two and started jogging before it became fashionable. He still runs three miles every day and, when not hiking, follows his other great passion – flying his own Cessna aircraft with Derby Aero Club.

Married with three children, Don lives in Mickleover, near Derby. He is a patron of the Derby Heritage Development Trust.

DON SHAW

EBURY
PRESS

1 3 5 7 9 10 8 6 4 2

Copyright © 2004 Don Shaw
First published in Great Britain in 2004 by Tideswell Press
First published by Ebury Press in 2005

This edition first published 2006 by Ebury Press,
an imprint of Random House,
20 Vauxhall Bridge Road, London SW1V 2SA

Random House Australia (Pty) Limited
20 Alfred Street, Milsons Point, Sydney, New South Wales 2061, Australia

Random House New Zealand Limited
18 Poland Road, Glenfield, Auckland 10, New Zealand

Random House South Africa (Pty) Limited
Isle of Houghton, Corner of Boundary Road and Carse O'Gowrie,
Houghton 2198, South Africa

The Random House Group Limited Reg. No. 954009

www.randomhouse.co.uk

Printed and bound in Great Britain by Bookmarque Ltd, Croydon, Surrey

A CIP catalogue record for this book is available from the British Library

Cover illustration by Jason Ford
Cover design by Two Associates
Interior design by seagulls.net

9780091908751 (after Jan 2007)
ISBN 0 091908752

To Liz and the family,
with love and thanks

CONTENTS

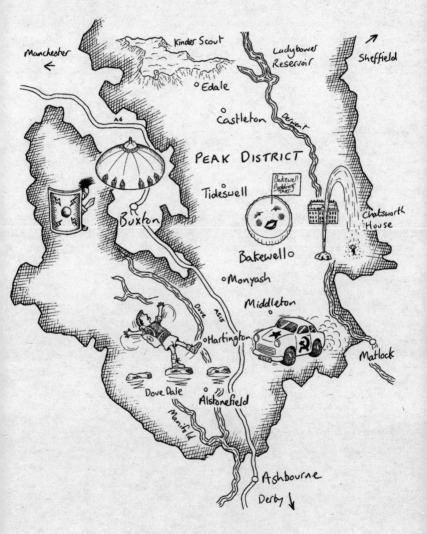

Map of the Peak District

1
JANUARY

'm taking out a one million pound lawsuit against you for deceit, malpractice and personal injury!' Even with the car windows shut, Freddy had to raise his voice to make himself heard over the blustering wind. Behind him, Phil 'Gruppenführer' Stevens cackled delightedly and punched the air.

'I told you, Freddy, it's a wonderful day. Listen to that wind!'

'It's not a wind. It's a gale. You're insane,' Freddy growled, white-knuckled at the wheel.

'Freddy, the rules are clear ...'

'Yes, rule 1.' Freddy hardly paused. 'No hike shall take place if the forecast suggests lives may be put at risk.'

'Rule 4a.' Phil was always a shade quicker than Freddy at fictional rules. 'The *navigator* decides if the weather is suitable.'

'But I won't enjoy it.'

Phil cackled again. 'Freddy! There's nothing in the rules to say you've got to enjoy it!'

'Ah yes,' Freddy sighed, 'pain is the game. Of course. I'd forgotten.'

Earlier that morning Freddy had phoned in protest. But Phil

had spoken patiently to his backsliding subordinate. 'In bad weather, Freddy, it's how good you feel *afterwards* that matters. Look in your rule book, Appendix A – "understanding your body on the hike".'

'Gruppenführer, have you looked at the appendix to rule 1? Should the navigator become insane all rules are invalid except Appendix C, which emphasises the necessity of saving life and preventing distress.'

'Didn't catch that last bit. Tell you what I'll do. I'll bring you a slice of Ruth's special ginger cake.'

There was a pause as Freddy pondered this. 'Hmmm, the sticky ginger cake?'

'Absolutely. Just the thing to keep the cold out.'

Freddy wasn't going to jump in straight away – would this be enough to overcome his dislike of bad-weather hikes? But he paused just long enough for Phil to nip in with: 'Great! Well done, that man. It's your turn to drive. Pick me up, usual time.'

En route to Phil's house, I sat in the front passenger seat while Freddy told me about their breakfast-time conversation. I could picture the scene: Freddy standing in his kitchen waving one arm in distress, and Phil in his conservatory enjoying the racket made by the wind. The greater the noise the greater his delight. Freddy, six feet tall and with arms too long for his cuffs, has a large, bespectacled and sensitive face and trousers that sag in the wrong places. He remains stoical in the face of life's misfortunes, one of which is Phil.

Phil is the same age as Freddy, sixty-four, but is several inches shorter and looks much younger; he is every bit a compact dynamo. In his youth he was a rugby scrum-half and he still behaves like one, quick and alert, always on the move. How he managed in his working life to meet the demands of being an air-traffic-controller I would never know. Freddy reckoned that holidaymakers who knew him found out when he was on duty and ensured they booked a flight on his day off.

Each Thursday, hike day, Freddy calls Phil if the weather looks unpromising. He makes his protest but gets nowhere, as Phil always calls on my vote to secure a majority of two to one. 'It'll clear up, the forecast's good.' It's spoken like a mantra but he's sometimes right.

It is difficult for forecasters to be accurate about areas of hilly country like the Peak District. The northern part is called the Dark Peak, with its grim gritstone edges and outcrops. The softer, white limestone dales of the South, pretty as a picture and easy to walk, form the White Peak.

Today we rocked along the A515, the stone-walled road that crosses the high ground of the White Peak between Ashbourne and Buxton. The wind rose to new heights of fury, jostling the car and prompting a moan of terror from Freddy at the wheel. Sheep were being driven down from the hills, cattle clustered together for warmth, farmers battened down loose boxes, and traffic slowed to a crawl.

'Jeez!' The car blew perilously close to the nearside wall. Freddy laughed in bewilderment. 'What am I doing here?' He glanced at me. 'It's your fault, Don, why do you always side with the fascist?'

Phil cackled in the back. Freddy was right. Although I didn't enjoy foul weather I felt the rewards from all the good days were worth the price of a bad one. We never missed a hike except for holidays, thick fog or impenetrable snow. Today, Freddy had a point. It looked as if we were in for a battering.

Freddy and I had been friends ever since the Beatles laid down the path to peace and enlightenment in the sixties. We met at a draughty Co-op hall in Nottingham, where two young disciples of the Maharishi had relieved us of fifteen pounds each, after which we were told to stand in front of a hat-stand decorated with roses and given mantras to chant. Neither of us were blessed or relaxed by transcendental meditation. Freddy was the most disappointed.

He had wanted something to ease the pain of the glue factory where he spent the whole of his working life, ending up as technical manager. Freddy was old before he was young. He began talking about retirement when he was twenty-one.

Freddy would have led a miserable life if he hadn't been blessed with an oddball sense of humour. Before retiring from his job in the glue factory, which he often likened to the sulphur mines, he sought his entertainment in various ways, one of which was making himself into a kind of Billy Liar – he would imagine blowing up the factory and, for extra pleasure, hurling the works manager into the great glue-mixing machine. Since retirement, he got much of his pleasure from needling Phil.

Phil's mode of dress was a favourite topic. In cold weather, he wore an ancient red beret in honour of the two years he had spent doing National Service in the Parachute Regiment. On warm days Phil would dress in a brown shirt with khaki-coloured shorts, map and binoculars slung round his neck and sunglasses perched on his army forage cap. The first time he and Freddy went on a hike – just before their retirement two years earlier – Freddy said that Phil looked like Rommel, the German Field Marshal who had fought the British in North Africa during the Second World War. He did, indeed, look ready to step into the nearest tank to begin the defence of El Alamein. Freddy called him 'Gruppenführer' (group leader) because he liked the guttural sound of it. Freddy liked to josh Phil because it enlivened the hikes – and Freddy hated boredom.

After a while, we turned left off the Ashbourne to Buxton road and arrived in Alstonefield, smug in its status as frequent winner of the best-kept village competition. At its heart is a classic village green with trees and an ancient pub with trestle tables outside. But its attractiveness is also a drawback, with many of its cottages bought by bonus boys from the City. They dash up the M1 at weekends in Range Rovers, their Barbours and sparkling wellingtons normally used only when the going gets tough outside Harrods.

Once we had parked, Freddy stared at the string of accessories emerging from Phil's rucksack: a bright yellow waterproof cover for his hi-tech compass, a pair of long-life Paramo all-weather trousers, followed by a strange-looking pad of insulated material that looked like part of a NASA heat shield. Freddy reacted to the latter with predictable horror. 'My God. What's that?'

'It's a bum-warmer for sitting on cold wet stones.'

'Where do you plug it in?'

'You don't. Your body warms it and it warms you back.'

Freddy put on his Oliver Hardy face. 'Well, I had this for Christmas.' He produced a cheap little compass. 'Out of a cracker.' He pointed at my new gaiters and Phil's new boots. 'I shall expect you two to do a *pas de deux.*' And with that we pulled our hoods over our heads and went into battle.

The road from Alstonefield led straight into the easterly onslaught. Heads dropped into chests, tears sprang from eyes. 'I move –' Freddy gasped – 'I move we sack the navigator. Who said this would stop? Con man! What do you say, Don?'

'Absolutely,' I sided with Freddy to keep him happy.

'Out of order,' Phil shouted. 'The navigator can't be sacked. Who'd navigate? You two couldn't find your way out of a super-market.'

We left the road and followed a steep footpath which led down into Wolfescote Dale, so named because a certain Mr Wulfstan had once lived there, not because it had been a wolf's lair. Even Phil took care on the descent, which was almost vertical.

The wind dropped as we reached the riverside and crossed by a stone-flagged footbridge. A statuesque heron stood near a small weir staring at the water. From the riverside spread the steep-sided woodland of ash, sycamore and thorn, with only a whisper of wind blowing through them. The comparative silence after the roaring hilltops was like entering a museum after a heavy metal concert.

Freddy looked at his watch. 'Coffee break,' he announced.

Phil hated early breaks. 'I refer to Appendix B,' he said. This rule, created by Phil, stated that by unilateral agreement of one member of the trio all other rules could be waived. He was usually the only one who used it.

Freddy objected. 'Rule 4c. We can stop within ten minutes either side of any hour.'

'Appendix B,' Phil snapped, killing all rules, and carried on walking.

Freddy sighed, but there was no referee. Phil was the navigator and hike-master supreme. Freddy muttered and followed on behind.

Ten minutes later we reached a clear stretch of grass without interference from nettles, brambles or bushes. Phil stopped and took out his bum-warmer. Freddy looked at it with distaste, spread out his spare over-trousers on the ground and sat down. The mid-morning snacks appeared. Phil handed over the promised slab of ginger cake and watched Freddy bring it to his lips. 'Hmmm,' he murmured, luxuriating in the taste, his head tilted backwards and eyes closed. Phil shook his head and polished off a small banana.

'How are you getting on with Dr Strangebugger?' Freddy asked, both to put off the moment of departure and to open up one of his favourite 'needle the Gruppenführer' topics – Phil's health.

Phil grunted. Dr Strangebugger, as Freddy and I called him, was Phil's health guru from Liechtenstein, who, from his rented attic in London W2, had ordered Phil to have blood tests for glucose absorption, liver function, haematology and biochemistry, sending him to some curious clinics in the medical neighbourhood of West One. His blood had been extracted, spun, analysed and counted by no fewer than five laboratories.

The doctor had also suggested that Phil should forsake the public amenities of the Peak villages and hamlets and pee in the open instead; this was something to do with creating an electromagnetic feedback from soil to body. He had advised Phil to walk without boots and socks as a supplementary means of absorbing benefit from the soil. Clearly he had never visited the Peak District, where walking barefoot is a pleasure only to be pursued on the lush lawns of home.

Freddy brought this up now. 'Can't understand you, Stevens. Strangebugger tells you to pee on the ground and walk on the ground in bare feet, and then you go and separate your bum from the ground with that thing.'

'Bums can get cold and wet.'

'So can your feet.' Freddy always wants to have the last word. We gazed at the river. The Dove, only ten feet wide in many places, flows, tumbles and splashes its way through some of the prettiest and wildest dales in England: Beresford Dale near Hartington, then Wolfescote Dale, Mill Dale and finally Dove Dale, the latter made famous by Izaak Walton, the seventeenth-century father of modern angling.

A dipper swam underwater and then came out to sit on a stone and bob up and down. Phil and I took out our metallic indestructible thermos flasks, more Christmas presents, which Freddy spotted with distaste. 'Oh God,' he said. 'More hi tech.' He produced his destructible Argos plastic flask and shook his head soulfully. 'You two …' The Puritan spoke. It was not the cost that mattered, it was the principle of the thing. Freddy's mobile came from his son, who had replaced it with something more modern. His video came courtesy of a dead aunt. He decried Classic FM because of its commercialism and bitty excerpts. And he was wary of any film that had been hyped too much. But his Puritanism – as with Phil's masochism – did not extend to food.

During morning breaks we tended to discuss minor issues, such as Freddy's old MGB roadster with its thermostat problem. More serious topics, like Freddy's search for the meaning of life or Phil's plan to slash health costs by forcing the nation to exercise as he did each day, were reserved for when we drove our legs forward on the hike.

Freddy's job had meant attending to a Thai manufacturer's worries over failed joints in their furniture products after the latest delivery of glue. Phil's concerns had dealt with the safe separation of departing and arriving aircraft, and I would sit in front of my word processor and think hard about what I might have for lunch.

Now retired, we have so much space in our lives that anything and everything is used to fill it. Freddy, when not on a meaning-of-life search, has a compulsion to pull up manhole covers in his driveway and examine the drains. Phil is obsessed with his body, stretches it to the limit and stuffs it with pills. I sit at my computer and listen to a deep American voice declare: 'The printer is out of paper.'

'It isn't,' I scream. 'You stupid idiot. It's jammed … jammed!'

After our break we entered Mill Dale, taking the footpath on the left-hand side, steep banks of woodland rising to the hilltops on both sides of the dale. This is a good 'talking' footpath, wide enough to allow a three-way conversation. 'I've been thinking,' said Freddy. 'Have you thought that if there were no one on earth at all, nothing would exist because we define existence through our senses? And, if you push it further, you could argue that if I was the only person on earth I might not be here.'

'Well, you're not, Freddy. You're not with us, you never are.' Phil cackled. Freddy was too deep in thought to take any notice.

'Somebody, through the five senses, must detect reality. Reality must be felt or seen. Take some intelligent being, millions of light years back. We don't exist in their existence.'

'That's because they don't know about us!' Phil exclaimed. 'Try the converse. A hippo's in my conservatory. It's there because I don't know about it. Is it there?'

'Yes, it could be. That's possible.' Freddy said. 'If you don't see it there because you're miles away somebody else might have seen it there. You can say it's unlikely, but no more than that. You can't say a hippopotamus is not in your conservatory if you're not there.'

'Excuse me while I cool my mind.' Phil put a piece of chewing-gum in his mouth. His voice lowered to a flat monotone. 'I see. OK. There's a hippopotamus in my conservatory. How did it get there and who feeds it? Ruth, when she's watering the flowers? "Ruth, don't forget the hippo's supper. God, there's hippo droppings on the carpet again."'

'You're not freeing your mind,' said Freddy. 'I'm not saying there is a hippo in your conservatory. There probably isn't, but –'

'Probably! You'd better get off home before Jean gets back. Get that crocodile out of the bathroom.' Phil grinned at me.

Freddy waved his long arms about, and clenched his fists in frustration. 'I'm talking about the nature of reality and not your perception of it. You don't listen.'

'Yeah, you show me the hippopotamus, Freddy. I'll photograph it and sell it to the *Sun*. Great.'

Freddy shook his head, and said no more.

We approached the river bailiff's house at a turn in the river. It was surrounded by hills, adjacent to an old water mill and a small hump-backed bridge. Freddy said it was the kind of house a bank manager might have owned before the Delhi call centres took over.

The black and white bargeboard around the gables, and the front garden edged with neat low fencing, shouted 'suburbia'. By contrast, the mill house on the other side of the river – recently renovated from its derelict condition of crumbling stonework, faded boards over door and window, and eaves that sagged and sprouted grass – looked 'right', even charming. It had been built in the seventeenth century with traditional grey stone. It belonged there, Freddy said. The house didn't. Freddy said it should be taken down and re-erected in Godalming.

Here, though, within this majestic fold, lay a problem. Harold the bailiff only had to glance out of his window and would be sure to spot us passing by. Such was his hospitality that he would try to lure us into the warmth of his fireside, whisky bottle on the table, while we listened to his tales of the riverbank. The hike was surely doomed. Freddy would be difficult to extricate. We walked quickly past the house, but were caught out.

'What are you lot up to, you daft beggars?' the familiar voice boomed out.

We stopped and turned round, affecting surprise. Harold stood in the open doorway, a big man in his late sixties, six feet tall and broad at the shoulders. A wide leather belt kept up his baggy corduroys. He held a mug of tea in his hand.

'Come on in and get some whisky down you.'

'Happy New Year, Harold. Sorry, can't stop. Thanks all the same.'

'Don't be daft, come on in.'

Harold's tales of water, poachers and wildlife were always worth a diversion. On a previous hike we had come across him with a party of scientists who were searching the Dove for white-clawed crayfish, a 'priority species' as far as water cleanliness is concerned. They were relieved to find the crayfish in sufficient quantity, proof that the river was unpolluted.

'How's the Manifold doing, Harold?' called Freddy, ignoring Phil's impatient attempts to move on.

'There's signal crayfish in, not a good sign, but we've still got the white-clawed. We've got action plans – for the other rivers as well. We keep up the battle!'

With this news we waved firm goodbyes to Harold, who boomed heartily at our silliness. 'Blooming barmy, you lot, you'll catch your death.' And with a wave and a laugh the human St Bernard went indoors, back into the sensible warmth.

Freddy said that Harold would be proved right. 'I can see the headlines now: "Peak tragedy, three hikers perish. Maniac leads friends to their death."'

'You stick by me and I'll keep you alive.' Phil was nonchalant.

'That's the trouble. If I weren't sticking by you I'd be safe at home by the fire.' Freddy took a mint out of his pocket and stuffed it in his mouth.

Phil saw it. 'I'll report you to Jean.'

'You're not my friend, Stevens. When's lunch?'

'It's not ten minutes either side of the hour yet – it's only quarter to. You know the rules.' Phil stepped on to the steep banking bordering the road, glanced up at the hilltop 150 feet above his head, and then began to scramble up the grassy slope, working his legs and arms like a lunatic.

Freddy cupped his hands to his mouth, 'Oi, Stevens! We had an agreement. No running off any more!'

Phil pretended not to hear as he concentrated on breaking his record for the climb. He has 'personal bests' for many of the great hills of the Peak District.

Freddy shouted upwards again, 'I've resigned, Stevens! It's all over. You'll have to find some other poor devil. Hike's over. Come on down!' Phil waved a hand in derision. After a rueful pause we started the climb. We had no choice. Phil was navigator. Where he went, we had to follow.

It was Phil's passion for exercise that had turned the hike into a severe test of body, akin to sado-masochism. He chose me, an ex-schoolmate, as his first victim. He then set his sights on Freddy, whom he met when both their wives were working together for a local charity. Freddy resisted fiercely, but Phil refused to give up and probed his weakest defences.

On Black Wednesday, as Freddy called it, Phil had turned up at Freddy's house and persuaded his wife Jean to pass Freddy into his care. He told her the hike would be a pleasurable healthy activity. Jean has a cloud of frizzy red hair and a snub nose in a round freckled face. Freddy refers to her as his 'ginger pudding', but not in her hearing. She is the daughter of a pub landlord and has seen two men suffer heart attacks, chaps who preferred leaning on a bar counter to doing push-ups in the gym. So she was receptive to Phil's idea of a weekly hike. 'Oh,' she said when he made the suggestion, 'of course Frederick will go.' She called him by his full name because Freddy hated it. It gave her dominance. 'He needs the exercise.'

Phil was now on the upper part of the hillside, so steep that he had to use his hands as well as feet.

Freddy shouted at him, 'I invoke Appendix D, Stevens! An unscheduled climb up a hill has to be met with an equally long walk downhill. Are you listening?'

Phil gave no sign of having heard and launched himself at the summit like a dervish. At the top he turned to grin at his companions labouring far below.

It was a familiar and depressing sight. No glorious cast of sunlight over panorama of hill and dale would ever cause Phil to take in the view. We had endured two years of this manic behaviour before Freddy could accept that he might not, after all, be killed by Phil through hypoglycaemia or cardiac arrest. However, although I was fitter than Freddy, I shared his doubts about accompanying someone who could push his pulse rate up to 180 beats per minute.

Freddy stuck his hand in his pocket and brought out half a bar of dark chocolate. He broke off a piece and popped it in his mouth, a customary response to Phil's wilder behaviour. Strangely, this regular recourse to an edible comforter never seemed to alter his waistline.

Ten minutes later we reached the top, the wind at its strongest. I bent my head forward, pushing against the gale. The cold was intense. No sign of Phil. 'With any luck he's fallen off,' said Freddy. Then Phil materialised out of a dip in the ground and caught Freddy looking at him queryingly. Phil shook his head. Clearly he had failed to beat his personal best.

We began the descent, the smell of wood smoke blowing from Milldale hamlet, bitter sweet in the cold air.

'So you didn't do it then?' Freddy asked Phil, giving me a sly grin.

'No, three seconds slower.' Phil kicked a loose stone downhill.

'Three seconds older in a year,' tutted Freddy. 'Tch!'

Phil had explained his theory a long time ago. If he had climbed the hill in the same time as the previous year it meant – to him – that he had not aged biologically. If he had beaten that time it meant he was younger. It was a serious business.

We walked towards the tiny stone hump-backed bridge that links Mill Dale with the northern entrance to Dove Dale. This is an original packhorse bridge – so called because it is just wide enough for a single horse to cross laden with full pannier bags, but so narrow that Izaak Walton's character in *The Compleat Angler* said of it, 'Why! A mouse can hardly go over it.' Beneath the bridge lay one of the stone wheels from the mill that had once stood there. An array of mallard ducks waddled out of the river towards us. Their trick is to surround a picnicker, look starving, and win crumbs.

We passed Maureen's cottage, from which she dispenses drinks and snacks through a small hatch between the windows, closed this cold day. Her husband Donald appeared from the rear of the cottage, carrying logs for the fire. He smiled in recognition. 'By 'eck as like, you must be crackers.' He put down the basket and gestured at us to join him at the side of the cottage.

Beneath a flapping cover stood a large motor car. He removed the cover and there, resplendent, was a shining Rolls-Royce. 'Got it at auction, once owned by the Duchess of Argyll. Twelve grand. Not bad, eh?'

We looked inside the limousine, absorbing the luxurious interior. 'What do you get to the gallon?' asked Freddy, conscious of the thirsty engine.

'That I don't know. No idea.' Donald shook his head as though the question was far too technical to answer with any certainty.

'Oh well. How often do you use it?'

'Use it? You mean *drive* it?' Donald stared at Freddy. 'Good God, no! I don't drive it. You'd get loads of hassle if you drove it.'

We stared at Donald. He continued to look surprised.

'Flippin' 'eck, no, you don't drive it. You'd get folk spitting at it. Chucking things. You know what they're like nowadays.'

'You must use it sometimes.' Freddy tried not to sound bewildered.

'Yeah, I use it when I go to the garage, to fill her up.'

Pause. Freddy chose his words carefully and spoke slowly. 'But if you don't drive it, how can you burn the petrol that makes it need filling up again?'

'Oh, it takes a gallon just to get to the garage.'

There was a pause. We nodded slowly. Phil looked dubious.

'That car is the best in the world. Wouldn't you like to own something that's the best in the world?'

Phil and I said yes, of course. Freddy nodded. He hadn't the heart to say no. He had other ideas about car ownership, which would come as a surprise to Phil and me. But he was not yet ready to announce them. And pressing matters were at hand – food, namely.

'Donald should get a knighthood. That car's greener than a moped,' Freddy said as we sat down on the wooden bench in the nearby hiker's shelter and opened our lunch boxes.

Phil had prepared his own lunch, a small but tasty concoction sealed in a small Tupperware bowl. Bits of walnut and apple vied with small pieces of crunchy lettuce and tomato for space and Phil ate slowly so he wouldn't finish before Freddy and me. Inside my box was a sandwich of farm-cured ham in brown granary bread, still warm when picked up from the village bakery that morning. Freddy had a home-made pork pie, which he nibbled slowly, making contented 'mmm' sounds as he ate.

A goosander, brilliantly coloured, sat in the water, uninterested in the mallard ducks that waddled out of the water to besiege our position. Phil took no notice of them, his face in a fixed frown. 'What's the point of a car standing still?'

Freddy shrugged. 'The point is, it won't add to global warming – and it's cheap to run.' Freddy chuckled at the thought.

*

After we had finished lunch we resumed the hike, entering Dove Dale by crossing over the packhorse bridge. Ahead of us, Freddy disappeared behind some bushes for a pee. Phil took his opportunity. 'Freddy? Don't forget to hit the soil, not the stone,' he called. 'You need your electro-magnetic feedback.'

'You should ring up the Department of Health,' Freddy retaliated. 'I bet the only degree Strangebugger's got is an MA in con-artistry.'

'And what happened to you when you went private for your prostate operation?' Phil lifted his eyebrows with a triumphant gleam in his eye.

'I was sent there by the firm. I wouldn't have paid for it,' said Freddy earnestly. His principles were at stake here.

'I know that, but the catheter stopped working. And there was nobody on night duty who could fix it, so you had to do it yourself. I'd rather have Strangebugger than your private hospital.'

'Balls,' said Freddy.

'No, a bit further up,' said Phil.

We walked further down the dale. This had first been discovered by the pre-Victorians, who would arrive in their silk top hats and mount donkeys for a trip along the right-hand side of the river. Lord Byron found its 'nobility unequalled by any sight in Greece or Italy'.

The second group to discover it was my gang from the working-class Chaddesden district of Derby. For us kids it could be either cowboy country or jungle, where Gary Cooper shot the bad guys or Tarzan leapt from rock to tree. It used to take us three hours to reach this remote and dangerous place. Nowadays, you can get there by car in thirty minutes.

After a while we reached Dove Holes, a set of large caves extending back under the rocky cliff for several metres. We have often watched rock climbers, spider-like, move beneath the high cave ceilings and always marvelled at their feats of prowess and strength. Today the caves were empty, but festooned with red and yellow climbers' ropes pegged into cracks in the rock. We passed by, following the curve in the river, then crossed a wooden bridge to the other side.

We picked our way up a rocky gulley. Freddy heard it first – Vivaldi's 'Four Seasons', appropriately enough the Winter movement. As we climbed out of the gulley it came to an end, replaced by a chatty male voice. This was Classic FM – Freddy's *bête noire*. We drew nearer to its source, a transistor radio perched on a partially built stone wall.

A man was at work filling in gaps in the stone wall, near him a pile of rocks from which he made his selection. It was a dry stone wall, no mortar needed.

The waller had his back to us so we could watch as we walked closer without embarrassing him. He picked up a piece of rock, looked at the place where it was to go and dropped it, obviously not satisfied with its shape. He picked up another from the pile, which went into the wall like a key into a lock. He was small and stocky, a grey balaclava covering his head and face. With at least three sweaters and two pairs of trousers on, he looked rather like the Michelin man of old, his chest an enormous balloon. He turned round and saw us. What we could see of his face looked like raw steak from years of wind and sun.

'Hallo,' he shouted. 'You're the first hikers I've seen today.'

'I'm not surprised. Most people aren't crazy.' Freddy glanced at Phil with a grin. This brought a deep rumble of a chuckle from the waller. I noticed that two fingers on his left hand were missing.

Phil lined himself up with the wall and admired its straightness. The waller was grateful for the compliment.

'When I put down a rock,' he said, 'I'm putting down hundreds of fossilized sea creatures, three hundred million years old, eh? Did you know that?' He said that the craft had died out in the early years of the twentieth century when farmers, to save money, had repaired their own walls. With the National Park had come a revival of the craft through subsidies.

We thanked him for his explanation and left. 'You know what he is,' I said. 'He's a direct descendant of the old rural trades that were going in Shakespeare's time. Most of them died out around the Second World War. It's a pity, isn't it, that they can't bring back the others.'

'Such as?' asked Freddy.

'Well, there was the hurdle-maker for one.'

'I hated hurdling. I could never jump hurdles,' Freddy said. 'I was too fat.'

'Hurdles were fences, not for jumping over,' I said.

Freddy was thoughtful. 'We took a wrong turn in the eighteenth century. Instead of factories we should have built more farms. And I wouldn't have had to work in the sulphur mines.'

'No,' Phil said. 'Freddy, if you'd been alive then, do you know what you'd have been?' He answered his own question. 'A poor peasant. You don't know how lucky you've been.'

'You know what you'd have been? An inmate of Bedlam,' retaliated Freddy. As we trudged towards Stanhope hamlet he quoted the disparaging couplet passed down through the ages: '"Derbyshire born and Derbyshire bred, strong in the arm and weak in the head."'

'Wrong,' said Phil. 'The word was "wik", which in local language means "quick", which we've got to be else we won't see where we're walking.' At that he set a cracking pace over the darkening fields.

We saw her on the road towards Stanhope hamlet. A bitch border collie, shaggy-haired and sitting on a stone wall belonging to a house. She watched our approach.

When we reached her she jumped off the wall, crossed our path and jumped on to the left-hand wall, trotted along a few yards, then leapt down to cross the lane and jump on to the right-hand wall, then walk the parapet once more before jumping down to repeat the sequence all over again. The criss-crossing ritual went on and on. How did we reward her? I told her we hadn't any biscuits, but she wasn't put off and carried on with her performance, a true star.

After walking half a mile we began to issue commands: 'Home. Go back! Go on, home! Go home!'

The dog pulled together the two white patches over her eyes in a kind of frown, then turned away as if to say, 'Don't give me that old stuff. Let's get on with it.'

She changed her ritual. She no longer walked on the wall but on the footpath. She would plod on a dozen steps, stop and glance round to ensure we were following, then walk on again, to stop once more – and so on. Finally in exasperation I ran after her and shouted: 'Stop, come here.'

All she did was look at me drily as if to say: 'Do me a favour and go and play in the traffic.' The hike continued with our new recruit. In the gathering gloom we must have looked a strange group, three men shouting and beseeching – a dog. We walked across a hillside towards Alstonefield. From here – presuming she lived at the house where we had met her – she would have a mile, at least, to walk home.

As she stopped to turn round once more I made a sudden run, grabbed her by her ruff and braced myself for a bite. I need not have worried. The dog stared at me with wide, sad-looking eyes.

'Go – HOME! Now look, dog …' I stopped as I felt something, a cord around her back, buried in her shaggy hair. I ran my hand the length of the string, felt underneath her belly and pulled the string round to bring a square of plastic into view. It was a hand-printed notice. In the dim light I could just make out the words: 'PLEASE SAVE MY LIFE. SAY "GO HOME JENNY".' Jenny placed a paw forward, a gesture that she wanted to be off again.

Having failed to persuade me, she bowed her head and pulled at my arm. I stood a yard away, and pointed towards home and safety. In as masterful, calm and steady a voice as I could manage I declared: 'Go home, Jenny.'

Jenny stared at me in wistful sadness. My arm remained pointed. Then she accepted defeat, turned and galloped back towards home. We could just see her as she entered the lane and disappeared into the gloom.

We carried on with our own homeward journey. Phil was in fast-step mode. A hike for him is never a good one unless he exhausts himself. Freddy and I strode behind and ruminated on the remarkable Jenny, the serial hiker hijacker. 'How many hikers had she collared before they put that card on her?' I asked.

'Were we taking her for a hike or was she taking us? ' Freddy wondered. 'I reckon she was taking us for a walk. Maybe she's a reincarnated hiker.'

Phil had heard enough. He turned round. 'You guys are off your heads. That dog enjoyed the walk. An animal is a bunch of conditioned reflexes, that's all.'

We climbed the steep hill towards Alstonefield. It had started to snow. We trudged past the old Post Office, now a café. Then we passed Jean Goodwin's art shop and rounded the corner to see our car in a corner of the village green.

The George had just opened. Through the small paned window of the snug we could see the bright log fire throwing shadows around the unlit walls. It was a tempting sight. Within a few minutes we were sitting on a polished wooden bench, sipping Burtonwood ale and staring into the flames.

After a while Phil's head drooped, but then jerked back as Freddy barked out a sudden laugh. 'That dog,' he said. 'I'll tell you what she's doing now. She's sitting by the fire, just like us, laughing her socks off at conning some more idiots.' Freddy looked at Phil. 'Like you conned us into this hike.'

Phil murmured something unintelligible.

Freddy chuckled at the idea of a dog being in control of humans. 'Just like you said would happen in the aircraft of the future, Gruppenführer.'

'What?' Phil stared at him.

'The dog,' Freddy said. 'You told us the plane of the future would be flown by a pilot and his dog. The pilot would be there to feed the dog and the dog would be there to bite the pilot in case he touched anything.'

We were still laughing about it as we drained our glasses and headed home.

2

FEBRUARY

Rain, driven by a cold north-westerly, rattled against the conservatory windows. Phil, as usual, sat there eating breakfast, a meal which had become the big one on hike days owing to the increasing demands he was making on his body. Not only was he running up hills but he had taken to dashing around the neighbourhood for an hour each evening, followed by a hundred press-ups, fifty sit-ups, and a variety of stretching exercises and crunch-ups of the reverse, cable or hanging variety, all this to keep at bay his dreaded sixty-fifth birthday, which sat on the late September horizon. It all added up to a lot of calories, Ruth said. Conse-quently, hike day breakfast was substantial even by American standards.

Porridge, laced with maple syrup, was followed this morning by an omelette and two sausages. On other mornings he might have English muffins and a baked egg, often making our mouths water with his tasty descriptions of the muffins leaking butter and dripping with a generous layer of home-made orange marmalade – all very odd because for the rest of the week he eats like a monk, a few oats and an apple.

Phil's container-load of pills were lined up in orderly fashion on the table. He had just popped the first tablet with a slurp of cranberry juice when Ruth came in, still dark-haired despite being over sixty, slim and neat, with beady bright brown eyes. She said, with a wry smile, 'Guess who's on the phone?' No need to announce who it was at 8 am on hike day.

'This rain isn't going to stop. Have you seen the forecast?' Freddy, of course, with his inevitable complaint.

Phil swallowed a 500-milligram tablet of glucosamine sulphate, long-term reinforcement for the padding between his vertebrae, worn and compressed by rugby tackles and parachute-jumping in his youth. 'Yes, Freddy, I have seen the weather fore-cast. It is bad but –'

'Gruppenführer, you can't take us out in this.'

Phil positively tingled at the thought of hiking in heavy rain. It would be a good test for his new waterproofs and, of course, would meet his never-ending desire to face all that Mother Nature could chuck at him. He knocked back a selenium tablet (Strangebugger had told him that we didn't get any from plants grown in British soil). He appealed to Freddy's logic. 'Freddy, you've got the waterproofs, you'll stay dry, so what's the problem?'

'The problem is, Gruppenführer, I won't enjoy it.'

'As I keep telling you, who says you have to enjoy it?'

Freddy and I suspected that Phil's masochism was a result of his father's experience as a jungle fighter in the Second World War, when any soldier who dropped out through sickness had to take his chance alone. Although suffering from dysentery, the thought of being left to the mercies of the Japanese soldiers was enough to make Phil's father cut a hole in his trousers and walk on. We suspected that Phil felt the need to match him in the tough-it-out stakes.

'Aaaaa-gum-ah!' Phil had difficulty trying to swallow a dose of calcium (for his bones).

'Do I hear a death rattle, Gruppenführer? You still alive? Oh dear.'

'Freddy, you know if we miss just one hike for rain we'll miss a lot more. Discipline will be gone, the hike will go downhill.' Phil was at his most sympathetic.

'Hah, downhill! Now we're getting there! I've been telling you all along it's the only way to hike!'

'Freddy, the hike is nailed through the calendar, inviolable.' Phil's tone was understanding, but firm. Down went a vitamin E tablet.

'I'll hate it. What's the point of having to hate something? Anyway, rule 2 states that the hike shall only take place if all members enjoy –' He broke off as Phil cut in.

'No, rule 1: the hike will take place unless there's snow you can't walk through, fog you can't see through –'

'And a lunatic you *can* see through,' chimed in Freddy.

'Think how good you'll feel afterwards!' An antioxidant capsule was next in the queue to invade Phil's stomach.

'Get out of it, Stevens!'

'I've taken the vote, Freddy. Don's going. I'll pick you up at the usual time, OK?' Phil put down the phone and tossed back his daily dose of vitamin C. It gave him great pleasure to hear the rain lash the conservatory windows.

Forty minutes later he beamed at Freddy, sitting next to him in the car, like fathers do at children who are being taken to the dentist and need a jolly-up. 'So,' said Phil cheerfully. 'How are you getting on with the "meaning"?' Freddy looked at him blankly, but said nothing. Phil grinned smugly. 'I've got something for you, Freddy, something that will change your life.'

'Oh God,' said Freddy dismally.

'No, seriously, something to cheer you up. I'm not telling you, it's a surprise.'

Freddy sighed, his face growing longer. Phil tutted. 'I give up. I think up all these hikes for you to do and you stay in can't-do-that mode. What can I do? You might as well be back in the glue factory if that's how you feel.'

*

We arrived at the parking place in Chelmorton, a street in the tiny old lead-mining village situated on high ground to the south-west of Taddington Moor. Freddy poked his head out of the car door and, shocked, immediately withdrew it.

'It's madness. It's wet, cold and windy out there!'

'Outside, my squad!' barked Phil with a grin. 'Marvellous, Freddy, eh? Wind and rain!'

Freddy took a deep breath. 'For those who are about to die for the aggrandisement of a madman.' He clambered slowly out of the car, pulled the anorak hood over his head and looked around. Nowhere on God's earth looks nice in rain. Grey stone cottages in summer look warm and welcoming, in wintry rain forbidding. A black dog, a mongrel with a rear foot missing, limped towards the car, its coat flat and shiny, water dripping from spikes of fur.

'Does anything strike you as odd about this place?' Freddy asked us.

Phil glanced around. 'No, what?'

'There's not one sign of life here. What conclusion do you draw from this?'

Phil shook his head, 'That we're here and nobody else is.' He sat in the driver's seat, with the car door open and his legs outside, as he put on his boots.

'Exactly! And what do you think that suggests?'

Phil shrugged his shoulders. 'That it's wet. They'd rather be indoors.'

'Precisely! Could that suggest they are sane and sensible and not in the grip of a lunatic?'

The dog sniffed around Freddy and, with a delicate balancing act, managed to cock one of its three legs against the outside of Phil's car door, unnoticed by Phil. Freddy looked on with approval.

Phil stood upright, boots on, stamping his feet. 'Backbone, backbone! Tonight you'll eat with gusto and sleep like a log!' Phil clapped Freddy on the shoulder. 'Get your gear on, come on.'

The dressing game in wet weather: balance against the car side to pull on over-trousers. When they're half way up you fall over with both feet trapped, unable to move. It's impossible to stand so you pull them on lying down, a frustrating and undignified business. Then comes the anorak zip. Yes! Who will invent a zip that doesn't require millimetre accuracy lining up the two catches with the runner? With frozen hands it's well nigh impossible. It all looks wonderful in *Backpacker* magazine, which assures you that you will stay warm and cosy encased in your protective gear – but this assurance is conditional on other factors that don't find their way into the advertisements.

Phil led us uphill out of the village, trudging against the wet north-westerly, towards Sough Top, part of Taddington Moor. The wind gathered strength with the climb, so that we had to lean at 45 degrees into it to make progress. Nature took a back seat today. To blazes with flora and fauna, the only thing we looked at was the ground ahead, and the only noticeable features in the background were limestone walls. Freddy shouted to make himself heard. 'Stevens, I know you're mad but why aren't we hiking in a dale somewhere out of this?'

'This is what it's all about,' Phil shouted back.

'About what, torture?'

'No! Keeping up to the mark!'

'I don't want to be kept up to the mark, the action's now for three million.' Freddy dug his head into his chest to protect his eyes from the sting of wind-driven rain.

We reached Taddington village at eleven-fifteen, and the A6 main road a few minutes later. An approaching BMW towed behind it a cloud of spray, and we caught a glimpse of a young guy behind the wheel in the white shirt and conservative tie of the company man, his dark jacket hanging up behind his right shoulder. The spray merged into the general murk as the car sped off towards the spa town of Buxton.

'That was a capsule of civilisation,' groaned Freddy. 'He's warm and dry – and what am I doing?'

'Ah, yes,' said Phil. 'But he's probably listening to Classic FM. Out here you've got the music of the elements. Much nicer.'

'I'd listen to Classic FM. I'd listen to heavy metal. Try me.'

'Cock,' said Phil. 'Absolute cock. He does forty thousand miles a year, blood pressure, ulcers, car pollution, stress, little word going round the MD wants him out, wife wants kiddies in private school, has to work like stink to get the dosh – come on Freddy!'

Freddy was oblivious to all but his own plight. 'There must be a number you can call. Hikers' Anonymous. I am a hike victim. My tormentor is Gruppenführer Stevens alias Attila the Hun.'

Phil ignored him and turned down the footpath heading towards Blackwell village. We crouched behind a stone wall out of the wind for our coffee break. Jean had thoughtfully provided Freddy with a slice of Thor cake, a variety of griddle cake traditionally cooked by Peak women as a winter warmer. It is named after Thor's cave in a hillside near Wetton, and consists of oatmeal and flour mixed with candied peel, coriander seeds, butter and treacle. Freddy found some comfort in its rough sweetness. At the same time he rolled the hot coffee cup around his cheeks, humming softly in pleasure. 'Glory be, warmth. Your death sentence, Stevens, has been commuted to life imprisonment in a secure psychiatric hospital. I'll visit you from time to time and bring you a *Backpacker* magazine, taking care not to get too near the bars, of course.'

Phil broke his silence. 'Freddy, If you'd been in the Paras you'd have learnt what physical hardship is all about.'

'Oh, of course, forgive me, I never had those delights. But you were paid for it. Here, *I'm* paying for it.'

We followed Phil on the next leg of the hike. I felt a slight stiffness in my legs, a surprise after a stop of only five minutes. An hour later, after a northern loop near Millers Dale, we were a mile to the east of Blackwell, having arrived at a deserted bus shelter.

Freddy was quick to open his flask and drink some more hot coffee. He shivered as he pretended to scrutinise the bus timetable. 'When's the next bus? I can't see one for February. Or is it one a year? I want it *now*. I'm tired and cold and I want to go home.'

Phil was not optimistic. 'If you get a bus this side of Saturday I'll be –' he broke off as a bus pulled up slap bang in front of the shelter. 'Well, blow me.'

The sole passenger on the bus was a woman. She looked down at us in distaste, no doubt because of our drab and dirty condition. She had shoulders that would not have disgraced a front-row rugby player and a nose a parrot might envy. She wore a green hat with a feather and clutched a large cardboard box on which she balanced a colourful teapot, the type used by canal women of old. Freddy offered up his lunch box to her, for no reason that I could fathom. Phil put both hands up, grinning. 'He's not with us,' he mouthed at the woman.

I was forced to laugh, and was glad of the excuse. It was difficult to find anything else to laugh about in such depressing weather. The woman drew back in horror, and the teapot nearly slid off the box. The bus drove off with its flustered, outraged passenger still glaring at us. Freddy shivered as he opened his lunch box and took out a cheese and pickle sandwich.

'I don't feel too good.' Freddy said, starting to eat.

'You're nesh.' Phil used a Derbyshire expression meaning soft.

'Nesh is better than dead. "Hikers found stiff as boards. Gruppenführer's brain removed for medical research."'

'In which case,' said Phil, 'you'll be doing the board walk.'

After lunch Phil led the way out of the shelter, Freddy pointing a finger at him. 'No good will come of this, mark my words, Gruppenführer.'

'Rhubarb, rhubarb! It's a great day!' Phil was in an ebullient mood, the stronger the wind, the more intense the rain, the greater his pleasure. I wasn't complaining of the cold like Freddy, but I felt a sense of isolation – and alienation – which intensified as we walked through the deserted village.

The afternoon section of the hike took us back to Taddington Moor, at 1,500 feet above sea level as high as Dartmoor but, being much smaller, nowhere near as threatening. It would take about an hour to cross in a south-westerly direction, given our average walking speed. We were halfway across the moor, Phil leading. I followed with Freddy a few paces behind me.

After a few minutes I sensed that he wasn't keeping up and turned round to find him twenty yards adrift, pushing forward one leg at a time in a purposeful, determined act of will. He lumbered a few feet more, then stopped to lean forward and place his hands on both knees. 'I'm knackered.' His face was slack with exhaustion. 'I've felt bad for an hour. Worse since we had lunch.'

I looked back again to see Phil forging ahead, unaware of the drama behind him. 'You serious?' It was a reasonable question, knowing Freddy.

'No, I'm not serious. I'm having fun. I like being frozen.'

I hesitated, then: 'Phil!' I shouted. Phil turned round, peering back at us through the sheeting rain. 'Freddy's not too good!'

Phil nodded drily with a 'tell me something new' expression but, seeing my concern, walked back.

'He says he can't move.'

'What's wrong, Freddy?' asked Phil, resigned but tolerant.

'I'm character building, you know, what you go in for. Think it's called suffering. Can you see my legs? I've mislaid them.'

'They're where they always are. Now stop pratting about and come on!'

'Can't. Bury me here.'

'Freddy. Seriously.'

'I am being serious! I can't move my legs!' Freddy let out a soft sigh and lowered his head once more. Phil hesitated, then took Freddy's right arm and placed it around his shoulder. 'Take his other arm, Don. He's got a bit of hypothermia.'

We worked out that, at the rate we were going, it would take the best part of two hours to reach the car. We helped Freddy across the moor, the three of us linked together like grotesque competitors in a double three-legged race. Freddy complained of no pain, only an increasing numbness in his limbs and an overwhelming desire just to lie down and quietly go to sleep. Left to his own devices, this would be an eternal sleep.

There's no stopping hypothermia once it has a grip and no reversal, except by an applied, exterior source of heat. It would be no good asking Freddy to slap his arms across his chest or jump up and down, even if he had been capable of such exercises. A hot drink might help to keep his central body core warm but wouldn't reverse the process. In any case, we had finished all our coffee. His waterproofs worked, and were keeping the rain out. Berghaus Gortex boots kept his feet dry. But the enemy was within, having slipped through his defences like a Trojan horse. It was like a deadly virus, spreading throughout his tissues, a race against time. At our slow rate of progress we were now about thirty minutes away from the nearest road. Freddy's eyes began to close.

'Freddy! Wake up!' Phil jerked his arm to rouse him.

'I am awake. I'm just closing my eyes.'

'Well, don't. Why didn't you tell us how you felt!'

'I did. You didn't listen to me.'

We reached the road and looked left and right. There was no sign of any vehicle.

Phil made up his mind. 'I'll fetch the car. Keep him moving.' Phil set off in the direction of Chelmorton, jogging awkwardly in his hiking boots. After about a hundred yards he stopped to shrug off his rucksack and gestured at me to pick it up. He set off again, able to jog more easily. Freddy muttered something to me.

'What?' I asked.

'I said mobile phone.' He was right. We always left it inside the car in case of breakdown, never thinking we might need it on the hike. It was all down to Phil's macho attitude. A mobile was for the high street, not for blokes in the Peak. Freddy and I drew nearer to the rucksack. 'Whatever happens,' I said, 'you've got to keep walking. Just concentrate on keeping those legs going,' I ordered.

'What legs?'

It was ridiculous. We were in the Peak District, not the Cairngorms. We weren't even in the north of the county where the Dark Peak offers some scary moments, especially on the high ground of Kinder Scout. You wouldn't feel embarrassed about sending for mountain rescue on those hilltops. But this was the White Peak, the soft southern hills. Help was always at hand. Wasn't it? I picked up Phil's rucksack and carried it over one shoulder. 'Keep going, just don't stop.' My first sense of isolation had changed to one of apprehension.

A road without traffic. The stone walls, normally warm- and friendly-looking, now took on a blacker tinge. And the air was colder and wetter than ever. Freddy said he had a weak feeling in his stomach, a sizzling sensation in both temples and pressure inside his forehead.

Above all, there was a numbness creeping through his mind. Every few minutes I looked at my watch. 'How do you feel now?' I asked the question for the umpteenth time.

'Buggered.'

'Good. Tell me when it's more serious.'

Half an hour passed of slow trudging, looking and hoping, but the noise of wind and rain on my hood made it impossible to hear an engine before the first visual sign. Now I was fearful for myself, my limbs growing heavier, my head gripped in a cold vice. I had just about given up when – joy! A plume of spray headed towards us. But the car that appeared out of the spray was not Phil's. It was a Jaguar, a sleek, black, big-engined job. I edged Freddy away from the centre of the road and waved my hand, flagging it down.

The car braked quietly, the driver's window sliding down before it came to a standstill. I stepped forward and caught a warm waft of Gucci after-shave from a handsome, olive-skinned face. The young man wore a pale blue shirt, a yellow and red silk tie and a soft and supple beige leather jacket. He had a golden stud through his ear. Clearly he wasn't a company man. He didn't speak but looked us over with a faint smile of curiosity.

'We're in trouble,' I said. 'Freddy here's got hypothermia.'

The driver looked down at our lower halves, at our boots plastered with mud and our filthy, soaking trousers. The window slid slowly upwards and the car drew away. I poured a rapid burst of mental machine-gun fire through the rear window as it disappeared.

Forty minutes had passed since Phil left us. There was a farmhouse about half a mile away over the moor. I could just see its wet tiled roof, but there was no sign of chimney smoke. What if I raced there only to find the place empty and then came back to find Freddy unconscious at the road side? What then?

There was still no sign of Phil, but another vehicle was approaching. This time, please, please, let it be Phil. It wasn't Phil. The shape of the vehicle, high and stumpy, indicated a four-wheel drive. I dragged Freddy to join me in forming a human road block. The driver would have to swerve on to the grass verge to go round us. Death or glory, let it come.

The vehicle arrived – and came to a halt. Now, there are times in life when you are stopped, literally, in your tracks. To say I was gob-smacked would be an understatement. The driver had a black beard, his face a welcoming smile of enquiry. That was the only normal thing about him. He was wearing a uniform. Fine, okay, if he had been the Waldorf Hotel doorman wearing his top hat and tails, or even a Morris dancer with bells round his knees, it would have been plausible. Scenarios could be devised, imagination could be stretched to embrace such a thing – but an East German soldier, from the days of Communism? Driving a Trabant border patrol vehicle?

I remembered what the patrol soldiers were called – Vopos. They were soldiers of the German Democratic Republic charged with the job of dissuading anybody so foolish as to try and leave their paradise for the decadent west. They were not popular chaps on either side of the Wall. The grin on the Vopo's face was at odds with the light blue uniform. It was even less appropriate given the AK47 rifle at his side. To add to his menace he had lost an eye, which placed him midway between cavalier raffish and south sea piratical. Maybe the Peak Tourist Board was having trouble with hikers defecting to the Yorkshire moors and had hired a hit man.

'Hallo,' he bellowed from under his steel helmet. 'Have we got problems?'

The rifle suggested that he had his own private way of dealing with problems. Yet he spoke English with a Derbyshire accent. And East Germany had disappeared in the merger with West Germany, and with it had gone the Vopos.

Hey, but why was I worrying? It was a vehicle with a driver. Solving the mystery of an East German border guard equipped with deadly rifle somewhere to the west of Chelmorton, and in direct contravention of our strict gun laws, could be dealt with at a later date. I told him what had happened.

'Get in.' The Vopo looked concerned.

'Thanks.'

I hesitated as I saw the rear passenger head room largely reduced by the pressure downwards of a pool of water on the canvas roof. 'Hold on.' The Vopo pushed up the roof, splashing the water on to the road. We got in and he let in the clutch. We lurched forward.

'Sorry. Can you stop?' I shouted over the rattle. The Vopo braked. I explained what had happened, that Phil was in Chelmorton. We would need to go there first. My outline of events was punctuated by the Vopo's utterance of the Germanic 'Ja', mixed with a sympathetic English 'Good grief'. After I'd finished my tale he shouted 'Wunderbar!', executed a three-point turn in the road and we were off with a tinny roar from the tiny 2-stroke engine. We rolled, rather than drove, at forty-five miles an hour towards Chelmorton. I felt it was time to ask our Vopo how he'd come to be so dressed and driving such a vehicle. Perhaps he was a film extra, but extras are not normally allowed off set, not in costume.

'You'll wonder what I'm doing dressed up like this,' he called out over the engine noise. I said I had some interest in the matter.

'I'm the world president of the Trabant Association.'

'Really?' My astonishment was genuine.

'I've just been up to Buxton to have my photo taken for a charity do.'

I was glad it was nothing more violent. I asked him about the legality of the rifle.

'Disabled. It's part of the vehicle, clipped on here, see?' He showed me its anchor point. 'Better than any thief alarm, eh?'

I had to confess that it had some value as a deterrent. I wanted to ask him why he'd chosen to be world president of that particular car club. Given its lousy reputation, perhaps nobody else wanted the job. But I wasn't going to be so mean-spirited towards our Good Samaritan and held my peace. He told me that his name was Graham.

We arrived in Chelmorton. Phil's head was under the bonnet of his car, which was positioned so that the rain swept the back of the vehicle and not the engine compartment. He ducked out as he heard the announcement of our arrival, similar to the sound of peas rattling inside a tin can, and stared in disbelief as the Trabant, its headlights shrouded by black anti-air strike deflectors, came towards him. And then he stared at Graham. There was no time for explanations, as if I had any. I made the introductions and said we needed to get Freddy to Graham's house, where there was a fire.

Phil climbed through the canvas to sit beside Graham, cast a bewildered glance at the helmet and uniform, then turned round to address me. 'The car won't start. I've sprayed all the electrics with WD40 – no use. I was about to ring 999 and get an ambulance.'

'He won't need an ambulance,' Graham said with assurance. 'When he's warmed up a bit I'll give him a spot of healing massage.'

Freddy gave him a wary look.

'Where do you live?' I asked.

'Middleton,' he replied. 'Middleton-by-Youlgreave.'

Ten minutes later we arrived at the village and crossed a large sloping square of hard ground, once probably a green, with many trees around to soften the greyness of stone walls, houses and the square itself. One of the houses, with an impressive early Victorian façade, had a nineteenth-century date carved above the doorway. On the upper side of the square stood a small memorial to the crew of a bomber aircraft which had crashed nearby during the Second World War. Beyond this was a leafy lane that meandered down to the Bradford river. Off the lane was a house with a low-loader vehicle and a lorry parked outside.

Graham drove through the gateway and stopped almost immediately, unable to proceed owing to – what would you call it, a Tribune of Trabants? A Triumph of Trabants? And with its reputation as a contender for the 'worst car ever built' award – maybe a Trash Heap of Trabants? A double row of them stretched around the yard: yellow, blue, white and red Trabants.

As if to counter any suggestion that this wasn't a farmyard, a couple of geese waddled belligerently towards us, their heads raised. But when they saw Graham they veered off sideways with a hiss and a clutter. 'They're my best burglar alarm,' he said and hurried towards the back door to the farmhouse. 'I'll get the fire stoked up. You get Freddy in.'

Apart from the Trabants, the yard was chock full of rabbits in cages, cockerels, busts of Socrates and Queen Victoria, car wheels and tyres, empty propane bottles, oil cans, a garden gnome, an old tractor, batteries, a bike, plastic cans and a blacksmith's anvil. A greenhouse served as a store-room. In addition to the Trabants were two caravans, a car transporter and a lorry chassis. A notice was stuck on the back door of the house. It said: 'Jesus Christ. He's the real thing.'

A few minutes later we were sitting in the living-room in front of the fire. Freddy lay propped up on a sofa with a blanket wrapped round him. This came off every ten minutes for an application of healing hands and a vigorous massage. In between times he munched on thick buttered toast laden with honey and sipped Horlicks from a mug bearing a Trabant logo.

Graham puffed contentedly on a black pipe. He told us that he had been badly injured in a quarry accident in which he had lost an eye. At that moment I would have believed anything he said. If he had announced that he was the ambassador to Bhutan I might have raised a mere twitch of an eyebrow, but no more. So it was no surprise when he told us that he sang tenor in his local church choir, as did Freddy, a fact which helped him relax. The good Vopo was normal after all, and not likely to strangle him.

Graham broke off to bring Freddy nearer the fire and give him one last pummel, then picked up his pipe again and sat back in his rocking chair. 'Nowadays,' he said, 'this place would be better known if its secret had been revealed.' Wreathed in smoke, he luxuriated in our perplexity. What secret? Phil and I were eager to know, and didn't notice that Freddy had fallen asleep. Graham poked his pipe at the fire. 'A former lady-in-waiting to the Queen lives here. She used to have Prince Charles and Diana staying with her at weekends.'

We murmured our surprise.

'Yup, they stayed here just round the corner. And nobody knew about it except the local people here. The paparazzi never found out.' Graham told us that he saw the princess more than once, passing his house. He had watched her face, reflective and melancholy, yet bearing a hint of that familiar shy smile as she went down to the fishing pools and the wooded footpath alongside one of England's lesser known rivers.

We listened to the ticking clock and the crackling fire, and breathed in the rich aroma of Elliman's Athletic Rub mixed with pipe tobacco. Graham tossed me a magazine, open at a particular page. It was a German magazine devoted to the Trabant.

'Wilkommen Mr Graham Goodall!' it exclaimed in banner headlines. Another page sported a picture of Graham poking his head and shoulders out of a car on display. 'Herr Goodall bei der Geburtstagsparty.' But wasn't this odd? How could the united Germans extol the delights of a Communist car driven by only two cylinders and which belched forth smoke so appallingly? Wasn't the Trabant the most pitiable heap of mechanical trash ever to go under the Brandenburg Gate or down the Ku'damm?

'Hah!' Graham exclaimed with zest. 'They said the same about the Citroën 2CV when it was first made, the worst bit of French car manufacturing ever to go down the Champs Elysée! It became a cult car, why? Because the modern car has no character. Where else can you find a car with an engine less than 600cc, no bigger than a lawnmower box, with a 26 horse-power output and that does 72 miles to the gallon! Its simplicity is wunderbar!' But there was a downside, he admitted. An army general, now retired and living in the village, had noticed Graham flying the flag of the German Democratic Republic. Graham had explained that it was merely to indicate his position in the village to a visiting party of Germans.

More worrying had been the parish council's complaint to the Peak Planning Board that Graham's yard was an untidy mess. Middleton was an idyllic hideaway for village people as well as weekenders, and Graham's yard, to most of them, was a blight. It was true that the Trabants hardly went with the classic cars on the other side of the square, the owner being the president of a prestigious vintage car club. In a further coincidence, one of Britain's authorities on the classic Bugatti car was also a neighbour. Graham could hardly have chosen a better place in which to arouse resentment.

Freddy woke up in a daze and raised a bewildered hand, momentarily unaware of where he was. He had missed Graham's tale of warring car factions, which would certainly have amused him.

'I do have supporters,' Graham said quietly. One such supporter was a descendant of the Eyre family, many of whom had died in the Great Plague of 1665. She had helped Graham collect some of the many rabbits which had once escaped from his garden.

'Knee deep in them, the village was!' Graham boomed with laughter. The phone rang.

'Hah! Anita, mein Liebling! Wonderful! Ja! Wunderbar!'

We learned that the call was from his German girlfriend, who lived in Mohnesee, close to that Reservoir so niftily emptied by the Dam Busters squadron during the Second World War. He had met her on one of his Trabbie expeditions, and she planned to come over in the near future.

'Well, mein Liebling,' said Freddy to Phil. 'What are we going to do on our next hike? A walk up Snowdon in a force eight? A walk without any clothes on? There must be something else that challenges you and half kills me.' Freddy was restored, mentally as well as physically. It was time to take our leave.

Graham didn't hold us back. 'Kommen sie hier bitte, mein friends! Kaput no more!' We retrieved our kit from where it had been drying in a utility room and followed him outside. 'Now then, which Trabbie?' Graham waved his hand with the nonchalant air of a greengrocer with a fine spread of apples.

Phil chose one with a folded tent on top. This could be unfolded to provide overnight accommodation, the benefit being that it was permanently fixed to the rooftop so marauding animals would find it hard to jump into bed with you. But, in a closed society, where could the comrades go where wild animals were likely to leap into bed with them?

Maybe that was overlooked in the euphoria at the Zwickau factory when the first car sleeper was produced. 'Comrade manager, I have invented a tent car. It will put to shame all those western decadent motor caravans!' ('Jawohl, ist gut. I promote you to commisar i/c car roofs. Vorsprung Durch Technik!')

Graham turned the ignition key, producing a whirring noise followed by a splutter, a cough, three more splutters, another cough, a slurp and then an explosion, after which the engine rattled into life with the noise of a gravel-filled cement-mixer. A cloud of oily smoke enveloped Graham and cleared slowly to reveal a fist punching the air. 'You see, my friends. What other car would start like this!'

I could think of none, anywhere. We floated away on a suspension ideal for nautical travel as it reminded me more of a ship than a car. The car sailed forward gracefully, with the kind of sway you feel in a rowing boat, but with a suspension that could soak up the irregularities of a 'B' road in rural Derbyshire. Freddy sat in the front passenger seat, fascinated by the driver's natty trick of taking the whole engine out of gear by merely lifting the foot off the pedal. What genius of Communist thinking produced this petrol-saving measure? The drawback for western, boringly safety-conscious drivers of this free-wheel mode was, of course, the possibility that the car would simply run faster and faster at its first trip downhill, and that the old-fashioned drum brakes would fail to prevent it from smashing into the first stone wall it confronted. Graham assured us that the brakes would never get so hot as to be ineffective, another miracle which would no doubt have earned its creator the Lenin Order of Technical Merit.

We reached Chelmorton. Graham immediately stuck his head under the bonnet of Phil's car, singing the Magnificat in a rich tenor voice. Fifteen minutes later Phil leaned forward to rub away the condensation on the windscreen, just in time to see Graham emerge from the bowels of the engine, his hands oily. 'Start her up!' Phil turned the key. It fired first time to shouts of elation from us all. We showered Graham with compliments and thanks, stuffed our hiking gear into the car boot and, with Graham exhorting us to ring him or drop by at any time of night or day, climbed into the car.

Graham gave a final wave as we drove away. Freddy, having slept a little, had enough energy to rib Phil. 'Gruppenführer, today must go down as the most deadly I have ever encountered. I shall sue you for four million pounds for endangering my life. Do you understand the charge?'

'Not guilty, you came of your own volition.' Phil reserved his defence.

'Now we move to the second charge. Graham said there was a mountain rescue post in Millers Dale. You missed it. It was there on your Panzer map if you'd only looked. Sheer incompetence. I move you be fired. Seconder?'

'Yeah, let's sack the bastard,' I murmured.

'Appendix E,' Phil snapped back. 'Navigator can't be sacked.'

'Send him for retraining then,' said Freddy. There was a pause and then he muttered something to himself about Trabants. I caught the word 'onedown', but then he said he felt a bit sick and fell silent for the rest of the journey.

And so Freddy arrived home under escort. As we stepped through the kitchen door we were met by a waft of warm air and the rich aroma of a dark and wine-laced casserole bubbling on the hob.

Jean appeared and stared at Freddy, who looked a shambles, hiking trousers lop-sided, his woollen hat hanging to one side and his long face white with exhaustion. 'Freddy, for goodness sake, just look at you.'

No mention was made of his hypothermia. After a hot bath

and supper he sat in the recliner by the fire, sipping a glass of Pinot Noir and listening to Elgar's Concerto for Cello in E minor – but only for a while. Within ten minutes he was dead to the world and couldn't remember the next morning how he managed to wake up in bed.

3

MARCH

Spring arrived early for once and – hey nonny nonny no – we could see lambs gambolling on the hillsides. Over the high pasture came the orchestra of dunlin, curlew and lapwing. On a bright day the plateau remained bare and harshly lit, but down in the dales the hiker was welcomed by softly emerging splashes of colour.

Phil was, as usual, blind to all rural charms and at this moment had his mind on other matters – the market town of Ashbourne, to be exact. Ashbourne is our gateway to the Peak, thirteen miles north-west of Derby. It's built on a hillside and has a sturdy look about it as befits a hill-farming community. It has all the features of a fine old town: a row of antique shops, a country-wear store, a cobbled open market, an ancient pub and that 'feel good' essential, a chintzy shop and café. But it's a market town with a difference. It is a war zone at a certain time of year, namely Shrovetide.

On the way to our first hike of the month we drove down St Johns street, noting the boarded-up shop windows reminiscent of precautions taken during the blitz of the Second World War. Two armies would fight it out on the morrow. The battle would last forty-eight hours and the police would turn a blind eye.

The annual 'football match' has no rules, apart from forbidding actual murder and manslaughter. The goals are three miles apart, so three-league boots are required for kicking the ball. It's Uppards versus Downards, the number of players unlimited. Derby used to stage the game, but in early Victorian times it was branded as savage and banned. This civilising influence did not, however, spread to Ashbourne.

Phil stopped the car near the market place, dug into the glove box, and drew out a map of the Ashbourne area.

'What are you doing?' Freddy enquired.

'Just …working out where the goals are.' Phil was absorbed in his task.

'Why, are you coming to watch?' I asked.

'No, to play.'

Freddy and I exchanged glances. 'Come again?'

'To play in the game.'

'What!' Freddy, shocked, looked at me. 'You can't do that! It's rugger players, young farmers, jack the lads. You'll be a geriatric in a full-scale riot! The chances of survival at your age are nil. You have to be joking.'

'Not really,' Phil said airily. 'I'm probably as fit as most of them.'

'Fit is not the word! Your bones, your physical strength, won't be a patch on theirs. They'll shred you and tear you apart! Not only that, we'd lose our navigator – not that I'm bothered.'

'I do fifty sit-ups and a hundred press-ups a day, not to mention my six-mile run.' Phil smiled. 'It's amazing that I never thought about doing this. I used to play scrum-half. No problem.'

Freddy called me at home later. 'The lunatic. I talked to Ruth. She says he's bandaging his hands like a boxer and he's got a body belt to keep his kidneys in. Least we can do is pick up the pieces.'

The next day was cold and damp. The crowds waited in Shaw Croft, a car park in the centre of the town. The leather and cork ball was 'turned up' (tossed) at the crowd. It disappeared into a heaving mass of testosterone. The ball took twenty minutes to travel a hundred yards. A mob, made up of young farmers, amateur rugby players and lads out for a lark, filled the entire width of the street from the Green Man pub to the shops opposite.

Phil danced around the periphery, eager to get his hands on the ball. Dressed in tracksuit, bobble hat and gloves, he tried to judge the moment when one mass would gain an advantage over the other. Suicidally, he intended to stand in the path of the emergent team.

Nothing moved. The two packs were at an impasse, almost still, like tug-of-war teams with equal power. Then, unexpectedly, like toothpaste from a tube, the ball popped up. One arm struck it, then another. It bounced off somebody's head, another arm made contact and the ball looped straight into Phil's arms.

Phil recovered enough to be driven home, a bag of frozen peas clutched to his forehead, the part of his body that had taken the biggest blow from the mauling pack that hit him. He maintained that he hadn't been knocked out, merely dazed. We sympathised but didn't tell him what would have been the biggest blow of all – as he lay on the ground a St John's Ambulance volunteer had called over a colleague: 'There's an old gentleman here, somehow got caught up in the game.'

Freddy, on retiring, had hoped to grow a beard and wear unconventional clothes, no longer branding himself as a company man. Anything would do. He wanted to be amused by the effect it had on people. His dislike of commercialism in music and the arts, and his refusal to see popular films, gave him the image of a loner ploughing his single furrow in a world that bewildered him, but one he wanted to understand. Like ET.

On his journey home on the day of his retirement, Freddy had listened to his namesake Freddy Mercury sing 'I want to break free.' He applauded the sentiment. He had stopped at a wholesale surplus store and picked up a tweedy Sherlock Holmes hat with drop-down flaps. He tried to tuck it away for 'future use' but Jean had smelt it out. It went the next day, whisked off to the church jumble sale.

'Frederick, no. But no. You look ridiculous.'

Freddy couldn't tell her that had been the intention. He had to proceed carefully. He tried growing a beard but this fell at the first fence, or rather at the first sign of stubble. 'You have to stand closer to the blade,' said Jean, and bought a four-bladed electric razor guaranteed to take the hairs off a pig.

The third assault on convention was not yet a practical idea. The plan was to confuse the people he felt needed confusing, like his Porsche-owning neighbour. We sat in the Red Lion drinking Marston's Pedigree and munching crisps while Freddy tried to explain the importance of being able to go 'one down' socially in the midst of 'one up' people who believed he was really one of them. I pressed him for clarification.

'People have cars on their drives to show status. I'm the exception. I want to put a car on my drive that shows lack of status. It bewilders them. That's what's funny. They think I'm crazy – more fool them.' Ironically, it was an ill wind, literally, that had injected a high-octane dose of inspiration. If Phil hadn't forced him on that hike last month he would not have met Graham. He now knew what he must do: buy a Trabant and stick it on his drive – adjacent to next door's gleaming Porsche.

The sticking point was Jean. He approached the matter as a logical proposition, stressing the economy of fuel and cheap servicing. Anyway, she had her Polo, so why should she complain?

'Think what the neighbours would say. *Think*, Frederick!' Jean said.

He was unable to confess that this was the whole point.

'If it came loaded with gold-plated extras it wouldn't make any difference. That car comes on my driveway over my dead body.'

Freddy now had a name for his life-game, onedownmanship, the converse of the oneupmanship fad of his youth. He didn't engage in life-games just for fun. There was a deeper motive. By stepping outside popular thinking and behaviour, he believed he would increase his chances of making a breakthrough in his search for the 'meaning' – of life.

'Everybody's brainwashed,' he would claim. 'Television does it constantly. And look at the tabloids – one headline and the government's out. You have to stand outside to see through it all.'

He found little to inspire or assist him, so he pottered and gardened, and dropped in at the library just in case anything might have turned up by way of illuminating the 'meaning'. He had always appreciated Wordsworth, but was unhappy with his idea that all man needed to know was to be found in 'one impulse from a vernal wood'. It sounded too simplistic. Too romantic.

It was time to move on, but to what?

The next hike started at Middleton Top, the crest of one of the steep inclines on the old Cromford and High Peak Railway, now a footpath. Marked by a tapering brick chimney-stack, it is a reminder of the great age of steam. At its base is the old winding-engine which drove the black cables guiding the locomotives up and down hill. Next to it is a tourist shop, cycle hire point and car park. The railway was designed to connect the Cromford Canal and the Peak Forest Canal at Whaley Bridge across the 1,000-foot-high plateau. It is a masterpiece of post-Regency engineering, defying gravity.

Leaving the car park for the mile-long descent to the canal, Phil put his head forward in the dogged manner he adopts for his most apocalyptic announcements. 'Do you two know how much time we're losing? I mean losing. It's not a matter of wasting it, or dissipating it, but *losing* it.'

'Come on then.' Freddy stopped laughing. 'Prove it.'

'Right. Well, I couldn't understand why time seemed to go faster and faster. Then I read an article about the perception of time – which is entirely subjective. We don't see it or feel it – we just experience it. The brain chemical which gives a sense of time is called dopamine. The older you get the less dopamine you have and so life goes much quicker.'

'You've managed to get some? From Strangebugger?'

'Not available. Look, you are in a coma for a year. You come out of it. Time has stood still – for *you* as an individual and you've lost a year. It's the same thing with dopamine. If you only have three-quarters of what a child has then you'll experience nine months of living instead of a whole year. Why do old folks say "time flashes by"? Because it does – for them! It's to do with memory posts sticking up in your time line of memory. A child has new experiences all the time, so a day takes for ever. There are loads of memory posts. For us, hardly any.'

Freddy nodded. 'Let me think, what did Wordsworth say? "We'll talk of sunshine and of song and summer days, when we were young, sweet childish days, that were as long as twenty days are now."'

Phil seized on it. 'Brilliant. Fantastic. I never thought we'd sing from the same hymn sheet.'

'It was Einstein's Theory of Relativity,' Freddy said. 'He started it. You left earth for a year and when you came back it was two hundred years later and you hadn't put out a note for the milkman.'

'Oh God,' said Phil – just when he had thought Freddy was on board.

Freddy chuckled. 'What do we do, build a time machine?'

'Hell's blood,' snapped Phil. 'Do you realise that within fifty years our grandchildren will be given the option to live indefinitely? While you've been chasing impossible things like the meaning of life I've been researching practical things, more about life than you'll ever find out. We're going to be the second-to-last generation which won't get the option of hanging around. You know what ageing is? It's rusting, literally. Oxidisation – that's why we have antioxidants, red wine, broccoli, carrots, cranberries.'

Freddy grinned, 'Here lies Gruppenführer Stevens. RIP. *Rust-in-Peace.*'

I laughed. Phil's lips flickered but he tightened them against a smile. 'I've spent years racing about hilltops trying to squeeze out a few more years, and what happens? We're going to get blokes on welfare benefits who clog their arteries with junk food and smoke and drink like troopers and whose sole idea of exercise is getting up from the sofa to grab a bacon buttie – and all of them living longer than me! What kind of a deal is that?'

'But who in their right mind wants to live indefinitely?'

'Oh, well …' Phil gave up and waved his stick at Freddy's stupidity.

Freddy grinned at me behind Phil's back. 'The worst the Devil could give me is an eternity of hiking with you, Stevens. Stop running around, and make the best of it while you're here.'

'Typical,' Phil said. 'Typical. You, Freddy, spent a lifetime in the sulphur mines. What have you got left? I've worked out that you're losing a third of your retirement through lack of dopamine. You should be doing something with me.'

'Like what?' asked Freddy.

'When you go on a two-week holiday which week goes slowest? The first one, yes?'

We mumbled our agreement, at which Phil rammed his newly acquired, hi-tech spring-loaded hiking stick into the ground, sending a stone whizzing up around our ears. 'Now, the first week is full of fresh experiences – memory posts – so time goes more slowly or seems longer. In the second week you're used to the place and just repeating the first week's experiences, so time goes faster. At our age it's difficult to find new experiences so time speeds up *all* the time. Yes? Come on, am I right?'

'And the cure?'

'We go camping'.

Freddy paused. 'Camping.'

'Yes. New experiences. Stretching time.'

'Pain.'

'Not this type of camping.'

Freddy spoke slowly and deliberately. 'Stevens, I do not camp. The last time I went camping I fell into a bed of nettles. I woke up cold and damp. And I spent all night worrying that some nutter was going to come through the flap at me with an axe.'

'Freddy,' Phil spoke equally slowly, enunciating with heavy patience. 'These hills are distinguished by their lack of axe-wielding, marauding and homicidal nutters. We are not in the North American mountains, there are no mad hillbillies in Dove Dale.'

'Anyway, camping's for kids. What would I get out it? I know you, Gruppenführer, suffering of some sort is involved.'

'It is not!' Phil exclaimed. 'It would be wonderful. We'd hike all day over new ground, find a forest in the evening, drink beer around the camp fire, have a great meal. For breakfast we'd have sausages, eggs and bacon, and then another hike before we go home. The two days would be equal to three in our experience of it. I am adding an extra day to your life. You'd be crazy to turn it down.'

I had to admit that Phil's image of sitting around a fire smelling the scent of wood smoke and listening to the rustle of trees appealed to my imagination.

Freddy, however, shook his head slowly. 'Gruppenführer, whatever you say, I know that I will either die or experience hours of misery. I don't want to have an extra day if that's what it brings. And there are the logistics to consider,' he said. 'I don't think any of us could carry a three-man tent plus everything else we'd need. Even if we could, there's no way I'm getting into bed with you two.'

'We don't need a three-man tent. We'll carry a two-man and a single. You can carry the single.' Seeing Freddy's reluctance, he played his trump card. 'OK, this is what we do. I'll carry all the equipment, the food and the two-man tent, which you two can sleep in. How's that?'

'And where do you sleep?' asked Freddy, suspiciously. 'Under a tree?'

'No, I'll bivouac – as per army standard.'

Freddy paused. And then, curiously because it was entirely unexpected, he agreed. 'Okay, I'll do it if I can decide which day we go camping.'

Phil stared at Freddy. This was too good to be true. He had resigned himself to another backdoor assault via Jean. In celebration Phil ran down the remaining hundred yards of the gradient.

At the bottom of the incline stood a pair of preserved railway wagons that used to be hauled up and down the hills. We passed them to join Phil on the canal towpath and walked towards the High Peak junction of canal and railway, now a museum site at Cromford a mile away. Freddy asked Phil about his proposed bivouac.

'You just cut down some branches to make poles and lash the poles to form 'A' frames. Other poles connect them, and the bed is made of interleafed twigs, branches and leaves. It's dead easy.'

'Takes a long time, I would have thought?' Freddy seemed genuinely interested.

'An hour, maybe less.' Phil was pleased that Freddy had showed a change of heart. It boded well for his future plans.

Freddy said he would not decide which day to go camping more than a day ahead. The weather would dictate his choice. Phil never bothers about weather forecasts, which suited Freddy. A few days later, around lunchtime, he phoned me. He said that the Met Office had given him – at a small cost – a detailed forecast for the northern Peak over the next thirty-six hours. It was acceptable, and Phil had agreed to go. 'The Gruppenführer has called a briefing tonight in his garden. He's going to teach us how to trap and skin bears.'

I checked the Met Office website. The forecast for the next day promised a fine morning and afternoon but heavy rainfall across the entire Pennine range by early evening, just about the time we would set up camp. I thought this odd and called Freddy. He rubbished it. 'I have a personal forecast, precise. Don't worry, you won't get wet. We'll be in a tent, remember.'

When we arrived at Phil's house he had the two-man tent pegged out on his lawn. He pointed out, amongst the tent's various gadgets, the inner fabric fluorocarbon (to get rid of condensation drips), the ripstop fully-taped fly (to keep out Freddy's axeman) and the bum-warmer type of thermal insulation on the ground sheet. A far cry from the tents of our childhood. Then he switched to military mode.

'The route. We jump off from Edale, here' – he pointed his stick at the map on the patio table –'about eleven hundred, go up Grinds Brook, here, then straight on to the Snake Pass, where we bivvy for the night. Any questions?'

'We cross Kinder Scout? In March?' Freddy's tone was incredulous.

'It's only a few miles,' Phil said.

'Of no man's land, of enormous ditches, up and down, up and down. At that height? We could have a blizzard. You can die up there if you're lost. Look at those guys who froze to death, half a mile from the Snake Pass!'

For once Freddy was scarcely exaggerating. Kinder Scout is a moorland plateau, four square miles of lacerated peat bog which, at over 2,000 feet, towers over the western sprawl of the Manchester conurbation and Sheffield to the east. It has few landmarks and can cause a novice hiker to walk round in circles – even on a clear day. It is not a hike for the fainthearted.

Phil said he had hoped to cross the moor to the fir forest on the northern side, ideal for camping. 'My cousin in Canada's asked me over. I hoped to get some practice avoiding black bears when I go hiking there.'

'Black bears?' Freddy shook his head. 'What are you on about?'

Phil spoke stiffly: 'Black bears pinch grub from tents. You have to hang it on trees.'

Freddy's eyes narrowed, his anti-con laser penetrating Phil's skull. And then he broke into a grin. 'You devious sod. You going to Canada? That is code for *we* go to Canada.' He looked at me. 'You've noticed how he slips a project into your subconscious? Then resurrects the idea later on and you're partly conditioned to it?'

'All right.' Phil was abrupt, hurt but dignified, and spoke rapidly. 'I was going to invite you to Canada, some of it at my expense, but it doesn't matter. We can stick to doing easy hikes round here, as your tired old legs demand.'

The next morning we gathered at Freddy's to pack the camping gear into the Polo, after which Freddy went back into the house and returned with Montague, their dog. 'You're not bringing that animal?' Phil looked shocked.

'The kennels are full. Jean's gone to see her sister. He's got to come.' Montague hopped inside the car to settle next to my right leg. He stared up at me and growled softly. Freddy saw my look of trepidation. 'Oh, he'll be no trouble, he likes walks.'

'But does he like hikes?' I asked.

'Don't worry. He smells a bit inside the car but in the tent we'll have a ripstop nylon auto anti-smell tape between us, won't we.' Freddy smiled at Phil. 'You'll be fine, on your own, in your bivvy.' There was a pause. 'Seen the weather forecast?' he asked, casually.

It was at this point that I began to harbour a suspicion – it was the way that Freddy had spoken. He had asked the question so casually – and glanced at Phil with a smile so sly – that I felt it was a precursor to some kind of wheeze. But Phil was so busy packing away his rucksack that he noticed nothing out of the ordinary. In response to Freddy's question about the weather forecast he merely said, 'No, what is it?'

'Bit of rain. Nothing much. Got your axe?'

We headed north, bound for Edale village. From there we would climb up Kinder Scout. In 1932, this was the preserve of a grouse-shooting few, but five hundred ramblers, organised by the

Communist Party, took part in a so-called invasion. In fact only forty of them broke away from the main party and invaded the summit, but this action, known as the Great Trespass, became part of folklore. One or two of the ring-leaders were imprisoned, which made good propaganda for the Communists, but the National Parks and Access to the Countryside Act, passed in 1949, was largely the culmination of the work of apolitical bodies such as the Ramblers' Association.

We pulled up in the car park below Edale station and set off, Montague at our heels. Phil was almost invisible under a mountainous rucksack, attached to which were the tent, kettle, mugs, portable barbecue and frying pan, clanking as he walked.

Edale is a neat village, with suburban touches, and part of the walk through the village reminded me of Solihull, hardly warning of the wilderness just beyond. We came to the Olde Nag's Head pub, the last reminder of civilisation. 'Gruppenführer,' said Freddy, 'why don't we –'

'No.' Phil cut off Freddy's attempt to subvert his macho plan. He wasn't going to waste time in a pub when a physical challenge was only minutes away.

'Aren't we supposed to be enjoying this?' Freddy asked.

'Not in a pub, no,' Phil said.

Freddy muttered something under his breath and tugged hard at the lead as Montague lunged towards a rabbit. We walked through a tree-lined dingle and then over a low wooden foot-bridge into open grassland. The gritstone southern edge of Kinder Scout glistened in the sun, high in the northern sky. Just below the summit was a ravine, littered with rocks of different sizes, as if jolly giants had collected all the boulders they could find, bowled half of them downhill and scattered the rest around in frenzied abandon. A prominent sign on a wooden post told Freddy that it was lambing time and that all dogs must be kept on a lead. 'That means you, Montague, so don't pull,' ordered Freddy.

'Wilderness is happiness,' said Phil, gazing up at his Everest.

'Happiness is a pint in the pub and a warm fire,' Freddy riposted.

We plodded upwards, following the brook which drains the peat moor. Phil called the coffee stop on the hour. Out came the flasks and snacks. We sat amidst huge boulders, gazing upwards at the Devil's Ravine. On a dark day, when the water drops between the sheer rock faces, its name fits.

All around were exotically carved tors, remnants of rock which have been exposed over millions of years to wind, frost and rain, shaping an array of weird and wonderful sculptures. They appear not just on Kinder but all over the Dark Peak. At Phil's briefing session he had showed us a book of Dark Peak photographs, some of them exhibits carved by nature in this massive outdoor art exhibition.

Freddy said he liked them. 'A damn sight better than anything in the Saatchi Gallery,' he commented, adding, 'When is a joke not a joke? When it wins the Turner prize.'

It was a slow haul into the ravine. On the last stretch the climb was near vertical in places. Freddy looked down at the space beneath him. 'Oh Lord, help us never, ever to go anywhere with Stevens again.' Phil put down a hand to drag him up and over a boulder. Freddy puffed and groaned with the effort. 'Of course, this is what it's all about – pain. It's not you who's mad, it's me for letting myself in for it!'

We scrambled the last few feet to stand on the southern edge of Kinder Scout, looking back over the acres of sky, thirty miles, forty? Freddy gulped down half a bottle of Ashbourne Water in relief. 'It's going to rain,' he pointed to a ridge of dark cloud in the far west. 'But you'll be all right, snug in your bivvy.' Again the light tone and the mischievous look – at Phil's back.

We turned inwards to look over the moor. The wind blew keen and cold across the landscape. A first glance showed it as forbidding and desolate, a desert of peat bog. A maze of miniature ravines and gullies (groughs, as they are known locally) stretched out as far as the eye could see, the first sight of which would have astonished those invading ramblers three-quarters of a century ago.

This is the Lost World. You could be on the moon. People live on Exmoor and Dartmoor, but no one lives here. The moor can't be crossed in any straight line without dropping into, and climbing out of, these deep gullies, some up to eight feet deep and spaced only yards apart. Today we were walking around the edge of the plateau, a fairly easy journey.

'If only,' Phil said longingly, looking over the groughs.

'If only you were mad enough – which you are,' Freddy was in good spirits. He took a slim book from his rucksack, opened it and began to study. Phil looked over his shoulder. It was a wild flower guide, opened at the chapter dealing with moorland.

'Didn't know you were a botanist,' Phil said.

'You see, Gruppenführer, how much you miss with your manic obsessions?'

Every fifty yards or so Freddy would kneel down to take a close look at a plant, cross-checking with his book. He claimed to detect the presence of sphagnum moss and then, later, cotton grass and evergreen crowberry. He said we might be lucky and find Arctic cloudberry, rarely found below 2,000 feet. And was that bilberry? Phil puffed out his cheeks and tapped his stick impatiently on the ground. Then he cocked his head back and peered accusingly at Freddy. 'Are you up to something?' His tone became threatening. 'Freddy?'

'What? No. Why?'

'Are you trying to delay us so we can't pitch the tent in the dark and have to go home?'

'Gruppenführer, would I do that?'

'Yes.'

'I give you my solemn word we shall camp. Anyway, you've brought that thousand-watt storm lamp. You could build the Pyramids under that.'

'Hmm,' Phil looked dubious.

The westerly wind increased and over the next hour we trudged from landmark to landmark, finally arriving at the Pagoda, rocks that rise up to form a multi-storey tapering tower. We turned towards the apron of the great stage, overlooking the world, a Wagnerian setting in which black cloud gradually swallowed thin strips of red, purple, yellow and gold.

Freddy raised his arms. 'Can you hear that massed choir? The Horst Wessel? Götterdämmerung? Mein Führer, speak to your stormtroopers!'

Phil gave it a quick nod. 'Right, quick lunch. We're behind schedule. It's your fault, Freddy, with that book.'

The rain-bearing cumulus occupied more of the sky as we walked down Jacob's Ladder, a track laid with stone, on the south-west of Kinder. Jacob, who gave his name to the track, had been a jagger man, a carrier of goods using a team of pack horses, transporting mainly salt and wood between Cheshire and Yorkshire. I couldn't imagine a tougher job than walking up and down Kinder day after day in all weathers.

Freddy seemed to enjoy himself on the easy descent. The threat of rain, normally the cue for a whinge, was ignored. Further down the valley we came across a hiker's shelter, a simple hut with leaflets inside provided by the National Trust. We glanced briefly inside, but no one was there.

We broke back into Edale, from where we would set off for the camp site. Outside the pub a number of hikers, pints in hand, joked and babbled happily. Phil was anxious to push on; his axe had an appointment to keep with a tree. While he fed and watered Montague Freddy admitted he was puzzled. 'If you take your axe to a branch around here you'll be arrested for transgressing a tree preservation order. So where are we camping?'

'If we could get on,' Phil said, 'I could show you.'

Just beyond the church was the National Park Centre and,

beside it, an official camp site. It announced an entry fee of four pounds per person per night. 'Black bears not welcome,' Phil said.

'They wouldn't go in at four pounds a night,' Freddy chuckled and then broke into a belly laugh. Neither Phil nor I had seen him this good- humoured on a hike before.

We expected Phil to turn in through the gate to the campsite but no, he continued down the road towards the car park. 'Well,' he said, 'if you two backsliders had been up to it we'd have crossed Kinder and camped in the forest. Round here there's no forest. I've got permission to camp near a wood, but we've got to drive to get there.'

An hour later we had erected the two-man tent in a small meadow on the edge of a wood near the village of Hayfield, due west of Kinder Scout. And with the permission of the farmer, Phil had managed to gain access to a clump of trees he could hack about a bit.

Freddy and I sat in the outer tent, the flap open so that we could keep watch on the barbecue, sipping Boddingtons bitter. Three porterhouse steaks sizzled, crammed side by side on the small barbecue range, sending out drifts of savoury smoke over the darkening meadow. And the first spot of forecast rain had struck the tent. What was more, to Freddy's obvious delight, Phil was about to start constructing his bivouac.

The rain had started to pitter-patter on the soft roof. Freddy kept watch on the industrious Phil. 'Just wait,' Freddy whispered. 'Bang on cue. I love those weather ladies.' He then confessed, at my prompting, that he had pretended to search for wild flowers on Kinder just to delay the hike so that Phil's bivvy would not be up in time for him to shelter. The plot hadn't required exact timing for the rain to fall. If it fell later in the night Phil's bivouac would not be sufficiently waterproof, made as it would be out of local leaves and branches. There was a hope – a slight one and Freddy looked up at the sky as he said it – that if it rained heavily now it could bring unexpected joy. Freddy looked at Phil fiddling with what looked like light alloy poles taken from his rucksack. 'We might get lucky and it won't be up in time. Then he'll want to go home.' Freddy sank the remainder of his beer. 'I'd even give up the steak – oh the joy.'

By the light of a storm torch Phil emptied his rucksack of the remaining poles. Within two minutes they formed two 'A' frames which he set in the ground two metres apart. Then he produced a string hammock. Two poles ran through holes in the hammock and rested on the cross-pieces in the 'A' frames. He then took out a roll of polythene and spread it across the two 'A' frames born by the weight of a ridge pole. The whole bivvy was up in a few minutes.

Freddy's mouth was open, speechless. As Phil tied twine around the end bits to keep the cover from blowing away, Freddy managed to find his voice. 'Stevens, what do you think you're doing?'

Phil looked at him in all innocence. 'What do you think I'm doing, making my bed, aren't I?'

'But that's cheating. You said you were going to lop off branches! You were going to cover it in leaves and things!'

Phil secured his home-made tent. 'Didn't you know that the first rule in the army is: "Don't make life harder for yourself than you have to."' He dived under the polythene and climbed into his hammock. 'Ah yes,' he said, listening to the rain. 'This will do very nicely. Most comfortable. Not a bad design, this thing, eh?'

He slipped out of the hammock and stared at the barbecue. 'Hmm, can't wait. Now then,' he said, checking the contents of the grub bag. 'We've got the mustard, good. Now let's crack open some more Boddingtons.'

Freddy sat still and dumb – an onlooker at the feast. He said he didn't feel hungry, but he recovered from his disappointment and cheered up when the steaks came into the porch. All three of us sitting there was a rather crowded affair, but we managed to do the steaks justice as Phil lectured us on the arts of camping in bear country. 'It's all about keeping dry, warm and comfortable,' he said. 'Not letting things delay you too much. Getting on with the job.' He shot a knowing grin at Freddy.

Later Freddy, earpiece in, tried to listen to Bach's Goldberg Variations on CD, but the battery failed. Phil took a sleeping tablet. 'A Dr Strangebugger offering,' he announced. 'Quite harmless. Good for getting off to sleep in a strange bed.' And with that he went to his hammock. 'Night, fellers,' he said. 'Sleep well.'

'Look at the time,' said Freddy mournfully, staring at a thick wet hawthorn hedge. 'God, it's only nine o'clock.' We looked at each other. There was nothing much left to do except listen to the rain. Freddy said, 'I think I'll clean my teeth.' I said I thought I would, too. We shared the sole remaining plastic bottle of water.

Freddy wrapped Montague in a blanket and settled him in the outer tent, then zipped down the flap and crept into his sleeping bag. We waited for sleep. Five minutes passed. A gurgling sound came from the direction of Phil's bivouac. The gurgle became a wheeze, followed by a sharp intake of breath. Then another heavy gurgle, wheeze and a repetition of the whole process.

I had reached that moment of semi-consciousness prior to oblivion when Freddy spoke. 'There's a lump right under my back.' I shuffled my bag to the extremity of the tent. It wasn't enough.

'Bugger,' he said. 'The lump's sticking in my side now. We'll have to move the tent.'

Reluctantly I squeezed out of my sleeping bag, and grabbed an anorak. In the darkness and heavy rain we performed the fastest tent relocation in history, pulling up the stays and guys, and shifting the fly sheet and canopy to where the ground was flatter, all to the accompaniment of Phil's wheezes and snuffles.

The tent back up, Freddy settled Montague again while I took off my anorak and got back into bed. Freddy was about to crawl back into his own sleeping bag when he realised that the fly sheet was wet. 'Oh hell,' he said. He sat up, grabbed his towel and wiped it down.

Ten minutes later peace had returned and both of us lay silently trying to emulate Phil's achievement of sleep.

An owl hooted. 'Oh my God,' said Freddy.

There was a pause before Phil started up again – an orchestration of wheezes, sighs, whistles and snores, getting louder and louder …

'Bugger,' said Freddy, fiercely. 'Bugger, bugger, bugger.'

The owl stopped hooting. Phil's refrain ceased. Painfully I waited for the next symphonic movement. It didn't come. Fifteen minutes passed by. Tension ebbed until I was, by kind permission of Morpheus, Phil and the owl, half asleep.

A low whine emerged from Montague. It stopped, then started again, and didn't stop. 'Oh hell,' said Freddy. He shushed Montague. The whine increased in intensity and decibel level. 'Sod it.' Enraged, Freddy clambered out of the tent clutching his anorak and pulled Montague on a march around the field, hoping the problem might be a matter of canine toilet. It was still raining.

Freddy returned, dumped Montague, crawled back into his sleeping bag. and zipped down the flap. 'Remind me never, ever, to go camping again.'

I became aware that the night had ended. A pale light filtered through the orange roof. I turned over and looked at Freddy, who was awake, grey-faced and expressionless. There was no sound of rain.

Phil was outside, whistling tunelessly. We could smell coffee. Freddy crawled out of his sleeping bag and opened the flap, to be greeted by a lick from Montague. He unzipped the outer door flap and peered up at Phil crouching by the stove, stirring the pot. Dressed in his red beret and khaki shirt, he looked dry, clean and freshly shaved.

'Morning,' Phil said brightly. 'Had a good night?'

After breakfast we took a vote. By a majority of two to one the hike was curtailed. We drove home in silence.

Just before we reached Phil's house our leader spoke. 'Sorry about my snoring, fellers.' But, he asked, had the experience at least been a success in terms of stretching time? Freddy nodded. It had been more than a success, he said. Last night, time had not only stretched but had gone on stretching and stretching until it could stretch no more. Then it had stood – perfectly and resolutely, interminably and quite horribly – still.

4

APRIL

'April is the cruellest month,' wrote T.S. Eliot. He was correct as far as Freddy was concerned. For Phil last month's camping experience had been a wonderful piece of time-stretching, indelibly etched in his memory – and, unfortunately, ours. But whereas we had no desire to repeat it, Phil couldn't wait. Freddy stated that he wouldn't be seen dead near the place. 'I'd rather be back in the sulphur mines.'

'We won't camp. We'll just go up Kinder again,' pleaded Phil.

'Stevens, your death wish I support, but do it on your own.'

We were en route for a ten-miler starting at Hartington village, which nestles in a valley a mile below the Ashbourne-to-Buxton road. It has a large market place, with a duck-pond, a seventeenth-century hotel named after the poet Charles Cotton, and an Olde Cheese Shoppe – or at least that was how it was spelt until somebody realised that the Miss Marples tea-with-vicar, chintzy, thatch-roofed softy-southern village image it evoked was out of keeping with the reality of a hill-farming community.

We sat on a bench by the pond for lunch, surrounded by ducks. They were canny, enquiring, never overtly begging but ready to dive towards us at the first sign of a crumb. Freddy dropped them a small piece of Derbyshire fruit loaf.

A coach drew up and out trooped a party of thirty- to fifty-year-old men and women, dressed for a works outing, some men in suits and ties, some women in hats. They drifted towards the cheese shop, when one man detached himself and wandered over towards us. He swayed slightly in the breeze.

'How's you goin', then, lads?' He wore a white cap like a cricket umpire. His nose was bigger than his chin and he carried a teddy bear. This he waved at us with a chuckle. 'Won it in raffle, Waysgooze Dinner. Now, you don't know what waysgooze means, do you?'

We had to admit our ignorance. He laughed. 'Annual printers "do", Bulcroft printers. Now, where's Bulcroft?'

Before he could answer his own question he was hauled off by two mates en route to the cheese shop. Freddy was amused. 'Cheese and wine party or a wine followed by cheese party?'

Phil, dressed in a blue tracksuit bottom and white T-shirt, faced the site of his new garden rockery, between the fish pond and the shed which contained all the garden furniture. A large pile of rocks waited to be relocated to an area of banked soil.

He began his pre-rock-lifting exercises. First came the leg stretches and the waist bends, then he took particular care over his groin stretches. After five minutes of this he took off his watch and laid it with care on a low garden wall, noting the time. He turned to confront a fifty-kilo rock, spat on his hands, squatted, put both hands under the rock, took an inward breath and, with biceps and quadriceps bulging – rectus femoris, vastus lateralis (he knew all the names and how they functioned) – lifted the boulder to his chest, staggered with it to its intended location and dumped it.

Both arms went up in a victory salute. Later he checked the time by his watch. 'Hell's teeth.' Twenty minutes had gone by, when he'd only guessed fifteen. He took a small paper pad from his pocket and noted the discrepancy. This was part of his on-going investigation into lost time. After his statistical analysis, he would go on to objective tests.

His mobile rang – it was Dr Strangebugger with bad news. The price of dehyroepiandrosterone, DHEA for short, was to double next week. Phil should place a bulk replacement order now. Phil didn't hesitate. He had learnt that this mother of all hormones (including testosterone) might be essential in avoiding Alzheimer's disease and remaining physically strong. Women had HRT, so why not men? The hormone level in males drops dramatically in old age. Phil told the good doctor that he thought the benefits had started to kick in – hence the macho rock-lifting. He only wished he'd taken it well in advance of the Shrovetide game.

An hour later Phil lifted his fiftieth rock of the evening and turned round – to face Freddy, who had come up the drive unannounced. 'Building your own Kinder, I see,' he observed. 'Good idea, because you're not going up the full-scale version again.'

'Freddy, we'll only cross half of it.'

'No way.'

'Oh,' Phil sighed in a reluctant, conciliatory mood. 'All right, you can decide on the next five hikes. All of them with as much downhill as you can find, but first just one more Kinder.'

Freddy's laser probed. 'Five? As much downhill as I want?'

'Yes, absolutely!'

Another pause from Freddy. 'On these conditions: no camping, no rain, we stop when I want to stop and we have a pint in the Olde Nag's Head at the end.'

'Done.'

'Oh, and one more thing. No racing up Grinds Brook.'

'Copy that,' Phil said, using unofficial air-traffic-control jargon. 'You've got it.'

That settled, Phil targeted the heaviest rock of the day. With his buzzing new hormones and adrenalin going round like suds in a washing-machine, he hauled it to his chest, jiggled his feet towards its drop-point, let go and punched the air. He went in to celebrate and drank a pint of filtered tap water, followed by a glass of red Merlot – for its antioxidant effect, of course.

A Kinder hike meant an early start. At eight-thirty I picked up Phil and then Freddy. He got in the car excitedly. 'I've found it,' he said. 'Got it at last.'

'Got what?' Phil asked.

'The "meaning" – well, most of it.'

We were underwhelmed. Freddy had tried most of the 'ways to enlightenment' and found them lacking. He started in 1964 when we had both studied transcendental meditation for two hours each week. The word-hum the Maharishi disciples had given him as a secret mantra had no effect, perhaps because he had no hat-stand at home. No, they had said, humming at a hat-stand at home wasn't necessary. He could do it sitting in a comfy armchair. It was supposed to work by allowing a thought – any kind of thought – to slip into the mind, then gradually allowing the mantra to take precedence and finally replace the thought. This, according to the young disciples of the Maharishi, led the mind into a higher state of being.

The problem with transcendental meditation was that Freddy had preferred the intrusive thought to the hum. Ten years later, when he was still attempting TM, the image of his next-door neighbour's wife, a soft, buxom Marilyn Monroe look-alike, started taking over from the hum. As he had been instructed never to forcibly eject any thought or image it remained with him, leading to a lower, rather than a higher state of being. It became so distracting that he gave TM the boot.

We drove past the cluster of antique shops in Ashbourne. 'Now,' Freddy gave us the good news. 'I found a book on philosophy – here, would you believe.' He indicated the open market on our left: assorted stalls full of books, fruit and vegetables, collectable post-cards, clothing, kitchenware, antique brass work and flowers. 'I've never read any philosophy before,' Freddy said. 'I was put off by Bertrand Russell twittering away on TV. Have you heard of Kant?'

'Yeah,' said Phil. 'Cant and hypocrisy,' and he gave a vibrato chuckle.

Freddy ignored him. 'Kant says all philosophers want to know the meaning of life, why we're here, in what space and what time. I've been reading Wordsworth when I should have been reading philosophy!' Phil's head had swivelled round, a reflex action triggered by the mention of the word 'time'.

Freddy continued: 'Kant says we can't fully understand the "meaning" because if we knew it we'd stop asking questions. But man needs to ask questions, especially "what is reality?" However – this is the catch-22 – we can't find reality through reason because reasoning itself can never end, and we can't go on reasoning once we have the answer. Now, he does say quite a bit about time. He says –'

'Time!' Phil exploded, the wrinkles on his forehead lifting in excitement. 'I told you! I knew it! It's time that's important! What does he say about it? This is good stuff, go on Freddy!'

'He says that time must have had a beginning, else it can't be time. That's logic.'

'Freddy, you don't have to read philosophy to know that!'

'But then he says, being time, it can't have started because it must have always been going. It's a continuous conveyor-belt. That's also logic.'

'Hang on,' Phil tried to get his head round it. 'He's saying time has a beginning, then it hasn't. He's right about the conveyor-belt – we're on the end of it about to drop off.' Phil waved a hand in dismissal. 'I bet he says the same about space, it must have limits but, being space, it must also go on for ever and ever.'

'Gruppenführer, you have more up top than I gave you credit you for.'

'So why are you excited?' Phil asked. 'Where's the "meaning" in all this?'

'Well,' Freddy was re-energised. 'The fact that there is *no* point is the whole point! Kant says that all these contradictions prove that worrying about the "meaning" is unreasonable. We can't get to the bottom of it, ever. Life is meant to be lived and not enquired into! If we're to exist in the world we do it through our five senses, through experience.'

'Hah!' cried Phil. 'What did I tell you! Experience! Time-stretching! Time and the "meaning" are related! I've been telling you!' He was triumphant, vindicated by his greatest opponent in the time stakes, Freddy. 'That's why we're going over Kinder today. For a new experience, what time-stretching's all about! Kant is telling you that you need me!' Phil was ecstatic. 'Way-hey!' he whooped, then he calmed down. 'So the good news is also bad news, Freddy.'

'How do you mean?'

'The good news is you don't need to look for the "meaning", the bad news is there's no answer to it.'

Freddy frowned. 'Well, I suppose Wordsworth knew all along. He said there was "a tale in every thing. Let the heart, not reason, find an answer".' He spoke the words carefully and slowly, to give the words their full meaning: '"Thanks to the human heart by which we live, thanks to its tenderness, its joys and fears, to me the meanest flower that blows can give thoughts that do often lie too deep for tears."' Freddy fell into a contemplative mood and was subdued for the rest of the journey.

I'd heard him on the subject many times. He found it difficult to accept that the genius of creation couldn't be revealed in some form or other. Genius equals God, yes – but who created God? Why did God create man? Wouldn't He be happier without murderers, child molesters, terrorists and the like coined in His image? Freddy was convinced that the answer would lie in something simple, something he could visibly see, as the spiral-staircase shape of the helix had been demonstrated in the discovery of DNA.

You don't simply 'arrive' at the launch point for Kinder, Edale village. On leaving the Hope–Castleton main road you drive slowly over five miles of twisting country lane. For mile after mile Kinder makes no appearance. Getting there seems interminable. It's an experience – albeit in miniature – like that of mountaineers first having to trek through the foothills before reaching Everest.

When you reach Edale there is a real sense of leaving civilisation as soon as you step past the Olde Nag's Head and set foot on the Pennine Way. Depending on the weather forecast, doubts can – and do – creep in.

Forecasts for the Pennine range of hills – including the Peak District – are sometimes difficult to predict as high ground adjacent to low ground can result in changes in atmospheric pressure, air temperature and humidity, creating fog at one level and not another, precipitation on high ground and not below. Kinder Scout is situated in the middle of the Pennine spine. It can be a fair day in the Hope Valley and a wintry gale at 2,000 feet. You can pay the Met Office for an altitude forecast, including temperature, but I know of only one hiker who has bothered with it and that was Freddy, for his own nefarious purposes on our camping expedition. For others, especially 'extreme hikers' such as Phil, the unpredictability can be part of the fun.

We drove to the Olde Nag's Head and parked there. Phil whistled to himself as he put on his hiking boots. Freddy pulled on his overtrousers. He was happy, he said, with Kant. He'd only read a small part of the book and there might be a bigger picture to reveal. In this mood of acceptance he drank from his water bottle and moaned about the climb that was to come. If he allowed Phil to think he was happy about this hike he would be dragged back to Kinder every week.

Freddy had begun to expand his fantasy world. He told me he now saw himself as a resistance fighter in occupied country. Phil was the Gruppenführer in charge of that region and Freddy had to do all in his power to thwart him, which he did by posing as a collaborator. He would tell me these stories until my eyes watered. But his ruses didn't always work – his had been a classic case of 'the biter bit' as he tried to get Phil drenched on the last Kinder expedition.

We set off. Ahead lay the rocky stretch leading up to the high, dark ravine. After his experience of hypothermia Freddy had bought an anti-hypothermic vest but, being on principle against anything hi-tech, he got round this by describing the vest as 'functional'.

We were halfway up the climb when we spotted two young men leaping down the ravine towards us. As they bounded from rock to rock I was reminded of the flying Dovedale Dash runners, who pelt down the side of Thorpe Cloud each winter in a five- to six-mile race for the maddest and the fittest. These men flew down like consummate fell runners, with immediate visual recognition of what was – and was not – safe for feet to land on. As the men drew nearer we could see that they had shaven heads, wore maroon sweatshirts and soft boots, and carried small but heavy-looking rucksacks. They had square faces, wide jaws, big shoulders and thick necks. We blocked their bouncy drop through a narrow gully, which forced them to a stop.

After a brief greeting, Phil had them sussed. 'You army?'

They grinned at each other. 'How did you know that?'

Phil replied, 'I used to be in the Parachute Regiment. Second Battalion.'

'We're in 2 Para! When were you in?'

'Fifty-eight to sixty. National Service. Some sort of exercise, right?'

'Yeah, we're going up and down. This is our fifth time today.'

Freddy, hearing this, smiled wanly at the thought. 'You're going up and down here five times – *today*?' he said weakly.

'Oh yeah, we might even do six.' They were casual about it.

'Don't tell me,' said Phil. 'Let me guess. You're getting fit for a selection. Maybe on the Brecon Beacons?' He swelled with ego.

With a pat on Phil's back they were gone. We watched them fly downhill.

'They're training for SAS selection.' Phil looked upwards and bared his teeth.

'Don't,' said Freddy sternly. 'You are nearly sixty-five years old. You nearly died in the Shrovetide football game. Just be grateful you can still *get* up here, never mind run up.'

We resumed the climb, reaching Kinder top forty minutes later, and took off our rucksacks, sweating and in need of a breather.

Three women hikers sat on rocks twenty yards along our proposed footpath. They were all dressed alike, in high-visibility yellow singlets over dark blue Gortex jackets, and as added protection for their legs they wore light-blue neoprene gaiters. The uniform extended to their Berghaus rucksacks. Even their sandwich packs looked identical.

The youngest woman, around twenty-five, was staring rigidly at the ground between her feet, her body tensed, her face miserable. She had a small round face and long golden hair. In her hand was an uneaten sandwich. The two other women were older, one in her thirties and the other in her forties, the latter festooned with binoculars, a map-case, compass, hanging whistle, lapel torch and what looked suspiciously like a satellite navigational aid. Freddy and I exchanged knowing looks – here was a 'Mrs Gruppenführer'.

I glanced at Phil. He stood quite still, the breeze ruffling the grey hairs either side of his red beret, his eyes in zoom-shot, locked on to this vision of female leadership. She looked heroic, a Nordic queen, a little like the younger Vanessa Redgrave in her icy composure – her head held high, a few hard lines round her firm mouth, blonde hair tied in a ponytail, a tall and lithe figure that had been subjected to regular working-out.

Phil walked towards her with a jerky, robotic movement, oblivious of where his feet landed. He stumbled twice but recovered without taking his eyes off her face.

'Oh my bleeding heart,' whispered Freddy. 'Gruppenführer in love. What's he going to do, salute her or kiss her?'

Mrs Gruppenführer glanced sideways at the younger woman, whose chest heaved, her face wet. 'Penny!' she hissed. 'Buck up!'

Penny looked up and saw Phil. She wiped away a tear.

It is relatively easy in a crowded railway carriage to ignore someone crying, but it's exceptionally difficult when you're surrounded by miles of wilderness and they occupy the path you're taking. Our other difficulty lay in the fact that we were brought up to help ladies in distress. Phil stood in front of his dream-woman, his smile as silly as ever, hardly able to speak. 'Is she all right?' he croaked.

'Sorry – who? Oh, Penny! Yes, she's fine.'

Phil, mind-locked, eyes stuck, nodded. 'That's,' he cleared his throat, 'that's good.'

'We're on an exercise. Got to her a bit.' She had a low-pitched voice and spoke with the efficient delivery of the London urban professional, obviously privately educated but now trying to eradicate the traces to sound as though she'd started at the bottom and worked her way to the top.

Phil tried to concentrate. 'Is – is that a GPS?'

'Oh, that …' She followed Phil's eye-line down to the satellite navigation aid. 'Yes, yes it is.'

I could tell by Phil's facial expression and body language that he was desperately trying to think of something else to say, but his tongue had apparently jammed. She continued with her explanation. She was a team leader in a PR company, based at the end of a cul-de-sac in Covent Garden, tough territory where lunch is a sandwich at your desk and going home before seven-thirty at night is seen as not putting the time in. She was leading Penny and Sarah on this exercise in learning how to be 'proactive' in a difficult environment, a typical exec-speak term which has booted 'taking the initiative' out of the language. She introduced herself as Helen, at which Phil broke out of his trance to suggest we joined the ladies for lunch.

The two leaders sat together as fellow Teutons, while Freddy sat close to Penny and looked cautiously into her face. He opened his mouth to speak but seemed unable to get the words out. He glanced towards Helen as though to make sure she was not watching them. Freddy could guess the reason for Penny's depression. Of all people, he knew what it was like to be made miserable in the workplace. He'd embarked on a life-game to keep sane, but what had Penny got to help her through her work-life?

Helen, eating her sandwich, showed Phil how to deal with the sat-nav. 'You feed in the co-ordinates. At any time you press a button and it gives the exact position. See?' Phil tried to concentrate on his celery salad, but couldn't keep his eyes off her. She was so beautifully commanding. 'Did you meet those army lads?' Phil asked.

'Oh yes.' A deep little chuckle rose from the back of the throat. On her own Helen would have sorted out those boys and made men of them.

While Phil fawned around Helen I noticed that the mist, until now in the background, had edged forward in thin serpent-like coils of smoke over the groughs. It reminded me of the climax in *The Hound of the Baskervilles* when Holmes stands guard over the villain's house and the fog begins to roll in. 'Quick, Watson. By heavens, we may be too late!'

I spoke in less concerned tones to preserve Phil's dignity in front of Helen. 'Shouldn't we be on the move?' I asked timidly. 'It's getting a bit foggy.' The two steely-eyed Gruppenführers surveyed the moor, then turned to each other.

'Where are you heading for?' asked Phil.

'Kinder Downfall.' Helen glanced at Penny. 'That's if we're all ready.'

Phil made a peculiar noise, half way between a croak and a mew. The words came out awkwardly. 'That's a coincidence,' he said. 'So are we.'

Freddy's eyebrows leapt upwards. It was hardly a coincidence.

Most hikers returning to Edale, having climbed Grinds Brook, usually go via Kinder Downfall, the rough defile on the western side of the moor, and back to Edale via Jacob's Ladder. The top of the Downfall is a sheep mugger's paradise. Far more cunning than they look, they have worked out that it is a popular place for hikers' lunches and surround their victim. Two or three of them provide a distraction by coming up-close and intimate, while the third sheep walks round the back and dives in to nick the grub at your side. It's an amusing place – but only on a fine day. Today we'd be lucky to find it, let alone eat there. But then, Phil had a staunch ally with a sat-nav.

'Three hundred degrees,' Phil announced. We packed up and he set off commandingly, leading with Helen. He was so absorbed by her that she had to remind him occasionally to keep watch on his landmark, a stone outcrop. The forgotten armies trudged in their wake. In their togetherness the two leaders didn't seem to notice the thickening mist. It was now moving westward, towards our landmark.

'Phil!' Freddy pointed to the mist. Phil and Helen didn't seem concerned. They had more hi-tech expertise at their disposal than Armstrong and Aldrin on their journey to the moon would have dreamed possible.

You do not just 'walk' across Kinder. In turn you spring, sink, stumble, climb, scramble, jump and slide. In a quarter of a mile you've used as much energy as you'd use hiking five miles on the flat. Part of the moor is a black sponge cake, the rest of the top surface a thick green mass of heather and gorse. The spongy part can be like walking on a trampoline of springy ground. But then the opposite happens and, instead of 'lift', you're sucked down. Walking through the thick green top between the groughs is also energy-sapping, but the really exhausting bit is having to plunge into a grough and then being forced to scramble up the far side, then down again into another grough, and so on.

One grough too far. The landmark had vanished from view in

the fog. It was a white-out, visibility down to no more than ten yards. The poor bloody infantry came to a halt behind their leaders. Helen calmly raised her sat-nav to the heavens. Freddy raised his eyebrows. Phil stared at his map.

Penny caught my eye and grinned, slumped to the ground and shook her golden hair. The two Gruppenführers broke off their conference to stare at her.

'Do you two know where we are?' Freddy asked, not showing any deference to the Augustan leadership. Helen looked coldly at him. 'It's no problem,' she said briefly. She examined the sat-nav.

Freddy's laser pinged, registering a poser, first class. 'If it's not a problem,' he said reasonably, 'why aren't we moving on?'

Helen held her breath a moment, 'We are not lost,' she said coldly and deliberately. 'Just temporarily unsure of our position.'

'Yes,' Phil said, in as deferential a voice as he could summon. 'I can see that, but *here* by my reckoning is a quarter of a mile over there.' He indicated with a gesture.

'You two had better get your act together,' Freddy said it as much for Penny's benefit as his own. She grinned back at him.

Helen said nothing but opened and closed her mouth like a fish. Sarah, arms folded, was unable to stem a smile.

Penny took courage from Freddy, 'Being *here* is no help if you don't know where *here* is – I would have thought.' She gave a brittle laugh.

The drawstrings around Helen's mouth drew together in a flash. The icy unflappability vanished. Her cheeks reddened. In the space of an hour Penny had been transformed from a weepy, vulnerable little lady to an 'I-draw-the-line-here' individual. I remembered that Freddy had spoken to her out of earshot of the rest of the party. Her droll impudence was very 'Freddy-like'.

Freddy moved towards Helen and pretended to look over her shoulder at the map she was studying. 'Uncertain of our position means "lost" in my book. What do you say, Gruppenführer?'

Helen instinctively took the map from Phil to shield it from

Freddy. This was a red rag to Freddy's bull. He looked annoyed with Phil for kow-towing to her. Phil as Gruppenführer was never pompous or egocentric – mad, yes, but not coldly superior as she was. 'Bit of onedownmanship needed here, I think,' he muttered.

'What? What did you say?' Helen surveyed Freddy with puzzled disdain.

Freddy ignored her and spoke to Phil. 'You're navigator. Well, navigate.' Phil hesitated, embarrassed. He was very much in Helen's hands, literally, as that was where the sat-nav lay. But was the sat-nav the answer?

Freddy wasn't going to wait for the leaders. 'Let's split up. If one group finds the Downfall they whistle or shout.'

Phil grimaced, reluctant to leave Helen. But he had no alternative. He turned to address his troops – and then committed the worst sin of his career as Gruppenführer. Rule 1, sub-section 2: 'Never claim a subordinate's idea or plan as your own.' He even phrased it like Freddy had done. 'Each group looks for the Downfall. We know roughly where it is. My group will go on compass heading, Helen's on the sat-nav. If anyone finds the Downfall they blow a whistle or shout to the other lot.' Phil shot a glance at Freddy, a mixture of apology and guilt plus a shrug – 'I was about to suggest it anyway.'

In response Freddy gave Phil a dry Oliver Hardy look. 'Yes,' he said. 'General Paulus in that Russian winter asked the Führer's permission to withdraw. Turned down. Hitler promoted him to Field Marshal because, by custom, Field Marshals in defeat shot themselves. Paulus didn't and was captured. Hitler shot himself instead.'

'What's that got to do with us here?'

'Just a cautionary tale, Gruppenführer.'

'Why does he call you Gruppenführer?' Helen frowned at Phil and turned to frown even more at Freddy.

'We're going,' Phil pretended he had not heard. He flashed

his idiot's grin at her. 'Whoever gets to the pub first waits for the others?'

Helen nodded, with an unpleasant sideways glance at Penny and, I thought, a deprecating look towards Freddy. His remark about onedownmanship and the way he said it had unsettled her.

Penny gave Freddy a smile of gratitude as they set off.

Miserably, Phil watched Helen's slim, upright figure disappear into the fog. Was Rachmaninov's second piano concerto playing in his head?

'I'm going to tell Ruth about you, Stevens.' Freddy shouldered his rucksack.

Visibility was no more than two yards. Having lost the stone outcrop as a landmark, our only chance was to bump, literally, into the twin rocks marking the entrance to the Downfall.

During the next half hour we climbed, scrambled and slipped our way over what could have been a treadmill. In the dense clammy fog each grough seemed like any other. We sweated from an exercise that was exhausting and scary. Were we going round in circles? It was easy to understand how people had died in this place.

Every minute or so Phil put out a hand to bring us to a halt. 'Ahoy!' he shouted. We listened carefully but caught no reply either by whistle or voice. The only sound we heard was the creaking noise created by water squeezed into boggy ground by our footsteps.

'Gruppenführer, why are we going north *away* from Edale, when we could be going south *towards* it?' Freddy shot the question lightly. There was no need for heavy sarcasm now – the facts spoke for themselves.

Phil tried hard to sound casual. 'The Downfall's as easy to find as Grinds Brook and there are markers all the way down.' This last bit of information, he hoped, would keep intact his reputation as navigator.

But Freddy was in for the kill. 'What if we never find the Downfall, what then? Do they find our skeletons in six months' time?'

'Don't worry. We'll get there.' He looked at his compass. 'Keep to three hundred degrees,' he said, pointing into the fog.

'Three hundred degrees to where?' asked Freddy.

'The Downfall,' said Phil.

'You don't know that. That bearing's only correct if you use landmarks. We haven't got any. We could be miles off track.'

'We're bound to hit the western edge and then we'll find it. We just walk west until we do.'

'But what if we hit the western edge south of the Downfall? Or, what if we hit the northern edge? You might think we're on the western side.'

Phil had started to run out of excuses. He pushed his head forward, angry with Freddy, angry with himself. 'By my reckoning we've about ten minutes to go to the edge.' There was now a note of desperation in his voice.

We ploughed on for ten more minutes. Phil had started to slow down, not through exhaustion, but through lack of confidence. He referred to his watch every minute.

'Time's up, Stevens, admit it.' Freddy had set the same timing on his own watch. 'We're not "uncertain of our position", are we? We're lost.'

Phil paused, then clambered up to the moor surface, stared around and – faced with nothing – slid back into the grough. He sighed and ran a hand over his face. There was a long painful pause. 'Okay, we're lost.' It was painfully said, but drew no sympathy from Freddy. He nodded, climbed up the next bank, took off his rucksack and sat down on a clump of gorse. Clearly, Freddy's view was that Phil could have loyalty from his subordinates when all was going well, but if he should fail …

Phil desperately consulted his map, but it was no more than a show. He gave up, ran a hand over his face once more, then clambered up the bank and sat near Freddy. We had an enforced break, during which no one spoke.

The fog had a sinister quality of silence and claustrophobia.

Phil made a jerky movement of his head as he glanced behind, as if afraid that the Hound of Hell might materialise out of the fog. He was no longer Phil the brave. Perhaps failing in his duties as navigator had unnerved him.

Our questions were unspoken, but shared. What had happened to Helen and party? Would the fog clear soon? What if … my thoughts were cut off by the faint, but distinct, sound of a whistle.

Phil was on his feet and shouting, 'Ha-lo-ah!' towards where he thought the sound came from. Freddy cupped his hands to mouth. 'Ha-llo!'

Pause. The whistle blew again in two long blasts.

'Keep blowing!' Phil shouted. 'We're coming!'

Shouting, and rapidly shouldering rucksacks, we moved off to plough through grough and gorse, bog and shallow pools, guided by the increasing loudness of the whistle. Holmes and Watson moved towards their man. Would they arrive in the nick of time before the Hound got him?

We braked hard. In front of us, standing between the twin rocks marking Kinder Downfall, were Helen and Sarah. Helen took the whistle from her mouth.

'Thank the Lord for that,' Helen said. 'Have you seen Penny?'

On the way down Kinder Downfall Freddy tried using his mobile phone to reach mountain rescue. A 'no service' message came up. Helen also tried using her phone, with the same result. But did it matter? Even if the phone calls had got through, how could mountain rescue be expected to find anybody in this thick fog? They would just have to wait for it to lift. It wasn't a desperate situation, or so we hoped.

Helen said that she had been leading the way when Sarah turned round to find that Penny had vanished. No amount of shouting or whistling had located her.

As we traipsed downhill the world opened up. The fog had begun to lift, leaving us shrouded on both sides by a veil of yellow mist. But the wide stony track we were on could be seen winding downwards, well below us, a reassuring sight.

Phil pointed out that the footpath, part of the Pennine Way and starting at Edale – climbed either by Grinds Brook or Jacob's Ladder – is a 270-mile walk along the Pennine Ridge, through the Yorkshire Dales, up into Northumberland, across the Cheviots and into the Scottish borders. Phil became excited as he talked, temporarily forgetting Penny's plight. 'It's got to be one of the best hikes ever. You could do it in stages, say twelve miles a day. Now then, what's twelve into two hundred and seventy?'

'It's twenty-two and a half,' said Helen, shooting Phil a quick – and what she hoped was a modest – smile at her mathematical speed of calculation.

'Ah yes,' said Phil. 'So it could be walked in ...'

'Don't bother,' cut in Freddy. 'We've just escaped from being frozen mutton on it. I have no plans now, or in the future, to contemplate such an outrageous idea.' It amused him to see the effect this had on Helen. She had given him another dark look. Freddy represented everything she disliked, followers not leaders, peculiar people who resented natural authority, *onedownmen*.

Freddy tried his phone again, still without success.

We reached the tree line, crossed the packhorse bridge, then passed through the farmyard belonging to the National Trust. There was the hiker's shelter, once again empty. I could see that, for an exhausted hiker coming off Kinder in a wintry gale, the refuge could be a life-saver, proof that the Trust isn't all about stately homes. They'd also ferried up helicopter loads of flagstone to prevent booted feet from breaking up the crumbly peat on the Downfall footpath.

We came into the hamlet of Upper Booth, where there was a public telephone. Helen went straight for it, found the number clearly displayed in the booth and dialled it. We waited outside as she talked rapidly and urgently into the phone. She came out. 'Right,' she said. 'Mountain rescue are on the job.'

We finally reached the pub. There was the usual crowd of people outside, hikers all, sitting at the benches eating and drinking. Freddy headed straight for a space at one of the tables and sat down. 'Mine's a pint of the best,' he said to Phil with a hint of a threat. Freddy clearly believed that he was owed something. It had been one of his worst hiking experiences, not quite on a par with a sleepless night in a tent, but disturbing in more ways than one. As Phil disappeared into the pub he shook his head at me. 'Why do I do these things?'

Helen went up to one of the hikers, a tall man with an air of authority and the trappings of leadership: GPS, map-case and compass. 'Excuse me, I've just called mountain rescue. We have someone in my party missing on Kinder. Do you know who –' Her voice stopped in mid-stream. She was staring at Penny, sitting at one of the tables surrounded by hikers, a gin and tonic in her hand. She smiled at Helen with the same poise and confidence that had asserted itself after meeting Freddy.

Helen went straight to her, almost shouting: 'Where've you been! Do you realise –!' She broke off as she realised that the loudness of her attack had brought conversation around the table to a halt. Lowering her voice, Helen asked Penny to come to one side for a word with her. Then she remembered – 'God! Mountain rescue!' She marched quickly into the pub to use the phone.

Freddy and I greeted Penny in great relief. But why hadn't she called or cried out as soon as she saw the twin rocks leading to Kinder Downfall? Penny opened her mouth to tell her story but stopped as she saw Helen coming out of the pub, heading straight for her.

'Right,' said Helen. 'Do you realise what you've done? You caused me to call out mountain rescue. Hopefully they won't send us a bill. You disobeyed instructions. What did I tell you to do if you got lost?'

Penny remained cool under fire. She said that Sarah and

Penny's exercise had been a competition to see who would be the first to reach Edale via the Downfall. Well, hadn't she achieved just that, and so was the winner?

Helen's voice was abrasive in reply, 'No, there was no competition once we were lost! You knew that!'

'No I didn't. I wasn't told that. I thought we were supposed to use our initiative in difficult situations. That was a very difficult one, wasn't it? I came across the twin rocks and went for it. No one told me the competition was over.'

The hard lines around Helen's mouth bunched together. She took a deep breath ready to launch another fusillade and then stifled it, her chest rising and falling in anger; there was very little she could say. An icy atmosphere prevailed.

'Well,' said Phil, returning with a tray of drinks. 'We can celebrate.' He placed the tray of drinks on a table and looked up, catching the tension. 'Well,' he said again uncertainly. 'All's well that ends well?' His attempt at a chuckle faded as Helen stared at him as if he was mad. She took the pint of beer offered to her with a low and curt 'Thank you'.

After the drinks – an embarrassing interlude with no one eager to say much – we took our leave, offering quiet goodbyes and shuffling away two or three feet, lingering rather than making a clean break. Phil smiled awkwardly at Helen. 'Nice to have met you,' he said.

'Yes, sorry about my party,' Helen said stiffly.

Penny smiled at Freddy. 'Thanks,' she said. And meant it.

Freddy had a broad smile on his face as we walked to the car. Once inside he rubbed his hands together, grinning at Phil. 'Fabulous,' he said. 'Penny gave it her. A wonderful turn-over, as you chaps say in rugby. Don't you think it was a great upset? I mean, we don't want female Gruppenführers challenging you for the job, do we? What will the world be coming to?'

Phil grunted but made no reply.

'Now then,' said Freddy. 'We come to the debriefing. First, the question of your leadership. You reckon to be the best guide in Derbyshire.'

'Except that he wandered off into Staffordshire,' I added.

Freddy chuckled. 'Stevens. Don has made a joke. Do you know what a joke is? It's when somebody else slips on a banana skin. Like you did today – though that woman is a real poser. She needs a spot of onewomandownship. She is one heap of ego and we're –' he checked himself – '*you're* best rid of her.'

Phil said nothing. After all, he had become disenchanted with his erstwhile soulmate. She could not use a sat-nav properly and he had been forced into the humiliation of confessing he was lost.

April is a very cruel month.

5
MAY

We sat outside the George at Alstonefield. The remains of our lunch lay scattered on the table, together with three empty Burtonwood pint glasses. A grey and white Muscovy duck strolled up to the table, performed a circuit of reconnaissance and was rewarded with a few crumbs.

Normally Phil would be up by now – agitated, schedule-bound, time-important. Instead he sat and tapped his fingers on the table, staring ahead, slowly chewing the last of his carrot sticks.

Freddy rested his elbows on the table, a hand propping up his chin as he lazily surveyed Phil, as a headteacher might a difficult but troubled child. 'Don't you feel at peace? Doesn't your arid soul feel some blessing – warm day, village green, daffy duck – doesn't it call to something human in you? Or, to paraphrase Wordsworth, the memory of it will seep even into your purer being, with tranquil restoration. Isn't this memory what the soul needs in dark moments, like walking under a city underpass?'

Phil grunted. He had just received his notification from the Department of Health and Social Security of his old age pension, due to begin in September on his sixty-fifth birthday. Hence his gloom. The pension was a stigma and he had no way of dealing with it. He'd rather give up his pension and remain young.

'I bet neither of you two have heard of the String Theory,' persisted Freddy. I shook my head. Phil made no response. 'Well, the world's top physicists say it applies to everything in the universe. And there may be more than one universe – lots more.'

Phil grunted. 'Pay attention, Gruppenführer. Not only is there likely to be more than one universe – several, like slices out of a loaf of bread – but the boffins have also discovered that there is the possibility of travelling between universes. They reckon that the smallest particle (a graviton, smaller than an atom) might disappear in their enormous atom-crusher. If it does – and that's what they're hoping will happen – it will have slipped into another universe. Got that? *Another universe.* And that universe might be only *one centimetre away from your ear.*'

Phil grunted again.

'Now then, this is where you come in. There might be copies of ourselves doing what we're doing now, and madmen racing up mountains. I'm saying the time has come …'

'How much beer have you drunk?' Phil grimaced at Freddy.

'A pint. And you owe me one. Listen, even if this were true, all it does is explain the mechanics of it. It doesn't tell us *why* it happened, why these things exist.'

Phil sighed. 'Really.'

'Now this is for your benefit – if a graviton can slip in and out of different universes, why not you? You could have your dream – you could live for ever and ever.'

'Hmmm,' Phil responded with his deadpan tone. 'I'll have to look into that.' He knew when some time-stretching ideas wouldn't work.

A group of mourners led by the local vicar walked towards us from the direction of the church, the men wearing black ties, the women in sombre dress. To our astonishment they trooped into the pub. Minutes later we heard the sound of raised laughter and toasts.

Then the vicar emerged, presumably having had his token pint. Our curiosity had to be satisfied. 'Who died?' we asked.

'Old Mary,' he replied. 'She lived just down the road. She left a hundred pounds for the mourners to have a good time in the pub, and that's what they're doing.' It took a few moments for it all to sink in. I always felt that the Peak was our escape from the harsh realities of life, and this funeral, without the usual sad-faced tribe of mourners, maintained that happy deception.

We trekked past the church. The gravediggers were at work, rattling the coffin-lid with soil and stones. Piles of flowers, with handwritten tributes tied to them, lay around the open grave.

We walked down the steep, winding lane towards Milldale hamlet. The lush grass slopes on either side blazed yellow with buttercups. At the bottom of the hill was Donald's covered Rolls-Royce. Maureen waved to us from behind the hatch, as she served some schoolchildren on a break during their day's nature course. We waved back. All was right with the world.

Or so we thought.

An hour later the footpath took us towards a five-barred gate through which we had to pass into a farmyard, an ancient right of way. I always feel nervous crossing a farmyard with a right of way – and not just out of fear of a loose dog. One day, I often tell myself, a farmer will object. And there have been cases of farmers driven mad by crushing debt and loneliness.

A man leant heavily on the gate, evidently the farmer. He was in his fifties with a reddened face. He wore a greasy cap, an open-necked shirt and old trousers. By his side, to my alarm, was a long-handled axe, propped up against the gate. A few feet from the gate was a wooden post about twelve feet high. On top of this was a wooden 'skull', which sprouted a tuft of coconut hair and had implanted green glass eyes. A red light-bulb was wired and fixed into the cavity. Lit up at night it would be terrifying. He saw us looking at it.

'That's to keep 'em away – hikers.' The look on his face was deadpan. Then a cracked grin turned him into the crazed Jack Nicholson of *The Shining*. The farm was nowhere near as remote as the snow-bound hotel of that film, but it was the sort of place where, under stress, you could easily become unbalanced. It was set off a track, which was off a lane. The lane ran for a mile before you reached a proper road.

I looked at the axe. We had met our nemesis at last. This was Freddy's nightmare, a mad axe-man. A couple of swings might knock us out – then inside for the twelve-bore shotgun to finish off the job. Burial would present little problem. There would be a secret trench where he'd buried his previous victims. He could easily open it up with the digger attachment on his tractor. He would have bags of lime for dissolving our bodies, and grass sods easily available as camouflage. We'd be nicely rotted down with the rest of them, come Michaelmas.

And no one knew we were on this particular hike. Not even our wives.

'So what's the problem?' I said nervously.

'Problem? By giney,' he used an old Derbyshire expression. 'I've been here thirty years and it's never worse. I'll tell thee what the problem is. It's everything about it.'

He began to move his arms about, breathing hard, working up a passion. 'We're done for, aren't we? We don't need hill-farmers any more. Government's getting rid of us. We're neither use nor ornament.'

Thereupon he embarked on a tirade against ministers and bureaucrats, against red tape and lack of subsidy. Governments of all shades were rotten and corrupt, the European Union an excuse for light- fingered farmers elsewhere to make their pile while the British went to the wall. I glanced at the skull on the pole. He followed my gaze. 'Hikers, eh?' He picked up his axe. 'I get hikers 'ere as think I can mend walls in two minutes.'

So that was it. Hikers who lost the footpath on his land had climbed over walls, dislodging rocks. Like the squire or the parson of old he had zero tolerance for minor offences. Damaging walls, for him, was a capital offence.

He disappeared into the barn, clearly en route for his shotgun. He'd reckoned the axe wasn't enough against all three of us. He would be out with his weapon, lethal at fifty yards. We moved quickly through the gate, got halfway across the yard, ten yards, twenty – not enough. There he was brandishing a scythe. With one mighty swing he would cut through our legs. Instead, he laid the scythe against the side of the barn and looked glum.

'I can't afford the tractor. I've got to cut the grass with this. You lads want a glass of home-made lemonade – one pound fifty between you?'

What could we say? Freddy hunted for some change.

In mid-afternoon we arrived at Tissington village, about four miles north of Ashbourne. The village has been owned by the Fitzherbert family since 1466.

Sir Richard Fitzherbert, the present owner, is typical of the asset-rich and cash-strapped aristocracy. Tall, fresh-faced and with the candid charm of a man who owns much and can afford little (unlike the Devonshires to the north, who have turned Chatsworth into a commercial business), he pays for his repairs by wandering around the village on summer evenings as a tour guide for paying guests who enjoy rubbing shoulders with the gentry. But it's worth the visit, if only for the supper-of-all-suppers he provides afterwards. This takes place after the tour in a converted barn – a mound of pies, meats, fish, puddings, coffee, chocolate ...

As a Londoner he had enjoyed a different lifestyle, worlds removed from the inheritance of Tissington, but he took on the task in the late eighties in the spirit of his ancestors, conscious of his responsibilities to his tenants, conservation and history.

His honesty about the challenges he faces is appealing. He says the village post office was forced to close because his elderly tenants were averse to listening ears or watchful eyes as they collected their benefit payments in the tiny office. Instead they went to the more 'anonymous' Ashbourne post office. It's an ironic case of the aristocrat not having too much pride to reveal his financial problems, and his tenants having an excess and not wanting to reveal anything.

The focal point of the village is the Hall, surrounded by its cottages. You leave the Ashbourne-to-Buxton road, turning right through an impressive stone-pillared gateway, and with an air of expectancy drive down a long tree-lined drive with wide lawns on either side, and then over a cattle-grid. It's a surprise to find, first, a village and then Tissington Hall tucked away to the left, out of immediate view.

There is the ubiquitous duck pond, of course, and a couple of hundred yards from the Hall is the old railway station. Before Dr Beeching's axe in the sixties the line took villagers by steam train into Ashbourne, or north to Buxton. It's now the Tissington Trail, used by walkers and cyclists.

May has always been an optimistic time of year. Before the age of science and enlightenment the teenage girls of Tissington and other villages used to go 'nuts' as soon as the sun rose on 1 May. They dashed into the fields and splashed their faces with dew, reputed to have special properties to cure acne, freckles and other blemishes on that special day. There is no recorded instance of the treatment working, but hope springs eternal.

Other traditions, such as crowning the May Queen, still survive in some villages. Dancing around the Maypole, a fertility emblem, was temporarily stopped by Oliver Cromwell, who called it a 'stinking idol'. But, once reinstated by Charles II, it survived as a happy and colourful custom, which children still enjoy. Also long celebrated in Derbyshire is Oak Apple Day, marking the escape of Charles II after the battle of Worcester by hiding in an oak tree.

Of all the customs in the Peak none is more famous than the

Tissington annual 'well-dressing' event, which has its origins in the fourteenth century when the Black Death spared the village. In thanksgiving flowers were thrown into the six wells. Faith in the magical properties of the water was reinforced in 1615 when a spring and summer drought dried up most of the wells in the Peak, but not those in Tissington. In gratitude to the gods one of the villagers, Mary Twigg, revived the practice of offering sacrificial flowers to the water gods. This has continued to the present day. But instead of tossing flowers down the wells the villagers now use them to create dramatic and colourful pictures. Thousands of flower petals, pieces of bark, cones, seeds and leaves are used in the pictures, meticulously framed on a large board with a clay base acting as a fixative. There are six wells, each 'dressed' with a single picture erected over it.

We passed several helpers preparing the wells for the coming weekend, when thousands of people would arrive to admire the artistic creations of the villagers. A hired coach pulled up with a hiss of brakes. The travelling party of WI ladies, from Sheffield judging by the address on the coach, stared at the work going on around the well. Then the protestations began: 'The wells aren't finished. We've come a week early!'

The flustered male tour-guide was forced to his feet, amidst hands pointing to the unfinished well and exclamations and expressions of outrage. The guide backed off the bus, followed by a large woman with muscular arms. 'Is this what we've paid to see? Is it?'

The guide continued his retreat. The woman's body language suggested that a complete refund would be appropriate, and if he didn't cough up she'd drop him down the well. He took one more step backwards and then turned to face the well-dressers, either for protection or for directions to the nearest holy place of refuge.

Freddy would have stayed for the big fight but Phil reminded us of our schedule. Freddy made his protest: 'We're not in the army, Stevens. That was a first-class bout. I had money on Mrs Tyson.'

Later on in the day we walked through Dovedale en route to Ilam. Fishermen were ranged at intervals along the river banks, fly-fishing for trout. Their clothing varied from that of the rough-hewn farmer to the 'Sherlock Holmes look'. Every few minutes one of them broke his silent concentration to reel in and then flick out the fly into the translucent water.

Further up the river we came across our old friend Harold Barker and a fellow water bailiff, their Land Rover and low trailer parked at the water's edge. They unloaded a number of heavy water-filled plastic tanks, each packed with young trout. Their first task was to re-oxygenate the water in the tanks after the journey from the local trout farm. The water would have lost some of its quality during the journey and it was essential to improve it as soon as possible. An oxygen cylinder had been brought along for the purpose.

As Harold started to pump oxygen into one tank the other bailiff, using a net-scoop, opened the nearest tank, trapped some fish and gently lowered them into the river. The start of the second re-stocking of the year (the first had been in March) was under way. I was fascinated by the metamorphosis of the ugly flapping fish, caught in the net, into fluid, sinewy creatures once they were released into the river.

Around fourteen bailiffs cover the Peak and they work hand in hand, forming a River Watch. When the moon is up their eyes have to be sharply skinned for the bad boys. Night-time is best for poachers.

Harold told us the story of a Victorian villain who had fashioned a wooden board, a long piece of rope attached, from which dangled baited hooks on the ends of fishing line. The board was weighted to float sideways up and then dragged against the current. He caught so many trout that the judge gave him a month for every fish he caught. He was in prison for three years.

Harold recited the verse commonly chanted by children of the time: 'If the Keeper found on him a rabbit or a wire, he got it hot, when brought before the Parson and the Squire.'

We left Harold and his fish and moved off down the dale. Freddy said he was thirsty. He had used up his water and coffee supply. Might the Gruppenführer suspend his addiction to pain and drop in at the Izaak Walton en route to Ilam for a swift half?

'I don't believe it. What is this?' Phil grinned at Freddy. 'This is a serious hike. Pubs are out. Rule 10, sub-section 2.'

Freddy immediately went on the counter attack. 'You forget rule 14B. Any hiker suffering from dehydration shall be entitled to a drink of up to one pint purchased at any hostelry of his choice.'

'Appendix B. All rules suspended. Sorry Freddy.'

'You are the worst Gruppenführer I've ever met, you know that?'

We rarely visit pubs during our hikes, owing to the difficulty of extracting Freddy from their warmth and comfort. Peak pubs vary in atmosphere and quality. Some are genuinely inviting, both in their welcome and in their history and setting. One of the best of these is a pub called the Quiet Woman at Earl Sterndale. Built in 1610, the pub could be mistaken for an old farmhouse. At the back and side of the property is a large enclosure leading into a field. Scattered around are hen-houses, pens and fencing that hold and enclose various animals, including geese, ponies, cows and rabbits. Friendly Tamworth pigs scuttle around in both the enclosure and the field beyond. A sign says: 'Magpie traps for sale'. There is nothing remotely pretentious about the place.

The pub has a traditional quarry-tiled floor and is heavily beamed, with simple wooden furniture that gleams when the odd sunbeam penetrates the small windows. A central feature in the Quiet Woman is a long narrow table. The old saying 'have a drink on me' takes on real significance when you appreciate its use in the past, not as a table, but as a laying-out bench used by the local undertaker.

The pub sign displayed outside shows a woman dressed in Elizabethan clothes. Her head is missing and the caption declares: 'Soft words turneth away wrath.'

There are various explanations for how she came to lose her head. One has it that she was such a shrew that her husband, the landlord, chopped off her head to keep her quiet. Another says the landlord was so fed up with her nagging that he declared that, if he couldn't have a quiet woman within, he'd have one outside – and placed the picture outside accordingly. We prefer the latter explanation, although I was intrigued to learn that the landlord in 1895, Herbert Heathcote, was also a butcher.

The following week Phil drove us north to Monyash. The place name is Saxon, an old English word meaning 'many [an] ash [tree]'. It stands at the head of Lathkill Dale, five miles north-west of Bakewell, and was once an important lead-mining centre. From there we would walk to Flagg, a village known for its stone-walling competitions, and even more for its point-to-point races.

The main event is organised by the High Peak Hunt, and is a two-mile race over twenty birch-fences, a tradition that began over a hundred years ago. The beer tent has always been popular with a variety of 'characters', farmers, businessmen and landowners. There was the wicked bookmaker in 1938 who grabbed his satchel and hot-footed it over the hills to Manchester before the last race, pursued by a posse of huntsmen, villagers and outraged punters. My favourite story is of the lady who, in days of yore, galloped first past the winning-post and carried straight on out of the field, only to be whisked off by her lover, leaving her husband open-mouthed. He'd backed her to win and was too embarrassed to pick up his profit.

The footpath took us through a farmyard with a seventeenth-century date carved in the stonework over the barn door. A short lane ended at the road, where we turned right to enter the village and came to a sudden standstill: 'APOCALYPSE NOW', 'PLAGUE VILLAGE', 'ENTER AT YOUR OWN RISK'.

Such painted signs, some displaying the skull and crossbones, were on every house and cottage, standing out amongst the garden hollyhocks and geraniums. They poked out of the unlikeliest of places, some tied to poles, others stuck on cars and windows. No garden was without its statement of doom. The most alarming placard was inside a window perched next to two propped-up teddy bears. 'TWINNED WITH CHERNOBYL,' it screamed.

A grey-haired woman stood in one front garden, fending off a black-and-white springer spaniel which was trying to grab a stick from her hand. Freddy asked what was happening.

She stared at us. We could have been aliens. 'You've not heard?

We had to confess our ignorance.

'It's the national cattle-incinerator. It's working now. Look!'

We followed the direction in which her arm pointed. We could just make out a steel building with a chimney at the back of a field. 'For the last two years it's been destroying cattle, three tons an hour – and never stopped. Now it's slowed down a bit, but you can still smell it.'

We learned that the villagers were concerned about the danger of chemical emissions from the incinerator, and a potential increase in the rat population. The community had initially briefed lawyers to fight the proposed development, but had then been unable to find the twelve thousand pounds required for a judicial review in the High Court.

But why, Freddy asked, were the signs of protest still all around when it was a fait accompli? The incinerator was up and running, wasn't it?

'Leaving them up shows how strongly we still feel about it. I retired here,' she said, 'for a quiet life in the country. Fresh air and good neighbours. And what did I get?' And with a lift of her eyebrows she went indoors.

We walked towards the incinerator. A huge truck, its hydraulics sighing, approached and turned into the driveway. A man wearing a shabby raincoat and a woolly hat was sitting at the roadside opposite the gateway, a white mask covering his nose and mouth. He jumped to his feet when he saw us and waved his hands. 'No! Go back! You'll get it! The disease!'

'What's the problem?' asked Freddy calmly.

'The air! It carries the spores!' The man's eyes bulged.

'If that's the case, what are you doing here?'

The man stared unblinkingly at Freddy until a Nissan Trooper approached and stopped. A woman in a headscarf wound down the window and nodded her head towards him. 'Is Melvyn bothering you?'

She solemnly addressed our would-be saviour. 'Melvyn, time for your lunch.' Melvyn shook his head in a sulk.

'Come on,' she commanded. 'Get in.' She opened the passenger door and Melvyn got inside. 'Sorry about that. There's no problem with the incinerator. If there were do you think the government would allow it here?' She did a three-point turn and drove off the way she had come. We stared after her.

Whoever she was, she clearly didn't live in Flagg. We hadn't seen a building without its sign of protest. We walked past the incinerator. It boomed, the sound that a super-heated furnace with an after-burner makes, but there was no smell. Even so, I noticed that Phil held his breath as we passed by.

Later in the day, towards the end of our hike, high on the airy edge where the kestrels hovered and the curlews cried, we walked down one of the packhorse roads that seem to lead nowhere. As we left it and joined a lane we came across a couple outside a tiny dilapidated chapel, only big enough for a congregation of about ten. The man, aged about sixty, was chipping away at some old putty surrounding a broken window. He wore a collar-less shirt and a railwayman's black waistcoat from the days of steam.

The woman, with a hard, sour face and scraggy body, a small

scythe in her hand, was hacking at the nettles and briars that surrounded the building. She wore an old pair of rubber boots and a faded pinafore – such as my mother bought with her clothing coupons during the Second World War.

'Morning.' We always greet everybody we meet in the countryside.

The man stumbled out a 'Morning,' and then looked away. The woman maintained her grim silence.

A sign outside, freshly painted, announced that this was the church of 'the First Adventists'. There are many Wesleyan chapels in the Peak, many of them still in use. 'The First Adventists', however, were not of that faith, but of the church created by the American Baptist preacher William Miller. The 'Millerites' had forecast the end of the world with the Second Coming, pinpointing the day to between 21 March 1843 and 21 March 1844. The failure of the first prediction was called the First Disappointment. One could easily understand why. You've cleared out the attic, sold off the mangle, and prepared for Paradise – and it doesn't happen. But don't despair. A second date is announced, 22 October 1844. This time it's for real. You auction off the cottage and contents, including the new cow and the grandfather clock.

As midnight struck on 22 October nothing happened, so they waited until breakfast. When that passed with no cow and no milk – and no cottage – there was more than disappointment in the ranks. The church split four ways. One of them, the First Adventists, had not been heard of in recent times and so Freddy's conclusion was that our couple had re-created it to save themselves, a congregation of two at Armageddon.

'This faith business is dangerous.' Phil stomped across the windswept open ground between Flagg and Sheldon. 'What is faith? You, Freddy, you're a sucker for it.'

'Gruppenführer! Slow down!' Freddy said, hurrying along behind.

But Phil had seized on the chapel couple as the perfect example of blind faith leading to unhappiness. His energetic pace reflected the driving power of his argument – aimed at Freddy. He shouted question after question with his back to a strong westerly, making it difficult for anyone following behind to hear him. Phil was relentless. 'How can you cling to a bloke like Kant, who might be right or he might be wrong? He lived ages ago. The whole point about faith is that you haven't any proof. It's a leap in the dark.'

Surprisingly, Freddy made no reply. This allowed Phil to build on his attack. He put the argument forcibly. Wasn't it a matter of faith – of the kind that had sent the May Day girls into the fields in a frenzied attempt to get rid of their pimples? How could Freddy have faith in a philosopher who reckons things only exist in our perception of them – a hippopotamus that *might* be there if we hadn't *seen* it? And wasn't he worried that there might be a buffalo in his loo when he got home? Phil gave a cackle.

Freddy told me later that Phil's tirade had sparked off something that worried him, except he didn't know what that 'something' was. But it was there, a niggle in the dark tunnels of his mind. It was unfortunate because he'd enjoyed himself since discovering Kant. He felt he'd been relieved of pounding the treadmill on his troubled search. The best thing about Kant was that he denied neither God nor religion – you had it both ways with Emmanuel K.

A week later we set off on a hike starting from Youlgreave, heading west towards Arbor Low, an ancient stone-circle. Phil, with total disdain for sentiment, summed up what we had experienced so far this month. 'We've had a nutter at the incinerator, a village up in arms, a busload of killer-women, a mad farmer and two religious fanatics. It shows the Peak is not the Utopia you think it is. It's like anywhere else, populated with the baked, the half-baked and the generally insane. It's all a matter of how you look at it.'

We turned left off the country road a short distance from its junction with the Ashbourne–Buxton road to walk across fields towards the stone-circle. Known as 'the Stonehenge of the Peak District', it consists of a circular bank enclosing a partially silted ditch. Inside this is an area of flat ground, around the edge of which is a stone circle of large limestone blocks, each lying flat, not standing as at Stonehenge. We had by-passed the circle on previous hikes and never taken the trouble to visit it, mainly because of Phil's insistence on time-keeping. This time he had relented.

There are four stones in the centre of the circle, which has led some people to say that it resembles a clock face. Had it been a ceremonial site, or a religious centre connected with worship of the sun and the moon? Or had it been used to predict the summer and winter solstices? We stopped at the northern side of the circle for our coffee break, and stared at the stones in private meditation.

Phil scoffed at the idea that it had been some sort of clock. 'The guys who built this must have been daft to have hauled hundreds of tons of stone into a circle just to find out what time of day it was.'

Freddy was smiling. Obviously he had the answer. It was not a clock, he said. 'Arbor' means 'earthen fortification'. The circle was in use from the late Stone Age to the early Bronze Age and thought to date from the middle of the third millennium BC. How did he know? Simple, a local historian had told him over a pint in the Dog and Partridge.

Two men approached, carrying between them a large metal case. One was thin and academic-looking, with a narrow face, a dead ringer for Woody Allen. He wore a jacket and dark trousers with a white, open-neck shirt. His companion, plump and bald, wiped his perspiring face with a handkerchief, breaking off to flap it at us in greeting. 'Morning,' he said. Assuming we were there to meet him, he introduced himself as Colin and his colleague, Roger.

Roger's eyes grew larger, magnified through his thick spectacles. He opened the case, taking out a selection of electronic devices, none of which we recognised. His companion, still wiping his forehead, caught our gaze and smiled hesitantly. 'Sorry we're a bit late but we got delayed in Ashbourne, traffic hold-up.' He looked at his watch. 'We've got ten minutes, we're okay,' then added nervously. 'So long as we don't get beamed up by rushing it!' He chuckled at his own joke, his smile fading at his partner's lack of response.

Roger placed the electronic devices at intervals inside the circle. He stared at the sky, decided the time was right and cast out an arm. 'In here, everybody, please.' The sun shone from his spectacles. 'All ready?' He beckoned us into the circle.

'Excuse me, Roger.' Colin raised a hand half in apology. He was gazing uncertainly at us. 'Are you Ley Society?' Our body language was evidently not quite that of the members of whatever society he was talking about. As we hesitated he turned back to Roger. 'I don't think these gentlemen are with us.'

And then it clicked. Ley lines are straight lines drawn on an Ordnance Survey map, linking up all the ancient burial mounds and stone-circles around the country.

The sun blazed from Roger's spectacles. 'You've not come for the experiment?'

But before Phil could stop him, Freddy offered our services in the absence of their colleagues. Phil raised his eyebrows in a 'Here we go again with Freddy' expression. But he was trapped and allowed himself to be ushered into the centre of the circle and told, by Roger, to hold hands. At precisely 11.45, Roger said, the moon would be exactly one degree south of Mars. In that conjunction maximum power would be unleashed. He said we should imagine the ley lines set-up as a cycle wheel, the psychic energy radiating down its spokes into the hub of Arbor Low.

We waited patiently, Phil muttering to himself. I held Colin's left hand, Freddy his right. Roger and Phil made up the circle. I could feel no psychic megavolts, just Colin's clammy palm. After a couple of minutes Roger broke out of the circle to go round his instruments, one by one, taking notes. As he reached the last box Phil tried to see what he was writing. Roger slowly rotated his head, saw Phil at his side and quickly closed the notebook. He went round the circle again, collected his instruments and put them back in the metal case.

'Thank you very much,' he said in his reedy voice. 'Colin? Ready?'

'So what was all that about, then?' Phil sounded tetchy. 'We've helped you, so can you tell us what you've found out?'

'The readings have to be analysed first.'

'And?' Phil demanded more.

'The energy lines emit them. They're localised.' Roger's eyes loomed through his thick glasses. Then he was away without even so much as a 'thank you'.

'What a nerd,' spluttered Phil as we watched Roger and Colin haul their box away. Colin turned and gave us an embarrassed and apologetic smile.

This oddball duo brought Phil back to his earlier gripe. He said again that, of all the weird people we had met recently, the chapel couple provided the best example of misplaced faith born of ignorance. 'And don't forget, Freddy, that Kant lived before their particular beliefs developed. You should be looking at later philosophers who had the benefit of more recent knowledge. Philosophy can't happen in a vacuum. You've got to have some knowledge of life and reality – the more you have the better you're placed to think about things. Common sense, isn't it?'

Freddy later admitted that the submerged niggle that had worried him earlier had now surfaced. He was surprised to find it was really quite simple. Perhaps Phil was right. Maybe Kant *was* past his sell- by date. Freddy now felt he understood the nature of his problem, believing in ideas based on old knowledge, but how should he deal with it?

He went back to the library and this time by-passed Kant. He browsed through Hegel, Hobbes, Schopenhauer, Locke and Hume until, jumping into the twentieth century, he discovered a chap he'd never heard of, Karl Popper. Like Plato, he discovered, Popper reasoned that our sensory experiences were fallible. Freddy told me that, based on his sketchy understanding of Popper, Phil was wrong. A hippopotamus could be anywhere. Sensory perceptions would *not* help in building up human knowledge.

In one stroke Popper had demolished hundreds of years of philosophical thought. For example, he pointed out that Newton's theory of gravity, for centuries held to be a copper-bottomed, hard-forged truth, had been put into doubt by Einstein's thesis on the same subject. If such a thing could happen, the demolition of what had been held to be an iron-clad truth, what price the rest of our convictions – Muslim, Christian, Hindu or whatever?

If there was one phrase which summed up Popper's ideas it was: 'we don't know nuthin'. However, Freddy was comforted to discover that Popper did agree with Kant in one respect: the meaning of life was beyond human knowledge, so you might as well have a good time and forget all about it.

But *was* this a comfort? Freddy felt torn apart, pulled this way and then that. However much he tried, he couldn't shake off his deep-seated worry. He suspected that other people did know what the 'meaning' was, but kept it to themselves, or they would surely be as bothered as he was? He said he felt like Erickson, the Second World War corvette skipper in *The Cruel Sea*. He had gone through an agony of physical exhaustion, sweeping for the sound of the German U-Boat which he *knew* was down there. Like Erickson, Freddy was convinced that the 'meaning' was there somewhere, even if submerged beneath the waves of time.

A possible answer came from the most unlikely of sources, his local doctor's surgery. Freddy was on his way out when a diminutive oriental-looking man came in. He was dressed in a sort of Mao tunic, light brown but with no collar. The trousers were the same colour, giving an impression of sedateness and sobriety. Rui, as he was called, said he was a monk at the Tara Buddhist Centre in the village. Intrigued, Freddy offered him a lift home.

Ashe Hall, a Victorian red-brick building, stands in its own grounds. It began life as a country house, then served as a convalescent home for injured servicemen (my father had recovered there from his war injuries) and later, as it was called then, 'a school for delicate children' – but a *Buddhist centre*?

As they drove up the long drive, lined with beautiful giant redwoods, Rui pointed to the gardens on either side. 'I garden,' he said. They pulled up outside the house and Rui took Freddy inside, asking him to take off his shoes before they went into the meditation room, once a large drawing-room.

Freddy stood in the heavy silence and breathed in the scented air. He looked at the Buddha icons and the beautiful tapestry wall hangings, and read a booklet about the founder of Buddhism, Siddhartha Gautama, who said his life was empty before he discovered its *meaning*. 'Sitting under a Bo tree, he meditated, rising through a series of higher states of consciousness until he had *attained the enlightenment for which he had been searching.*' Freddy re-read the sentence. And read it again. He asked Rui for his explanation. The little man said, 'You talk to monk. I garden,' and went outside.

Freddy tentatively poked his head into the sitting-room – nobody. He looked in the kitchen and tapped on an office door. No response. He daren't go upstairs. But there must be monks about somewhere. Freddy put on his shoes and went outside. Rui was kneeling by the side of a herbaceous border weeding. Freddy went up to him. 'I didn't see any monks. Are there any here today?'

Rui was thoughtful. 'Monk meditating in bedroom. You come back?'

'Oh yes, I'll come back.' Freddy said it at once without thinking. He said goodbye to Rui and walked towards his car. *Would* he come back? He didn't fancy meditation, Buddhist style. He liked to have clear and straight answers. And meditation reminded him of the young men who had told him to hum at a hat-stand. At least there was no hat-stand in the hallway at the Buddhist Centre. But humming to Buddha? It wasn't an exciting prospect. Then he remembered the phrase he'd read over and over again – '*attained the enlightenment for which he had been searching.*'

He couldn't get that out of his head.

6

JUNE

We could see the flag of the German Democratic Republic drooping from the chimney stack as we laboured up the lane from the river. Graham was at home.

The hike was circular, as usual. Our route was to be Youlgreave village along the river Bradford to Middleton village, where we would pass Graham's house, then over the countryside in a wide arc through Lathkill Dale and back to Youlgreave. In all it was a distance of about nine or ten miles.

The scrape of our hiking boots on the gravel launched a pair of geese towards the low stone wall in a flurry and a flapping of wings.

Graham popped his head out from behind a row of pole-supported runner beans. 'Phil, Freddy!' He shooed away the geese, then stepped over the cabbage patch to reach the wall. He wore garden-stained jeans, a grey cowboy hat, a blue shirt and a boot-lace tie – John Wayne rather than Vopo. His face broke out into a wide smile. 'Freddy! Phil! Don! My friends, wunderbar! We must celebrate in Feldschlossen. I've not seen you for ages!'

Freddy, despite his Puritanism, was always ready for any liquid hospitality. I was happy to oblige, but Phil, as with Harold Barker and his death by whisky, shook his head in apology. The hike came first but, as he was thinking of something diplomatic to say, Graham had already waved away his refusal. 'And I have a crisis. I need advice.' He wiped the sweat from his forehead with the back of his hand.

Freddy put up a warning finger to Phil. Under no circumstances would he abandon his Good Samaritan role for a portion of hike. Graham's problem, by all that was fair and just, was also our problem.

Feldschlossen was turned down in deference to Phil's feelings, and the butterscotch smell of aromatic Dutch tobacco, mixed with the even sweeter smell of blackcurrant tea, permeated the house. 'Hmmm,' Freddy murmured, appreciating his drink, which he'd never tried before. All three of us drank tea and nibbled pieces of cake, while Graham puffed his pipe as he hunted through a pile of correspondence, bills and petrol receipts. He pulled out an official-looking letter. It was from the Peak Planning Authority. It confirmed that an officer would visit him at 2.30 pm – today.

Graham shrugged. 'I've tidied up the yard and got rid of most of the rubbish, but the Trabbies are still there and that's what people are complaining about. I've looked up the law on planning. I'm a collector in the same way as people collect stamps, but what defence have I got?'

'That *is* your defence.' Freddy exclaimed. 'Good God, is there a law against collecting cars?' He was Graham's champion.

Graham shook his head. 'But it's *where* they are, isn't it. The villagers don't like to see them. I can't blame them. And I've got some Germans coming – any time now. They might buy the Vopo car for an exhibition in Frankfurt.' Graham indicated by a gesture that it was all too much for him.

Phil looked at his watch. 'Well, if we cut back on the hike we could be here again – yes, before half past two. On the way round we'll try and think of something.'

Freddy looked at Phil in mock amazement. 'Gruppenführer, that's the first humane act you've made in your life!' He turned to

Graham. 'This man has made the greatest sacrifice possible, the donation of part of his hike.'

As we walked away from the village a Mercedes 500 saloon with German number-plates passed slowly by, three middle-aged men inside. Each of them scanned their surroundings. 'Your fellow countrymen, Gruppenführer,' said Freddy. 'Looking for your comradely flag.'

An hour later we had not reached any conclusion. Trabants, by any normal standards, were indeed ugly. And Graham's yard amounted to a car park. How do you defend a car park in what should be a picturesque village setting? Freddy said he thought it made for an interesting village. 'Vintage sports cars – Bugattis – Trabants – Princess Diana – bomber memorial. For its tiny size it's incredible.'

We reached the eastern entrance to Lathkill Dale. Freddy opened up his book of wild flowers. Phil frowned at him. 'We're supposed to be keeping to a deadline, you know.'

'No problem, Gruppenführer. I'm just looking for one flower.'

'One? You told us there were fifty-four wild flowers in Lathkill!'

'There are. This is one very special flower.'

'What's so special?'

'It's called Jacob's Ladder. It's very rare.'

Phil turned to look at him. 'I remember that time near Jacob's Ladder when you were trying to get me wet through. That was rare as well. Come on, your Vopo leader needs you – let's go.'

'One minute,' Freddy showed Phil the illustration. 'A bishop in 1499 dreamt he saw angels climbing a ladder, so he commissioned an image for one of the windows in the Abbey Church in Bath. It's still there but hidden away from the tourist path so it's not often seen. The flower has kept the bishop's dream going for posterity as it still lives on. See each angel with wings climbing the stem?' Phil looked at the picture and grunted, grudgingly accepting that Freddy was not up to his former delaying tactics.

'And it's in this dale!' Freddy enthused. 'You know those fences further up on the left before we enter the gulley – those fences protect it from humans and animals!' Freddy glanced wryly at Phil. 'That includes us, by the way.'

'There's no end of flowers in Lathkill,' Freddy continued. 'Bird's-foot trefoil, yellow rockrose. Look, there's one. And over there, look – that's a wild geranium.' He pointed to the side of the footpath. 'It's amazing, this place. We've done this hike a hundred times and we've walked like the blind. Isn't that incredible? And there are birds – there's goldfinches here – that's now an endangered bird. And butterflies! There's over twenty species.'

Freddy's excitement was a surprise, to both Phil and myself. 'And, what's more,' he said, 'I'm going to look for Jacob's Ladder.'

'Well, we're not stopping to search for it. Next time I might let you.' Phil was his old bossy self. 'A hike is a hike, not a nature ramble.'

Freddy tutted and sighed. Phil was beyond redemption.

I was impressed. Freddy was right. We were blind and ignorant. And, into the bargain, this new version of Freddy – Freddy the botanist – would add something to our hikes.

Izaak Walton fished in Lathkill Dale and described it as the 'purest and most transparent stream' he had ever seen. But by cutting through porous limestone rock over millions of years the river vanishes at one point to reappear further down as fishing pools. We passed by the largest of these, the water so clear that the river bed could be seen in a luminescent display of greens and blues, reflecting and deepening the colour of overhanging vegetation and trees. A couple of wagtails and a coot sailed serenely upriver. I blinked at the iridescent flash of a kingfisher nipping downstream.

We passed the spot where Carter's Mill once stood, used for grinding corn. Here, the river falls over a dam formed of tufa – a rock formation created by the deposit of calcium carbonate on rocky moss. It is only found in limestone streams and only in the purest of water. In the form of stalactites and stalagmites it occurs mainly in the north and west of the UK, and mainly in underground caves or petrifying springs, but rarely in an open river such as Lathkill.

In 1847, the peace of the Dale was interrupted by the construction of an engine house for a lead-mine, but the project was defeated by lack of water for the pumping wheel. It became derelict a few years later. Time has softened it as ivy grew around its massive stone-blocks, turning it into the semblance of a ruined castle wall. Later it was further enhanced by a surround of wych elm and beech.

Today it blends in with its surroundings, but poses a puzzle to the uninitiated. We sat on the smallest of the truncated stone piles at coffee break and turned our thoughts back to Graham. 'Why doesn't he play the tourist card?' I suggested. 'He calls himself the curator of an open-air museum, which is true – Trabants are museum pieces.'

Freddy and Phil agreed. It sounded sensible. But then Graham would have to apply for the yard to be recognised by a 'change of use' permit from the council. It was doubtful that he would get it. Freddy chuckled. 'I think we ought to have more collections like that, then I could form a onedownmanship club.'

We reached the western end of the dale, close to the village of Monyash, where the river splits into a number of shallow streams. Amidst the thick reeds which hide the waters are large, moss-covered stones, the remnants of a sheep-wash used first by a medieval monastery and then by farms until as recently as the 1940s.

Just before the gulley, on the left-hand side, were some wooden fences enclosing a grassed and stony area of about fifty square yards. Freddy stopped and pointed to a flower – there were a number of them. This one had tried to escape capture, part of it under one of the lower fencing rails. He bent down, pointed his finger and very gently touched the stem. The blue angels' wings shivered. Freddy, with his big hands and large face, was motionless in meditation. Phil was impatient, wanting to move on. But there was something about Freddy which held my attention – his gentle stare *into*, not at, the flower, wiped away all his ungainliness.

'Freddy, what are you doing? It's your saviour we're supposed to be helping. Graham needs you.'

Freddy waggled his right arm as he stood up. 'You have no soul. "Love this friend hath sown, within our hearts, the love whose flower hath blown, bright as if heaven were ever in its eye, will pass so soon from human memory." Treasure the best while you can.'

'Freddy, don't tell Graham that. What he needs is ideas, not poetry.'

'You know what Phil is short for, don't you,' said Freddy. 'Philistine.'

Phil grinned and led us into a narrow gulley half-full of boulders and rocks. Most hikers, unfamiliar with the place, think it was caused by a rock fall. Few recognise it for what it actually was, a quarry originally worked for a type of stone called Derbyshire marble.

We emerged from the dale and turned left over open fields leading back to Middleton. A skylark trilled in the warm air. We walked through a farmyard and passed a line of ancient stone feeding-troughs raised on a platform of slabs. Phil checked his watch and increased the pace to meet our deadline. And still we had no solution to Graham's problem. Stamp collectors are lucky – they can indulge their hobby without any fear of intervention. You can't stick cars in an album.

We arrived back in Middleton to find Graham in conversation with a middle-aged man who had a straggly moustache and carried a faded leather briefcase, presumably the planning officer. No sign of any Germans.

Graham spotted us, quickly excused himself and came over. 'He's not the planning officer. He's from the Inland Revenue!' he hissed. Apparently the tax man had turned up completely out of the blue, waved one of Graham's letter-heads and demanded an explanation.

The letter-head bore Graham's address and was preceded by a logo and, in large bold capitals, the words 'TRABANT CENTRE UK'. If this wasn't an invitation to trade, what was? 'I normally only sell cars surplus to the collection. But just before he arrived the Germans came and took the patrol car out for a trial run. And that's not surplus, it's the only one of its kind. If the Germans get back and say they want to buy it while he's here, he'll think I'm trading.' Graham grimaced. 'And the Germans aren't very good English-speakers. How I'm going to explain to them with him around I don't know.'

'I'll go and cut them off somehow, try and keep them away till he's gone. I'll say I'm a Trabbie lover and want to see the engine. I'll get them talking about something.' Phil dropped his rucksack on the ground, squared his shoulders and jogged off on his rescue mission, his jaw set in grim determination, though slowed to a lumbering gait by his heavy boots.

He left behind a deeply worried Graham, who had visions of the tax man faced by a returning trio of ecstatic Germans waving fistfuls of euros. 'So what's all this about then?' The tax man would shout his questions as the English do when confronted by non-English speakers. 'You – have – come – here – to – buy – this car – yes?'

'Ja, ja, ja! We come, ja!' Grins all round.

'You buy from Trabant Centre UK – yes?'

'Oh ja. From Herr Goodall, ja.'

'How – much – money – for – this –car?'

'Oh ja, we have money.' Out would come the notes with not an invoice or receipt in sight – payment in cash, no questions asked, right under the nose of the tax man. Caught red-handed.

Phil saw the Trabant swaying towards him and stood in the middle of the road to flag it down. The driver wound down his window. Phil approached him with an admiring smile on his face. 'Excuse me, is this a Trabant?'

'Yes.' The front-seat passenger with a lazy left eye surveyed Phil warily.

'Wonderful car – wunderbar!' Phil said effusively, his arms spread wide as he embraced the epitome of East German technology.

'No, no good,' Lazy Eye shook his head. 'Bad car.'

'Oh,' Phil grimaced. He tried desperately to think of something else to say.

'For exhibition – Communist things – the Berlin Wall,' Lazy Eye said.

Phil nodded. The driver, a Boris Becker lookalike, tapped the throttle sending out a cloud of oily smoke. The vehicle lurched forward. 'Halt!' Phil, his arm stretched out, jumped in front of the Trabant. It came to an abrupt stop. Boris glared at Phil through the windscreen. There was an exchange of dark mutterings inside the car. Phil had to allay their fears. He came round to the driver's window and decided to come clean. 'Look – Graham Goodall, you know him?'

'Graham Goodall! Yes!' They looked at each other in relief. 'You have Trabant?'

'No no, no. Graham sent me to stop you – going back to his house.' Phil spoke clearly and slowly. 'Tax man has come to see him.'

'Taxman?' They exchanged glances. Boris frowned. 'Taxman here in Middleton?'

'Yes. Tax man is here, mit Graham.' Phil managed to remember the word for 'with'.

'Taxman is in Koblenz, not here.'

'Sorry? Koblenz is in Germany.' Phil was baffled.

'Ja. Koblenz is in Germany'.

Phil shook his head. 'No. Tax man – money,' Phil made a counting gesture with his fingers. 'Money – for tax man. Not in Germany – here.'

The three men broke into German, gesturing and talking as one. Boris put his hand up to silence his passengers. 'No. Not possible. Taxman is good man. Taxman play football.'

'What?' Phil asked sharply in best farce tradition. Boris, in halting English, tried to explain that Taxman was a footballer in Germany, a good footballer and would not be in England looking for money.

'You come to Graham, please,' he commanded. Phil got in the rear seat and with a roll and a sway the Trabant sailed off towards Middleton. Boris shook his head once more. 'Taxman never … not take money … he is good man.'

A Ford Mondeo overtook them, the driver a young man in a white shirt and tie, his jacket hanging behind his seat. It could be the planning officer!

Phil looked at his watch. It was almost half past two. He sighed and sat back. The outcome was beyond his control. He tried to puzzle out the connection between the tax man, a footballer and money. And then it came to him. He opened his mouth to speak and then thought better of it. Anything he said only seemed to make matters worse.

The tax man sat at the roll-top desk in Graham's study, going through Trabant invoices and records. Occasionally he took a sip from the cup of blackcurrant tea which Graham had offered in an attempt to create a human bond. Graham had hovered for a bit before leaving him on his own as an indication of his complete lack of guilt.

Freddy and I stood in the lane, a second line of defence should Phil fail to keep the Germans away.

A Mondeo car came round the square and parked behind the Mercedes. The driver got out, gave us a cursory glance and then walked into the yard, casting an eye over the collection of cars. He was fair-haired and fresh-faced, in his thirties. He hesitated as he looked at us and was about to speak when the shrill clatter of the Trabant drew our attention. It had arrived back with Phil inside.

As Graham emerged from the house, the Germans got out of the car. Boris strode into the yard to confront Graham.

'You have Taxman the footballer here?'

Graham grimaced. 'Footballer?'

Phil jumped in. 'There's a footballer in Germany, called Taxman,' he explained. He looked at Boris. 'I think they've confused him with somebody else.'

A group of pigeons decided to relocate themselves from the rooftop and took off over our heads. A white blob landed on the young man's shoulder. No one thought of telling him.

'Excuse me.' He addressed Graham. 'I'm from the planning department. I gather you're Mr Goodall?'

'That's me.' Graham looked despondent.

'I'm from the council. Planning.'

A bewildered Lazy Eye looked from face to face. 'Where is Taxman?' he asked.

The tax man had just left the house and overheard the remark, 'Excuse me,' he said with injured pride. 'I'm not a tax man, I'm an officer from the Inland Revenue.'

Everyone started to talk at once. The Germans exchanged views in German. The planning officer said 'Look here' several times.

The tax man asked if he could be allowed to speak.

Freddy asked Phil what on earth was going on.

Phil exclaimed, 'Just a minute. I know what's happening.' No one listened to him.

'Stop!' he shouted.

Everyone fell silent. 'Now,' Phil spread out both hands slowly and deliberately. 'I am now going to explain simply, please listen carefully.' He said that there was a tax man – revenue officer – present. The Germans had confused him with a German footballer called Taxman and they had mistakenly jumped to the conclusion that he was being bribed by Graham to throw a football match.

The Germans digested this information. The planning officer frowned, anxious to get on with the job. The tax man peered intently at Graham, his untrimmed moustache quivering. The pigeons flew back over our heads and settled on the roof.

Freddy seized the initiative and addressed the tax man. 'Mr Goodall here is lending these gentlemen from Germany one of his cars. He paused. 'They're from the Trabant Association in Germany. Graham is world president of the club.'

The tax man said 'Aah', in a long drawn out sigh of comprehension, smiled and nodded his satisfaction. The Germans smiled back at him, wondering what he found amusing. He picked up his briefcase. 'It's clear to me you're not trading, Mr Goodall. I'll be writing to you shortly. Bye.' He shook hands, hesitated, smiled and patted one of the Trabants on its bonnet. 'I can't see anybody wanting to buy one of these.'

He walked back to his car. In the pause which followed, one of the Germans turned to Graham with a beaming smile and said in a loud voice, 'We like Trabant. We buy.'

The pigeons fluttered. The revenue man stopped in his tracks for one precise beat and then revolved slowly to stare at Graham. Ten minutes of explanation later, he shook Graham by the hand and, for the second time, said he was satisfied and would be writing to him to that effect.

After he had gone the planning officer, who seemed to have caught the generous mood of officialdom, took Graham aside. 'All I came to check on was the state of the yard. We can't stop you keeping these cars because it doesn't come under our planning laws. This was once used as an overflow parking area for a garage in Youlgreave so you don't even need to apply for change of use. What you must do is keep the place tidy.' He glanced around – the bust of Queen Victoria had disappeared, along with the propane gas bottles and the rest of the jumble, since our last visit. 'Well, you seem to have done that. Keep it up.'

*

After his departure we sat outside around a white ornamental table, partly shaded by the house, the terrace stones sun-warm under our feet. The geese circled overhead on their watchful patrol. Graham brought out some celebratory Feldschlossen and a plate of pretzels, and told us of days gone by.

Each year the villagers drove their sheep down Stinking Lane, a winding stony path running down by what is now Graham's house. The lane was so called because the animals went down to the sheep-wash by the riverside, smelling strongly, and returned as sweet as roses. At noon the process came to a halt for the village feast. Stone jars were pulled out of the cooling river and from them beer or homemade lemonade was poured into flagons and mugs. It was as jolly and heartening a country celebration as anything out of Thomas Hardy.

The Germans talked about their homes in Koblenz, a picturesque town at the junction of the Mosel and Rhine rivers. We toasted ourselves, the hike, the Trabbies and Graham. The Germans, after hearing his account of Diana's visits, proposed a toast to Her Majesty the Queen. Before they left, they presented Graham with gifts from his various friends in Germany: a silver Trabbie miniature steering wheel, a Trabbie watch, a Trabbie pen and a Trabbie pocket knife.

We drove away from Middleton. 'Oh ja,' Freddy imitated Boris. 'Vee did gut. Vee not talk about zee war.' He then broke into the old Beatles song (he remembered all of them): 'Tax man'.

As we neared home, he fell into silent contemplation. We had celebrated Graham's victory and had also seen a Trabant, the ultimate in the art of onedownmanship, the only one of its type in the United Kingdom, going for a song.

Was it a massive gallows, maybe, designed to despatch as many miscreants as possible in one go? Or was it part of a giant rack, a medieval torture machine? We were on our next hike and standing in front of a huge wheel standing in a field close to Sheldon village, near Bakewell. The wheel was balanced horizontally eight feet from the ground. It looked like a device capable of causing all sorts of outrageous pain to the human body.

'It's not many as knows what that is.'

We turned round to find an old man with a walking stick. He had a large strawberry of a nose and wore a cap. He nodded at the machinery. 'That's for pulling up the lead ore. They've kept it there to show how it used to be in the old days.'

This was the Magpie lead-mine, its upper works preserved by the efforts of the local history society. The lead industry began with the Romans. They were, truly, an amazing lot. Without much understanding of strata they dug into the hillsides chasing outcrops of galena. By the fourteenth century lead-mining was so productive that surplus lead was exported to Europe.

Chatsworth House, built in the late seventeenth century, was partly funded by the sale of lead, the rights to which the Dukes of Devonshire had owned since Elizabethan times. Together with seams of copper, coal and large amounts of stone, wealth was concentrated under the ducal feet making them, in turn, the richest aristocrats, and Derbyshire the richest county (one reason why it has more stately homes per square mile than almost anywhere else) until the middle of the eighteenth century, when lead-mining fell into decline. Who said that money was made only south of Watford Gap?

The smaller family-run mines, such as the Magpie lead-mine, were viable until the seventeenth and eighteenth centuries, when ever-deeper mining led to flooding. The high cost of pumping out water led to the miners selling their labour – and mines – to entrepreneurs who exploited them, particularly the children, whose working conditions were arguably worse than those of the chimney boys. Working for a meagre wage, they and their fathers toiled in the deep, wet and dangerous tunnels. Many gave up and lived in even worse poverty. *The Times* newspaper reported that it was 'impossible to conceive the vast depth of misery which exists ...

many of these poor sufferers had their children in bed when visited, whose bedclothes had not a vestige of either linen or flannel about them.'

Daniel Defoe, in his book *A Tour Throughout the Whole Island of Great Britain*, completed in 1727, describes how he stood at the top of one mine-shaft, nothing more than a 36-foot square hole in the ground which plunged vertically to a depth of over seven hundred feet. He looked down in horror. Out of its depths a creature came into view, slowly clambering up the wooden ladder fixed to the sides.

What Defoe saw was not a workman returning home from his labours, but 'a skeleton, pale as a dead corpse, his hair and beard a deep black, and his flesh lank, something of the colour of lead itself, looking like an inhabitant of the dark regions below, who had just ascended into the world of light.' How he had managed to haul himself over seven hundred feet from the bottom was a mystery. The climb alone would have taken forty minutes.

It wasn't the kind of job you would jump at. Nevertheless, there were still some family businesses working lead veins which were capable of returning a profit. Such were the Magpie and the Maypitt at Sheldon.

The old man told us the dark story of the Magpie mine. A hundred and seventy years ago the family owners of the two mines found they were working the same vein of lead ore. It was not unusual for miners to break into other workings, and disputes were usually settled by meetings of representative miners who would judge claims in the back room of local pubs. The Magpie dispute was difficult to solve because both claims had merit. In the meantime the families fought each other above and below ground, lighting fires with the intention of smoking the enemy out of what they considered to be their tunnels. Finally, one day in 1833, the Magpie miners lit an underground bonfire and added sulphur. They knew the draught of air would take the fumes into the Maypitt workings. Three men, two brothers and their father, were killed as a result. Five Magpie men were sent for trial at Derby Assizes. They were acquitted as a result of the difficulty in identifying the culprits, and because the Maypitt miners had acted provocatively by having lit similar fires.

Nevertheless, it was a remarkable verdict in an age when a simple burglary could mean a death sentence. It is said that the widows of the dead men put a curse on the mine, and the creaks and groans of the timbers underground became the voices of the dead.

There is one hike I know so well I could walk it blindfold, but only in my imagination – it has some difficult bits. I have hiked it man and boy for half a century.

It starts at Ilam, just west of Dove Dale, follows the river Manifold northwards, then over the hills to Alstonefield, down to Milldale, south through Dove Dale and back to Ilam. It's our stand-by hike, which we were doing today as time was short. Freddy and I used to walk it on bank holidays in our youth, spurning all others – too busy or too idle to work out new hikes – just content to be out in the fresh air and enjoying a glass or two at the George at lunch-time. That was until Phil, the navigator, came along with his new hikes and painful regime.

Ilam Hall, at the side of the Manifold, is our jump-off place. It's been a youth hostel since 1934, originally built by industrialist Jesse Watts Russell around 1820. The first time I stayed there was with my gang from Chaddesden, circa 1950. One of our enterprising lads discovered a cache of tinned American army 'K' rations that had been dumped in undergrowth at the back of the hall. We opened the tins with pocket knives and dined on chewing-gum and shortbread. I was sick as a dog. Was it past its sell-by date? I have hated shortbread ever since.

The Hall is built of blocks of stone which have turned an unattractive grey-black over time, but is a much more cheerful prospect in the context of the surrounding woods, river, parkland

and church. Just below the Hall the river cascades over a sizeable weir. It was here that Russell built a 150-yard stretch of promenade. This is Paradise Walk, twelve feet wide, bordered by a low wall and a bank of trees and shrubs, mainly ash, wych elm, yew, lime, sycamore and beech. It is easy to imagine the formally dressed dinner guests of over seventy years ago as they promenaded, drinks in hand, taking in the spectacle of the huge bank of trees beyond the stretch of lush meadow by the river side.

The water here is deep, whereas only half a mile upstream the river seems to have dried up. In fact it's simply gone underground and reappears close to the weir in a series of 'boiling holes', through which the underground water forces itself upwards to rejoin the main course. A well-meaning Victorian – a spiritual descendant of King Canute and with more money than sense – tried to concrete over the gaps through which the river went underground. It was a case of pouring money down a hole.

Enclosed by railings at the side of the Walk is the 'Battlestone', a large upright stone about six feet high by two feet. It was unearthed around 1820, when Ilam village was re-built. It is thought – there is no proof – that it commemorates a Saxon battle against the Danes. The Viking Great Army had invaded the North and Midlands from 874.

The footpath follows the river until it reaches a tiny brick-built cottage with a handkerchief-sized front garden, full of hollyhocks and beans, and through which the walker passes close to the cottage window. There used to be a painted sign fixed to the gateway demanding a toll of two pence per person. But the occupants of the cottage allowed wind and weather to obliterate the sign, and the post with the coin-box on top now leans over at a drunken angle. Had the cost of re-painting the sign and re-setting the coin-box outweighed the income from it? Today Phil said we should pay our dues, knowing there was a toll charge legally due. Freddy, the anti-establishment man, refused to pay. 'If there's no sign and if the cost of repainting and fixing the post is too much for them, then we don't pay.'

Phil put his two pence in the box. 'We'll compromise. That's for the three of us,' he said.

Further on, surrounded by fields full of sheep, we climbed up the steep hillside towards Castern Hall, an imposing house of square proportions, built in smooth stone with a stable block at the rear. The present building is William and Mary. It replaced a former house built in Henry the Eighth's reign.

On Freddy's first hike past the Hall, some time in the fifties, he had stopped to peer at the top-floor windows on the footpath side of the house. On a careful inspection he had realised that a few of them were not windows at all, but painted to look like them. He had laughed out loud. What kind of oneupmen were they in those days? It would have been better to have left the wall alone. Freddy did some research and pinned the reason down to a tax on windows introduced in 1696 by King William (a nifty way of raising revenue, and one which, said Freddy, could be *seen through* as such). The tenant, who could not afford the tax, had obviously removed some windows and filled in the gaps with walling. As time went by one of the family descendants, or tenants, had painted the stonework to resemble the original windows. In the latter part of the twentieth century we had witnessed the stone-work being removed and real windows put back in their place.

As we reached Castern Hall, Freddy pointed towards the windows. 'They tell you about the people here. The missing ones show they were broke, the painted ones show they were vain, and the replacement windows show they had common sense!' And then a thought struck him. Excitedly he smacked his hands together. 'Just realised! The painters weren't oneupmen at all! If I paint windows on our blank wall facing the neighbour think how bewildered he'll be! It's great *onedownmanship!*'

The idea continued to give Freddy great amusement as we wended our way round the Hall and towards Alstonefield.

*

Freddy went back to the library and found a book by Brian Magee, *The Confessions of a Philosopher*. It was bang up to date compared with the other stuff he'd been reading and Magee wrote in terms he could understand, perhaps because he'd had a wide experience of life. He had been a Member of Parliament, as well as a university professor and music and theatre critic. Freddy was intrigued to read that Magee felt that great music (Mahler, Mozart, Wagner) and great theatre (Shakespeare) had 'something to do with … the question of *life's meaning*.' Each of them, Shakespeare, Mahler and Wagner combined, according to Magee, had dealt with the totality of human experience. In his view no other single writer, painter, poet or composer had managed to achieve that.

Freddy didn't jump in the air when he read the words 'life's meaning'. He was getting used to setbacks. But, encouraged by the reference, he decided to give the trio a go, even if just to be satisfied that there was nothing there. The great Bard bothered him, however. Despite wanting to enjoy Shakespeare he felt alienated by the archaic language. He had great difficulty trying to understand all those tortuous soliloquies. Poetry was different. There were far fewer words in a poem than a play and Freddy could dwell, absorb and finally comprehend.

Freddy felt even more dissociated from the Bard when he was forced to attend the local Shakespeare Society's offering, in which Jean's brother Max was acting. He had persuaded Jean to go and watch him and she had yanked Freddy along. Freddy couldn't remember the play, nor did he want to. It was in one, early, scene that he completely switched off. His recollection of the actual dialogue is fuzzy.

But it went something like this: Servant appears. Addresses boss. 'He is without my lord.' There should have been a pause between 'without' and 'my'. Coming together it came across as 'he is without his lord'. Who was without his lord? Freddy had laughed out loud at the thought, turning heads and mortifying Jean. Although it didn't measure highly on the Freddy scale of misbehaviour, Jean said he was getting more infantile the older he got. Instead of a retirement home Freddy would be better suited to a nursery.

He decided not to start with Mahler. Magee said he had 'lived a life' while listening to one of his symphonies. Freddy had been to Birmingham some years before to watch Simon Rattle's hair jump and down as he conducted Mahler's Fifth, but had no experience of having 'lived a life' during it. It was beautiful music but he had not felt drained by an 'emotional experience', as Magee had, nor was any light shed on the mystery of the 'meaning'.

What he would do, Freddy decided, was to give Wagner an airing. Now here was a man who wrote big music and Freddy had a big car journey to make, to collect an MGB part from a place in Hull. He bought a CD of the *Ring* operas and his intention was to play it on the journey, choosing bits of the four operas that caught his fancy – 'bleeding chunks', as they are known in the music business. Later, at home, he would wait until Jean was out of the house, lie down and surrender himself – and see what happened.

It was a hot day on the run north and he wound the window down. He had just come up to a red traffic light near Hull when the second Act of *Die Walküre* began. He turned the volume up, trying to drown himself in the excitement that the music provoked – wave upon wave of rising emotion, the bass-baritone voice of Wotan and the soprano acrobatics of Brünnhilde surging towards its dramatic conclusion.

The traffic light appeared to be stuck, and restless drivers were honking their horns for someone to make a move. Freddy turned his head and saw a Golf GTI alongside. The young guy inside also had his windows down, letting out the ear-splitting 'thump thump thump' from a heavy metal band. Wagner and Iced Earth was a confusion too much for a driver behind. He switched on his own music to drown the cacophony. And now they had rock and roll as well as Iced Earth and Wagner.

A weary-looking man with a lean sharp face climbed out of an old Citroën in front of Freddy and walked back to him, choosing him as the least likely of the disc jockeys to cause him grievous bodily harm. He bent down and whispered: 'Do you mind?' or that's how Freddy thought he heard it. In fact it was delivered in a scream: 'Why don't you turn it up! I can't hear it!'

'What?' shouted Freddy.

The lights had changed. Traffic was on the move. Horns were blowing behind Freddy's queue. The man went back to his car. The heavy metal guy grinned at Freddy and zoomed off.

The second act of *Die Walküre* came to an end. The Citroën had not yet got going. The line was stuck.

All that Freddy could hear were horns blowing. In that moment he rejected Wagner. He was too dramatic, he told me later, arousing passion and excitement which contributed nothing to meaning. He said he had thought of diminutive, peaceful Rui at the Buddhist Centre.

He returned home, listening to the Beatles.

7

JULY

We lay on our backs in the sheep-cropped grass north of Hartington, becalmed by the humid air and the buzzing of bees. Lunch, for once, had been a lazily indulged ritual. Phil was the first to rise. He poked me with his foot. Then I heard Freddy murmur, 'Gruppenführer, do not kick me. Why can you never enjoy a moment of peace?'

A crack, a sizzling sound and, three seconds later, an aerial explosion that echoed down the valley provided the answer. We were on our feet so fast, and packing away lunch boxes and flasks with the rapid motions of figures in a silent film, that I felt momentarily dizzy. I glanced upwards to see towering cumulonimbus clouds, heavyweight cauliflowers in the sky.

'We used to say thunder was God moving his furniture,' Freddy said, breathing heavily with the speed of effort. 'I believed it was true until I was nine. Why is it that practically everything we were taught to believe in as kids has been knocked down?'

'No discipline,' Phil answered promptly. 'Kids could be –'

'Kids could be smacked by teachers,' Freddy chimed in.

'Every male had to do a stint of –' Phil struggled with his rucksack.

'Military service,' Freddy said, as we exchanged grins. It was a litany we knew by heart.

'Sunday school was the norm, legislation favoured –' Phil did not seem to notice the send-up.

'The police – not the criminal.' I put in my pennyworth. We scurried away from a nearby tree, a potential deathtrap – even at thirty yards' distance – if lightning struck it.

'You've missed something, Gruppenführer – respect for the elderly,' Freddy shouted over a rumble of thunder.

'That's right. No race problems either. And –' Phil was interrupted by a lightning strike to our left. A pause, then came the loudest crash of thunder yet.

'And no consumer society, so nothing to nick!' Freddy shouted. 'Here endeth the lesson!' Cheerfully he added, 'Hooray!' I joined in his laughter. Phil was too busy gazing cautiously upwards to notice. A jagged strike of lightning cracked the sky to our right. Under attack from both sides, we hurried into an open field for safety. The hilltops flickered to an electric dance. Hailstones – yes, in July – began to pitter-patter all around us. Within a minute they were drumming and bouncing off the hard baked path, and within two minutes our boots crunched through a bobbly white carpet.

As quickly as it had begun, the thunderstorm was over. We had come to a part of the hillside where the land fell steeply away to form a deep bowl, bordered on one side by a dense wood. The footpath was narrow, running along the lip of the bowl. Without warning a scatter of large raindrops thudded into the white footpath. We tore off our rucksacks and scrambled to put waterproofs on, but the weather-god had the jump on us. The rain beat down. No time to fiddle with zips and bits of Velcro. All I could do was huddle over and clutch my flapping anorak tight across my chest. A car-wash would have found it hard to compete with the amount of water dumped.

The deluge lasted three minutes, and stopped abruptly. We

cautiously removed our dripping anoraks and stood upright to find that the bulging woolpack clouds had magically shrunk, almost to nothing. The hot noon sun hit our faces. The weather-god had wandered off, his moment of fun over.

'Sssh!' Phil motioned us to stop moving. I turned my head slowly and followed his gaze down into the bowl. A large dog-fox had ambled out of the wood and stood motionless, staring at a small flock of sheep. We were in a direct line between the fox and the sun, so it was unlikely to see us. We were not betrayed by our scent either, as the faintest of breezes put us upwind of the animal.

The sheep were on the move now, some running while others, less mobile, struggled to get clear. One of these had a lame hind-leg and had great difficulty in making its escape. It tried frantically to climb the bank. The fox moved carefully towards his target, eyes fixed. I had a flashback from a moment in Kenya when a lion, viewed from the safety of our safari vehicle, had walked slowly towards a herd of kudu. Its quiet concentration was embodied in the fox.

The enfeebled sheep had only seconds to live, the distance ten feet and closing. Six feet – I thought I could see the muscles bunching in the fox's hindquarters. The glint in his eyes reflected the sun. Had anyone ever been as close to a fox about to kill, insulated from it by wind and sun, as we were? There was a twitch of its ears. His muzzle wrinkled. He paused, and was still again. The sheep stumbled and slithered backwards, then looked at the fox, turned away once more and tried to walk up the bank.

Two steps forward, one back, its chances of escape nil. The fox crouched ready for the deadly leap. I drew in a deep breath. 'Tally ho! Whoa! Eh you! Gerrout of it!' We shouted our separate warnings. The fox jerked his head towards us in shock and, blinded by the sun, turned and ran back towards the wood. Before disappearing he gave a backwards glance and then shook his head, almost as if to say that hikers should know better than to interfere with nature.

In our hiking lives we have helped old ladies cross the road, returned lost children to their parents, rounded up cattle that had broken out of a field, helped catch sheep – and now we'd saved one from a fox.

An hour later we passed a farmhouse. The window frames and front door shone with a bright green paint. Above the doorway the date 1790 was carved on the stone. There was a large cattle yard and several outbuildings, mostly neglected and in disuse. The door to the stone barn leaned outwards, held by one hinge only. Old birds' nests drooped from the eaves and bindweed poked through gaps in the stonework. The yard was partially overgrown with nettles and weeds. Rusting bits of old machinery and parts – axle, tractor seat, mudguard, bonnet – lay against the barn walls. The covered open barn had part of its corrugated roof missing. Underneath were stacks of wooden crates, piles of breeze-blocks, broken concrete slabs and the wreck of an Austin Metro surrounded by black plastic binliners tangled up with rotting pieces of wood, wire, mouldy carpets and piles of moss-covered timbers. The entrance gate, made of tubular galvanised-steel, was in relatively good condition except that the wooden post to which it was attached had tilted slightly and the opening end of the gate touched the ground.

An early Land Rover, some fifty years old, approached and stopped, its diesel engine rattling like stones in a barrel. The vehicle had dent marks all over it and the mud of years had coagulated and hardened to form a concrete skirt halfway up the bodywork. The driver got out to open the gate. He was in his sixties, and wore a tweed cap and an oversized jacket. His face was angular with 'up' lines around the mouth denoting a cheerful personality. He showed crooked teeth as he spoke. 'How do,' he said happily. 'Nice now, eh?'

We agreed that it was nice now and watched him try to lift the gate. 'Slips an inch or two every day. I must get that post fixed. Do yer mind 'elping me lift it?'

The man in the passenger-seat seemed impervious to all this. He was round-faced, probably in his thirties, and smiled through the windscreen at nothing in particular. With his right index finger he traced a line across his cheek.

We helped the farmer open the gate wide enough to let in the vehicle. He drove the Land Rover into the yard, parked it and got out with his passenger, who stood looking at us, his finger still at his cheek.

'Most kind, gentlemen,' the farmer said, and then hesitated, with a glance at the younger man. 'I wonder if you'd do me another favour. You look educated gentlemen, as though you know a thing or two.' He hesitated again, indicating the younger man.

'This is Benjamin, my lad.'

Benjamin smiled. His finger traced a new line across his cheek. His father took off his cap, scratched his head and thought of the best way to put it. 'I just need a spot of advice. 'Ave you got a moment? Do yer mind?'

Phil looked as though he were searching for a way to object, but Freddy spoke for us. 'What's the problem?'

'I'd best show yer in the 'ouse.' We followed the farmer to the side door, which had been left unlocked, and passed through the kitchen and the dark square hallway into the living-room – surprisingly bright, but then we saw why. The age of the house suggested that it would have been built with oak beams and would have had an inglenook fireplace. It had neither.

In place of the inglenook was a minimal fire-surround made of machine-cut stone. The beams were boarded over and painted an egg-shell colour to match the walls. It was neatly done. The furniture consisted of an Ikea-style oatmeal fabric sofa and armchair and a low teak coffee-table. A Jacobean oak corner-cupboard with a fine dark rich patina was presumably a survivor of the original room. A couple of ceramic ducks were pinned to the wall above the fire-surround. It could have been any living-room on any housing estate in the country. I hoped the local conservation officer would never be invited inside. The farmer caught our look of surprise.

'I know what you're going to say,' he said cheerfully. 'Where's that old inglenook and beams gone to? Hah, well I got rid of 'em all. Good riddance, eh? I boxed them beams in meself and did the fireplace. Not a bad job. Aye, much better, lighter, modern – yer can't beat it.' He paused and his face fell. 'Hill farming's 'ad it, you know. Last year I earned five thousand pounds. That's all. I've 'ad to do jobs for the National Trust repairing footpaths to get some money in. You see, my problem –'

He broke off as Benjamin walked into the room and sat down in the armchair, a packet of crisps in his hand, facing the television. 'Now then, hang on – Benjamin wants the telly on.' He switched on the television. 'You see, Benjamin's not 'ad a good education since 'is mother died.' He pointed to a neat double row of the old large-volume edition of *Encyclopaedia Britannica* stacked along the skirting-board under the window.

'What I want to know is 'ow best to use these books 'ere, to get 'im to read. I bought these last week. Guess what I paid? You'll never believe it. Five quid. Five quid to take 'em away, the lady said. There's some nice pictures in it, get 'is interest.' He bent down to pick up one of the volumes. 'Now it says it somewhere, where is it? It says "*all the knowledge in the world 'ere*". I know they're a bit old but things don't change that much, do they?' He paused again. His tone changed, sounding troubled. 'You see, I've got to get some money comin' in, and what I thought was … well, I'd turn this place into making ice-cream.' He flicked through the pages. 'See, when I go, yer know, Benjamin will be on 'is own. But if 'e can read 'e can run the business, you see. And what I wanted to know from you gentlemen was, well, do you think I can teach 'im with these books?'

We mumbled: 'Should think so … give it a try … we're not teachers ourselves but …' and other get-out-of-trouble phrases.

Benjamin smiled at Blue Peter-clone TV presenters shouting

as they played a game for under-fives, not looking at his crisps but feeling for them in the packet, his eyes riveted to the screen.

'I've been to the bank just now,' the farmer said. 'I told 'em there was no really nice 'ome-made ice cream in the area. But they said they'd want this farm as, er, what do yer call it, coll ...?'

'Collateral?' I said.

'Yes, that's it! Collateral! Benjamin? You eat any more of them crisps and you'll get fat, and then where will we be?'

We managed to extricate ourselves with excuses about time and itinerary – three embarrassed men. Benjamin, judging by his devotion to the under-fives programme, would be a 'special needs' case, unlikely to respond to a reading lesson using the language of the encyclopaedia. At a simple guess, if he had reached his thirtieth year without learning to read there wasn't much chance now. And so we had taken the coward's way out.

I felt like the man who had lent a tin of paint to his neighbour and went round to recover it. He knocked on the door asking if Harry was in, and Harry's wife stared at him pale-faced. 'Haven't you heard? Harry died yesterday. Heart attack.' The neighbour stood paralysed for a moment, and then blurted out, 'Did he say anything about a tin of paint?'

We thought it would be some time before we came this way again. As it turned out, it would be sooner than we imagined.

After days of temperatures in the thirties the blow-torch over southern and eastern England had swung north and westwards. It is at times like this that escape into the Peak is a relief. There are always compensations in the sights and the sounds of the Peak in summer.

Most of the sixty-odd million people who inhabit this country only get the chance to use a fraction of their senses in the overinsulated, over-stimulated hurly-burly of everyday urban life. There are few places left in Britain where you are far enough away from aircraft and traffic to sense that pure silence, that heavy stillness in which each blade of grass, each stone and each puff of cloud, possess a luminous sense of being.

The same can be said of other sounds. Modern life brings with it a non-stop barrage of unnatural noises – car, television, radio, phone, strimmer, washing-machine – a mostly unnoticed source of mental and spiritual stress. Walking in the Peak, sounds are isolated and pure and calm the mind – the alien curlew's call from the moor, the far-off cuckoo in the spring, or the rushing noise of water, clear and crystal, cascading over the dark weir.

Sometimes Freddy and I stop as one, caught by beams of misty sunlight streaming through foliage in a wood, or we pause to stare at pink and white campion flowers magically illuminating a bank in Lathkill Dale, or, above the Derwent valley, lift our hypnotised faces at the wheeling glide of a peregrine falcon.

Phil, of course, is a hundred yards ahead by now, tapping his stick in frustration. 'I keep telling you. Hiking is hiking,' he says. 'And botany is botany – choose.'

We ask: 'What is this life if full of care, we have no time to stand and stare?'

There is a dell, near Longnor, well away from the beaten track and reached only by an old drover's way. In this dell is a tiny pack-horse bridge, underneath which tumbles the stream, edged by watercress and marshy flowers, trees and an old stone sheep dip. The medieval pathway, made of ancient stones and cobbles and just wide enough for the passage of driven sheep or cows, winds down a hillside to the bridge. It is like stepping back a thousand years, untouched and perfect. On one particular route it serves as our lunch stop – as today.

We sat in silence on the grassy bank, munching our salads and listening to the sound of tinkling water – until a faint engine noise could be heard, growing louder. Suddenly, a scramble-bike slid into view over the rough cobbled pathway, ridden by a man of indeterminate age, dressed in red leathers and a black helmet with an impenetrable black visor. He halted the slide, slithered in the opposite direction and then brought the machine back into line with expert ease. The bike was now ten yards away and, short of the bridge, dropped down the bank into the stream. The rider stood upright on both foot-rests, legs straight, as he negotiated his way around stones, the exhaust burbling. At the far side the engine note rose to a short scream as he lifted the front wheel high enough to place it on the bank. The bike rose up to settle on both wheels and then disappeared around the bend of the hillside, the noise fading – but not quite – into silence.

It took ten seconds before we gave simultaneous vent to our outrage at the desecration of our perfect place. 'The bastard didn't even come over the bridge.' Phil lowered his foot to kick the water, causing a splash.

'He needs hanging,' said Freddy.

'We ought to report that guy,' Phil said. 'Trouble is, I'd never remember the registration number. I can't even remember what colour it was.' He sucked his teeth in annoyance.

'Don't talk about memory,' Freddy said. 'I was at my nephew's wedding and what happened? I had to introduce somebody to somebody and I said this is – er, er – dithering, like an idiot, so I escaped – just remembered, I shouted, left my car lights on!'

'Look,' said Phil, 'nobody could have been more embarrassed than me. I was at a funeral – Ruth's dad. There was somebody I thought I knew and I kept thinking: I know you. So I asked somebody who he was and they said, "He's your brother, you idiot!"'

We packed away our lunch things and set off, still laughing at Phil's joke.

'Gruppenführer?' said Freddy. 'I'm more bothered about your legs than your brain.'

'How do you mean, you're bothered about my legs?'

'You don't seem to have run up any hills lately. Is it anno domini? Or have you, at last, come to your senses?'

'No, I'm doing it out of respect for your old legs, Freddy.' The footpath narrowed, forcing us to walk one behind the other. Phil always used to lead but recently I had noticed that he opted for bringing up the rear whenever a narrow footpath forced us to walk like this. Freddy had spotted it, too. He turned round: 'Why are you slacking, Gruppenführer?'

'Just a bit hot. I've put a bit of weight on as well.'

'You fat? I don't believe it. I was the one who was fat. At school all the budding fascists were knocking me about, but I bet you had a wonderful time learning torture at your Gruppenführer training school.'

'Freddy, I was bullied at school. I was small. Small kids get bullied, you know?'

'Ah, but I bet you were taught how to dish it out as well! You became the heroic games player while I read Billy Bunter. You'd play football on Saturday morning while I ran errands for my mother. If I had a pound for every kick, punch and skin-burn – they used to stretch the skin and rub it hard with their knuckles.'

'I did it with my fist,' Phil shot a grin towards me.

'Exactly! Did you get top marks for torture? And when we had the annual school cross-country race – of course it had to take place in winter – budding Gruppenführers like you had already finished while I was stumbling and throwing up at the halfway mark, hoping to die. One year I took a short cut. Why not? I was tail-end Charlie and what's the point of pain for pain's sake? Well, I was spotted by somebody – probably the history master's wife who lived there – I'd met her, a real Mrs Gruppenführer. The next day my name was called out in assembly. I was dragged on to the stage by my ear and shown off to the whole school for what I was, a no-good. The head said I would never be a team player. I was marked out for special treatment. Which I got.'

Phil clapped his hands. 'Stout headmaster. Exactly what you deserved, Freddy. We all pay the penalty for your shortcomings.'

'I hadn't noticed, Gruppenführer. If you ask me, I'd say your masochism has done for you. I'll be quicker than you soon.'

Phil didn't reply and I dared not turn round to catch

his expression. He retaliated quickly, though, changing the conversation. 'Freddy, when are you going back to that Buddhist place?' he asked.

'I thought I might go next week some time.'

'Well, don't forget to hum at the hat-stand as you go in.'

It gave me cause for thought. Freddy had aroused my interest in the Buddhist Centre. How many English villages can boast a Buddhist Centre, apart from Etwall? None, as far as I know. I asked Freddy if he minded if I joined him and he was only too pleased. The fun side of him was already at work conjuring up wild scenarios of villains disguised as monks working for a wicked tycoon, James Bond style. Monk sweeps should be carried out at regular intervals, he said. Tractors could be fitted with monk-sweepers, similar to the cow-catchers on the front of American trains.

I was still laughing as Freddy drove up the impressive drive. Freddy pointed out Rui, who was tilling the soil on one of the borders. He hesitated when he saw us, but when Freddy waved he threw up both arms, recognition shining from his face in a big smile.

As we waited in the large hallway, I picked up a leaflet on a side table and read that the 'Buddha Tara was full of compassion and a manifestation of the wind element of all the Buddhas'.

The receptionist went out and returned with an English man, who was shaven-headed and wearing the saffron and red-striped habit of the Tara order. She introduced him to us as Lab Sum. He looked about thirty years old and had a calm smile.

We went into the sitting-room. Lab Sum went straight to the silver tea dispenser which stood on a mahogany sideboard. The room bore no trace of anything oriental. Apart from the sideboard it was furnished with a chintzy sofa and two armchairs. Lab Sum poured the tea in silence. I broke it. 'When did you become a monk – er – Lab?' I asked, the image of a chemist's laboratory in mind. And should I have used his full name?

'After university. I was reading psychology,' he chuckled. 'Living on a grant.' He handed Freddy a cup of tea with saucer. 'That's how it began. We had a Buddhist group and I joined, went from there.'

Freddy warmed to him. 'And how has your life changed since then?'

'Well, as a student I satisfied all the usual cravings – drink, food – whatever I wanted. But now I have none of these things.' He gestured for us to sit on the sofa, handed me a cup of tea and turned to pour one for himself.

There was a pause as Freddy glanced at me. 'Don came along out of interest. I don't know why it is but I seem to be the only person who's worried about why I'm here on this earth and what it's all about. You look as though you've found the answer.' He broke off as he saw Lab Sum shake his head. He answered, 'No,' before sitting down in one of the armchairs, cradling the cup of tea in his hands.

'No?' Freddy's long face fell like a landslide.

'It's not something you can just stumble across, especially in the western workaday world. As a monk I can pursue it full-time but most westerners can't.' He looked at Freddy. 'You're anxious, aren't you.' It was a statement, not a question. Before Freddy could answer he continued. 'Feel your cup of tea, concentrate on its warmth.'

Freddy put his hands around the cup. It wasn't too hot. 'Just feel the sensation, how comforting it is.'

Freddy closed his eyes for a moment.

'Now smell it, breathe it in.' Freddy obeyed the instruction. 'Now drink some and feel the sensation of it passing down your throat.' Freddy sipped his tea, held it in his mouth as for a wine-tasting and swallowed it slowly – I did the same.

'While you were doing that were you anxious?'

'No,' Freddy said. 'You, Don?'

'No,' I said.

'Most people,' continued Lab Sum, 'I have to say in the whole of the western world, not just England – look to the future all the time. They don't live in the present. Would you agree?'

'Yes,' Freddy admitted. 'We hope for things to happen. That makes us anxious in case it doesn't.'

'You have just said a word we never use. Can you guess what it is?'

'Anxious?'

'Nearly – the word's hope. What does hope bring?'

'Ah.' Freddy nodded, indicating that he could see where this was leading. His own voice level had dropped. Lab Sum was so relaxed and calm that to speak to him in anything above a half-whisper would have constituted assault and battery.

'What happens,' asked Lab Sum, 'while you're hoping? What takes place in the mind?'

'Well, I suppose it's worry.'

'Looking forward produces hope that leads to fear. That's the other word that's not in our dictionary – fear. Like next week you may earn a lot of money if what you hope for works out – but then you fear it may not happen. So if you don't hope you don't experience fear, do you?'

'So it's all about the here-and-now,' Freddy nodded in understanding.

'And isn't that all we've got? We don't experience the future, do we, except in our hopeful and fearful minds?'

On the way home I read in one of the Tara leaflets that a meditation class, billed as 'The Art of Enlightenment', was open to the public the following Wednesday. I pointed it out to Freddy. 'Fancy going along?' I asked.

'Yes, why not. By the way, did you notice in their meditation room that they've got both chairs and cushions. If it comes to you and me tossing up for the last chair, it's mine. Okay?'

When Freddy got home Jean told him that a friend from his

school days had died of a heart attack. It reinforced Lab Sum's teaching about living for the present and not the future. Freddy was determined to go to the Buddhist evening class.

Freddy and I broke all taboos when we talked about the inevitable business of dying. We never touched on it in Phil's presence. Talk of dying, to him, was nothing short of treachery. But Freddy and I often talked about death, treating it as natural, not a taboo. We made up jokes like 'old hikers never die, they just trail away'. There were two ways of facing the final curtain, we decided. The first was to smoke and drink at will and adopt a relaxed attitude to life. Enjoy yourself. Like Sinatra, do it your way.

Another was to crumble gracefully, have a passive but enjoyable retirement and, at the end, get out as quietly as you can. Both my parents achieved this. There were no grand exit scenes. The last thing my father said to me was, 'Don't switch the light off.'

My mother did things in equal style. Told that she wouldn't last till morning, I sat at her bedside chatting to her friend. It got too much for mother. She said, 'Stop talking' in a petulant voice, as if we were simply chatting away at the cinema and had interrupted her enjoyment of the film. In both cases it demonstrated a life in the present. Both sounded quite happy near death.

Both exits gave me hope.

We sat eating lunch poised high on the hillside above Matlock Bath. Through a gap in the tree canopy beneath I could see the stone wall that separated the river from the road. It curved in a southerly direction towards the spa building around the bend.

My thoughts switched to Phil, who sat beside me. He had laboured during the climb and appeared tired. He had been uncharacteristically quiet during the morning. I was drawn to the conclusion that Phil had chosen this hike around Matlock, with its steep and long climbs, to set our minds at rest over his apparent lack of fitness on the last hike. Had it backfired?

'All right, Phil?' I asked.

He looked at me and grinned. 'No problem.' He stopped himself from saying something else and then quickly changed the subject. 'Freddy the Buddhist. Now, that'll be the day. Ruth's got a book of religious jokes. Want to hear a few about Buddhism?'

'Go on,' said Freddy patiently.

'I've reached nirvana – what do I do next?'

Freddy laughed.

I struggled. Phil looked at me. 'Nirvana is the end, the ultimate goal. There is no next!'

I laughed, as much at my slowness as the joke.

Phil looked at Freddy, who had his nose over his coffee cup. 'What are you doing, Freddy?'

'I'm doing what the monk told me to do.'

'Hah. He's wrong. You drink it through your mouth.' Phil chuckled. 'You know what Woody Allen said about Buddhists? He was amazed that so many Buddhists wanted to know the universe. He couldn't find his way around Chinatown.'

I sensed that Phil was resorting to humour to cover up whatever problem he had. If he had chosen today to prove his fitness he had made a mistake. As we began the afternoon stretch he trudged slowly as if the weight of his rucksack was too much to bear. Where was the masochistic delight? For the first time ever his troops were outpacing him, even having to slow down to allow him to catch up.

Phil, rather obviously, tried to distract us and cover up his weakness by cracking another joke. 'Buddhist monk driving a car, hits and kills a Catholic monk's dog. Says to him, "Sorry, my karma ran over your dogma."'

Freddy laughed out loud with me. 'Gruppenführer, brilliant. Whoever said the Hun had no humour stands to be corrected. Where do you get it from?'

Phil's jokes did something to allay our fears. But only for a time. He stopped, just short of a steep stretch of footpath, calling for an additional break. He sat on the ground and splashed some bottled water on his forehead and neck. This was unparalleled in the history of our hike. Phil had never allowed unscheduled breaks.

'You okay?' Freddy asked with real concern. There was a long pause during which I sensed that Phil knew the game was up.

'No. I'm knackered,' he said.

'Why?'

'Oh …' Phil shrugged. 'Not getting enough sleep.'

Freddy was astonished. 'Gruppenführer, not getting enough sleep? You slept for England the night we camped. It was us who didn't get any sleep!'

The story came out grudgingly as we hiked the last leg back to Middleton Top. For the last six months, Phil said, he'd been getting less and less sleep. At first he had ignored the problem and assumed it would go away. In youth it is possible to 'make up' for lost sleep. Not so when you are old, Phil had found. Worrying about not sleeping made it worse. Bedtime had become a battle ground, the bed developing a malevolent personality, the pillow its fellow conspirator.

He'd tried grannie's remedy of warm milk laced with whisky. And he had sat in an armchair saying to himself 'I am tired and want to sleep' over and over again. It didn't work, so he had said the converse, 'I don't want to sleep.' This mantra was – ironically – successful. He didn't sleep.

'So what does Strangebugger say about it all?' asked Freddy.

Phil shook his head. Strangebugger had referred him to some homeopathic remedies which hadn't worked. So he went to his GP and was given Temazapam, one of the common hypnotics that only work if you're not anxious. It had limited success and he couldn't face taking it for the rest of his life. He rattled off the various 'cures' he had tried – a visit to an acupuncturist where sleep turned out to be more than a pinprick away, a hypnotist who had relieved him of £150, herbal remedies, sleep tapes which played sounds of waves breaking on the shore, antihistamines for their side-effect of causing drowsiness, massage and aromatherapy. In the end he went back to the GP, who gave him a questionnaire to fill in and said that most insomniacs in his experience were just depressed.

Strangely enough, Phil's aggregate score bemused the doc, who was forced to declare that he wasn't depressed but, just to be on the safe side, had prescribed an anti-depressant, not for its intended cure but for its side-effect of inducing sleepiness. Amitriptyline had a fifty-year history of being a safe drug, was cheap to prescribe – and it worked. Phil had a full night's sleep. But – there was a price to pay. Phil said he was okay for walking on the flat, but climbing hills was another matter. His legs simply would not work. He couldn't go ten steps up a gradient of more than ten degrees without a prickling tide rushing from his legs straight up his spine and into his brain. His eyes inflated under the pressure. He felt he would either faint or burst a blood vessel. He wanted to ditch the little yellow pills but then, of course, he wouldn't sleep.

We began walking again. 'Hah zo, mein Gruppenführer, zat is vy you haf not kommen up zie hills! I vill now run up ein hill and grin down at you!'

Freddy jogged forward to press home the point that the tables had turned. But why hadn't Phil told us this before? We really didn't need to ask. It was obvious what the problem was. His pride was in the firing line. He'd hoped the side-effect of the pills would wear off before he was found out.

Later, as we arrived back at the car, Freddy had a brainwave. 'Gruppenführer, I haf ze answer. You kommen mit us to ze Buddhist meeting!'

Phil gave him a sceptical smile. Freddy wasn't put off. 'What have you got to lose?'

'I do not believe in reincarnation. You might, I don't.'

Freddy had overlooked this difficult aspect of Buddhist teaching. 'But if it's true, Gruppenführer, think! It's the ideal way of solving your time-stretching puzzle! You just keep coming back as different people – you could go on for ever!'

'Yeah? Knowing my luck I'd come back as you.'

Freddy pondered on the problem. He remembered seeing the Dalai Lama interviewed on television, and had thought him the perfect example of a human being who, in his own words, was 'committed to abide long enough to dispel the misery of this world'.

But how to get Phil to the meeting? What chink was there in Phil's armour? What ruse could he employ? Think laterally – what does Phil like most? Answer – curry. He persuaded Jean to invite Phil and myself for an early supper before the meeting. It would be a very hot curry, his favourite, Jalfreezi prawns cooked with fresh green chilli, capsicum and onion.

We ate outside on the patio, seated around Freddy's plantation-teak garden table, shaded from the continuing heat by a large colourful umbrella. After the meal Freddy suggested that we hikers went for a drink in the Plough and Rake. A pint to the good, Freddy casually mentioned the Buddhist meeting, which was in half an hour's time. Phil was in such a good mood following the delicious meal that he gave way, even expressing a mild interest. He said that, at the worst, it would be a laugh.

The Buddhist Centre windows were wide open as we drove down the redwood-lined drive. The polished sun still burnt at seventhirty. I could feel the radiant warmth of the building as we followed a queue of people into the hallway. A group had already gathered. They chatted to each other and in turn paid their fees to the receptionist sitting at a small table in a corner of the hallway.

Shoes were removed and placed in a rack. Lab Sum arrived and greeted Freddy and me, and we introduced him to Phil. It was time to take our seats in the meditation room. There were five rows of chairs behind each other facing a raised platform. The last row went back into the bay window. A few cushions had been placed in front of the chairs.

Clearly, for the majority of Buddhist followers, the journey to nirvana was helped by sitting comfortably. Phil looked about him with a faintly sceptical smile. He would not embrace anything weird, but the people present would not have looked out of place on a visit to a National Trust house.

About thirty people sat in the five rows of chairs, with one or two younger people sitting, legs crossed, on the cushions. Freddy, Phil and I sat in the middle of the audience. We were surprised to find Lab Sum joining us. As he exchanged greetings with those around him we wondered who would be taking the class?

The question was answered as a tall man of about thirty-five entered the room. He wore a grey suit, blue shirt and tie, and looked like a chartered accountant or a solicitor. He stood in front of the Buddha icon, bowed with his hands placed together and then recited a prayer, a foreign language to the three of us but joined in by most of the group, some of whom rented flats in the building.

The tall man stepped on to the raised dais and squatted down on a cushion to face the audience. He looked serene as he welcomed us, the new guests. He began with the art of relaxation.

We followed his instructions. 'Let the pressure go from the top of your head. Feel it dissipating down through the neck and shoulders. Let the shoulders droop. Let the tension go, down and down through the chest and back, to the stomach. Let it flow down, out of you, down through your thighs, down through the knees and down through the feet into the ground beneath. Let it all go.'

There was harmony inside the room. The drone of bees was heard through the open windows. Our tutor told us to concentrate on the tips of our noses, sensing the breath leaving our nostrils. 'Now imagine you are breathing in light and breathing out smoke. Fill your body with light.'

The room was silent. No clocks ticked. Apart from the bees the only other sound was the faint chug-chug of a tractor in a neighbouring field. Breathing was reduced through bodily relaxation to a minimum. The end of my nose became my universe. All around, minds drifted into a quiescent and unruffled calm. Thirty souls in close harmony.

The human digestive system, beyond the initial peristaltic motion, involves the production of hydrochloric acid in the breaking down of food into a substance called chyme. This passes via the pyloric sphincter into the small and large intestines, from whence the nutrients move into the bloodstream. At the same time the waste residue passes via the colon into the rectum.

All three of us, by dint of communal troughing of some very hot substances, were at more or less the same stage in this highly efficient absorption and waste disposal system. A triumvirate of stomachs filled with beer, chilli, capsicum and onion makes for a volatile concoction. Enzymes aplenty were deployed within to hasten the process.

The gentle silence was first broken by a melodious gurgle from Phil's midriff, followed by a high-pitched squeaking. Freddy then joined the refrain as second piccolo, emitting a high-pitched musical note rippling low down in the digestive tract. He had difficulty controlling a burp. I contributed to the refrain with a repressed bass epigastric note. Normally, this orchestra of sounds would not have been heard amidst general conversation against the background of everyday noises.

In that utter silence, that massed quietude created by earnest and sensitive souls in search of enlightenment, the sounds were magnified and resonated with a reverberation that was as disruptive of genteel reverie as it was excruciatingly embarrassing. The situation might have been confinable, even saveable, if the three sets of nutrient manufacturing machines had switched themselves off at that point. They didn't. They rose to a crescendo despite desperate attempts by the three instrumentalists to shut them down.

Beads of perspiration sprang from my brow. I could hear Freddy breathing in short gasps beside me. At that critical moment a phrase from one of the leaflets jumped into my head – ridiculous and appallingly funny in the circumstances: 'the Buddha Tara was … a manifestation of the *wind* element of all the Buddhas.'

Freddy farted.

8

AUGUST

The temperature in the shade was 28 degrees Centigrade. Under the sun it was more like 35. And we were hiking. Freddy had routinely called Phil to declare him insane, and having routinely failed to abort the hike, unleashed a fiendish wheeze to save the day. He told me in bits and pieces after the hike what had happened.

It began with his phone call to Phil. 'Stevens, do you know what the forecast is for today? It's going to be 32 degrees. You're not proposing we go out in that?' Freddy sat at his kitchen table, phone to one ear, looking at a coloured flyer headed 'Steam Fair' which depicted a large steamroller.

Phil sat in his conservatory, eating breakfast. 'The rule is quite clear,' he squawked in exasperation down the phone. 'Freddy, listen …'

'Gruppenführer, have you looked at rule 32a recently? Or even 50c para 2?' Freddy traced his finger along the picture, stopping at the roller's name-plate: 'Leviathan'. He had made his call on automatic pilot, his usual reaction to the outside temperature being either too hot or too cold for hiking. All his attention was taken by the picture and the memories which flowed from it.

'What's rule 32a?' Phil asked cynically. 'There isn't one.'

'You don't know rule 32a? I don't believe it.' Freddy's tone was mild. His memories of the steam age were sharp and clear.

'Freddy,' Phil said, 'you know it's only snow, fog and holidays that stop us, not the sun. Anyway, Don's going,' he added and drank his ration of cranberry juice.

Freddy smiled at the picture. He loved steamrollers with their enduring simplicity and honesty of purpose. He spoke in a distant tone: 'When we drew up those rules the earth wasn't warming at the rate it is now – and anyway what about your legs?'

'A lot better.' Phil quickly changed the subject. 'Come on, it's a beautiful day.' He hated showing weakness. He had high hopes that today might show his will to be stronger than the side-effects of the little yellow sleeping pills.

It was now 8 am. Freddy stared at the coloured leaflet in longing. He had told me many times how – as a child in 1945 – he had watched Hercules, a 12-ton steamroller, demolish a wartime concrete road-block outside the Gloria cinema in Chaddesden. Freddy had asked the driver for a ride in his cab. Not only had he been allowed to sit alongside the driver but also to sound the whistle, a moment never to be forgotten.

Freddy smiled nostalgically at the picture. The voice in his ear brought him back to reality. 'Freddy, are you there?'

'I'm here. I will go on the hike, but please make a note of my protest, timed ...' he glanced at his watch, '8.03 am, the fifth of August. '

'Right – wilko, good man. I'll pick you up, usual time, bye.'

'Oh, Gruppenführer? Just one thing – we *are* doing the Buxton hike today, as you promised last week?' He wore an anticipatory smile as he spoke.

'Affirm,' Phil spoke with the lingo he'd used as an air-traffic controller. He felt businesslike again. His pride had taken a battering on the hillside above Matlock Bath – and then, of course, had come the Buddhist debacle. The result had been a shocked group of meditators, an anguished monk and a drop-me-in-a-deep-hole wish experienced by the three hikers, who now kept their heads down while walking in the village. Phil said emigration was the answer – to the Rockies in Canada. Freddy saw real pain in that scenario and voted for Norfolk or Holland, somewhere flat.

The steam fair reminded Freddy that – if his plan were to succeed – he must tread carefully so as not to make Phil suspicious. But, then, any sane person would have genuine misgivings about hiking in temperatures more suited to lazing in the shade with a cool beer. Phil was manic, of course, and had to be countered at every opportunity so that he didn't descend into complete madness. Freddy saw himself as Phil's saviour. In fact wasn't that what he'd been all along since the first hike began?

As Freddy gazed at the picture of Leviathan a jolt in the region of his brain's sensory decoder sparked off the memory of *that* smell, the never-to-be-forgotten aroma of steam mixed with oil and smoke. Freddy closed his eyes, slowly breathed in through his nostrils and gently tilted his head backwards to savour the moment. He made a little hissing sound and pressed tongue against teeth. Just at that moment Jean walked in. 'What on earth are you doing, Freddy? Auditioning for the part of Hannibal Lecter?'

On the journey towards Buxton Phil glanced at Freddy in his driving mirror. It was odd that, despite the heat in the car, the usual stream of grunts, groans and accusations that would normally accompany such discomfort were absent. As we drove across Flagg Moor, a mile south-east of Buxton, we passed a field with a big hoarding sign which announced: 'STEAM FAIR'. Phil did not glance across. He was too busy trying to overtake a slow-moving tractor.

The field was full of steam engines of various types, rollers – giant and small, some static, others moving. There were about two hundred people – men and boys mostly – surrounding the exhibits. Freddy made a muffled sound, a catch in his throat, as he stared at them. I caught sight of a huge showman engine, with gold and gilt livery, and light bulbs fringing the cab roof, a glorious sight from the days when fairground rides were driven by steam. I was aware of Freddy craning his neck as we sped past. He stared as long as he could.

Three miles east of Buxton we turned right to join up with the A6, where there was a parking place opposite the entrance to Deep Dale. Freddy climbed out of the car puffing and sweating. 'Gruppenführer, I feel as though I've been in a sauna.' He made no further protest, how-ever, and drew his rucksack from the car boot.

'We'll be following the river for most of this hike so we should all feel cooler, Freddy,' Phil reassured him. 'But you ought to get a medal. Not a bleat or a gripe out of you.' He hesitated. 'Sure you're all right?'

'How do you mean?'

'You've hardly complained. Normally you'd be at me.'

'There you are then, Gruppenführer. You don't know what a good man you've got.'

'Absolutely. Well done that man.'

Freddy threw up an ironic salute at Phil.

'You don't salute out of uniform. Take that man's name, s'arnt major.' Phil was in an exuberant mood. His briefing was simple – we were to follow the river Wye through the gorge of Chee Dale – popular with rock climbers – and return via the dale-tops.

We sorted out our kit. Freddy foraged inside his bag, becoming increasingly panicky. Then he let out a dismal wail: 'Oh no!' He searched desperately in the car boot, then gave up. 'I've forgotten my socks!'

'Freddy!' Phil stared at him. 'Oh, hell's teeth. Now what? We can't go back and I presume you haven't brought any money with you.' He dumped his rucksack on the ground. Folding his arms, he looked wryly at Freddy. 'Sure you didn't leave them at home deliberately?'

'Now would I do anything like that?'

'Yes.'

'You are the most cynical person I've ever met. Would I come all this way only to have to go all the way back?'

'No, because the next thing is you'll suggest we go into Buxton for a –'

'For an ice-cream, yes, why not?' Freddy finished the sentence for him.

Phil blew out his cheeks in exasperation.

Freddy shrugged. 'The fact remains I have no socks. We can't go back to get them – too far – and we don't carry enough money to buy any. So what do we do?'

We sat three in line on a stone wall, pinned into silence by the heat. It was Phil who broke the spell. 'Now, I'm not going to order you what to do. I am going to be democratic.' He paused for dramatic effect at this unlikely concept, then continued: 'You two choose what you want to do and then we'll do what I want.' Freddy acknowledged Phil's humour with a dry smile.

'What about Haddon Hall?' I suggested. Haddon is the home of the Duke of Rutland and one of the most fascinating medieval and Tudor houses in the country. It was built over a period of four centuries, starting in 1180. It still has the original minstrel gallery that overlooks the Banqueting Hall, as well as a Great Chamber and a Long Gallery.

Freddy stopped me. 'Hang on. I told you, we haven't enough money.'

He rooted in his trouser pocket. 'Wait a minute,' he said, and produced a crumpled leaflet. 'I'd forgotten I had this.' He unfolded the leaflet advertising the steam fair. 'I think entry is free. It's only ten minutes away,' he said innocently.

It was too innocent for Phil. 'Freddy,' he said threateningly.

'What? What's the matter?'

'Come on. No socks, no hike, handy leaflet in pocket for Freddy's great love – the steam engine? Case proven.'

'I don't know what you're talking about!'

Phil made a 'tell me another one' gesture. He knew that Freddy's love of the steam engine was not surpassed, even by onedownmanship cars.

'The fact is,' Freddy said, 'I haven't got any socks. And if I haven't got any socks I can't hike. So we either go home or do something else. I happen to like steam fairs.' Freddy closed his eyes. He'd await our decision.

I smiled to myself. Phil had seen through his ruse right away. In the catalogue of great wheezes this one would be at the very bottom, as obvious a piece of chicanery as anything he'd ever had the bare-faced effrontery to produce.

Freddy's greatest wheeze had been a practical joke that – almost – had no ending. He had told me about it one night in the pub. Freddy and Jean had entertained six of her relatives one evening – a chore that could not be put off any longer. Freddy considered them incurable devotees of oneupmanship and, as such, the perfect target. After a drink or two he announced that the previous night he had awakened from such a vivid dream that he had remembered every detail of it. He had seen six numbers on a National Lottery card, and had written them down immediately. He had then gone out to buy a lottery ticket.

He warned his guests that he would not show by as much as a flicker of an eyebrow if he learned later that he had picked the winning numbers. 'The point is,' he said seriously, 'I don't want to ruin your evening. If you thought I'd won you'd all be jealous.' They laughed dutifully. Aunt Cynthia, who made no secret of her dislike for Freddy and thought him insane, curled her lip. 'I don't believe you,' she said. 'You're making it up.' Freddy, who knew she was weird – she bought bottles of Ashbourne water for making tea – merely smiled and shrugged. There were others who showed their disdain, like Jean's brother Max, a burly court bailiff who enjoyed serving eviction orders. He was contemptuous of Freddy's inability to get his trousers to hang properly. Max usually ignored Freddy, but on this occasion – just to be on the safe side – managed a weak grin and said, 'You won't want to talk to us any more.'

Nervous laughter accompanied the TV draw. The guests started to twitch as soon as poker-faced Freddy checked and rechecked his numbers. He did this six times and then walked out of the room without a word. After a few minutes Jean went to look for him. She returned to say he was not in the house. Max went outside and came back to say that Freddy was making a call from a public telephone box.

On his return Freddy was met by a barrage of questions. He simply smiled, spread out his hands and invited them all to share a bottle of champagne. The guests managed brittle laughs, attempted to 'hunt the winning ticket', and one or two of them made him giggle as they tickled him in a body search. Aunt Cynthia's face, at first a picture of distaste, lightened as she started to hedge her bets in case it was not a hoax. She even tried to smile, look amused and make sure Freddy noticed.

Freddy said that if he had won the jackpot, most of the money would go to charity. 'What would I need money for, after all?' Aunt Cynthia made a funny little sound and gave him a ghastly grin. Max gave him a hard stare. Freddy told them that – if he *had* won – they would never find evidence in any show of wealth. His life-style would not change. It was true. His onedownmanship was so entrenched that he might win millions, but still boast a clapped-out car on the driveway.

Freddy would have left his bewildered victims in the dark but Jean said that enough was enough and told them the truth, which immediately brought great relief. But Freddy made no confession, keeping up his mysterious winks and smiles. And so his guests left on that strange evening not entirely sure what had taken place. Whenever Freddy spots one of them these days he receives a haunted look.

As we sat on the wall awaiting inspiration, Phil dug idly

through the bag which contained his boots and socks. Occasionally Ruth would drop an extra pair into the bag by mistake. He let out a tiny exclamation and looked at Freddy, who had his eyes closed against the sun. Phil grinned at me as he brought out a pair of rolled-up green hiking socks and dangled them in front of Freddy's face, tickling his nose. Freddy opened his eyes – which grew wider in instant recognition of his doom.

And so the hike began, Freddy back in grumpy doom-laden warning mode. 'It's too hot. Gruppenführers who go out in this should be shot – no good will come of this.'

'Freddy, I've cut this hike down to four and a half miles. I can't do any more.'

'Yes, you can, you can abandon it. Show proper leadership. Think of your men suffering under a noonday sun … think of that ice-cream.'

The hike followed the river Wye, the chitter-chatter of blue tits accompanying Freddy's moans. He glanced up at a ledge on the limestone cliff and pointed out a common lizard, a brown flicker on the white rock. Then he stopped to examine wild flowers with the aid of his book. He pointed out wild roses, angelica and water crowfoot.

'Freddy,' Phil sighed and puffed. 'I've shortened the hike because of the heat and now you're stretching it out again!'

'Stevens, aim of hike: "to enjoy all the attractions of the Peak District".'

'Appendix B – overruled. Hike continues.'

'You have no soul.'

'You have no sense of duty.'

We crossed the river by a narrow pedestrian bridge, to be met by a series of stepping-stones under the cliff.

'You see how thoughtful I am?' said Phil. 'If I'd brought you in wet weather these stones would be under water.'

'The job of a navigator is to plot a hike you can finish. No brownie points.'

We stopped for our ritual coffee and ate a banana each, sitting on the river bank. Freddy removed his boots and socks to dangle his feet in the cool water. Phil and I followed suit. It was a welcome relief.

'Better than sex,' Freddy remarked, then added, 'as I remember it.' He looked down at his feet. 'These feet have tramped a thousand miles in the Peak. How have they managed to put up with sixty-four years of pounding about without fracturing one of their tiny bones? I mean, babies can turn up their feet and suck their big toes. At our age all you can do is look down and say, "Sorry, feet, you're on your own."'

He scooped his hand in the water and threw some at his face in one motion, then repeated the action, this time tossing the water at his neck.

On the re-start he fell silent. His pace slowed. Phil was forced to stop every hundred yards and wait for him. 'What's the matter?' he asked, after ten minutes.

'I don't feel too good.' Freddy spoke in a flat tone. Phil gave him a 'tell me a new one' look.

'No, I'm not joking, I don't feel good at all.'

Phil had heard it all before and ignored him. I was preoccupied with my own problems. The smooth, light frame of the rucksack against a shirt wet with sweat had begun to chafe my shoulders. We spoke little, bowed down by the oppressive sun now at its highest point of the day.

We trudged heavily out of the gorge, leaving the cliff's shadow for the baking heat. Shortly afterwards we came across a copse, bordered by a stone wall. Phil stopped under one of the trees to remove his rucksack.

I sat down, grateful for the shade and pulled out my food and another thermos flask – this time containing iced water.

Freddy sat slumped against the tree, his mouth open, breathing hard.

'You okay?' I asked.

He turned his head slowly, his face slack. 'I feel terrible.'

'How do you mean –' I broke off as Freddy's head dropped to his chest, his eyes darting upwards in their sockets. 'Oh my God, Phil!'

Phil stared. For a moment he thought this was Freddy the joker. But then Phil saw that his face had drained to the colour of chalk. Freddy fell sideways, stretched out on the sloping ground.

I was still rooted in shock. Phil scrambled to him and hurriedly placed two fingers over the inside of his wrist, felt for a pulse – nothing. A readjustment of fingers – nothing. Phil felt for the artery in his neck – nothing. He slapped Freddy's face, then felt it – cold as marble. He tried the other wrist – still no pulse. He put his ear to Freddy's chest. Still nothing.

Phil sat back. 'He's gone.' Back into action, in a last desperate act, he kneeled at Freddy's side, locked his hands together and was about to pump his chest ... and stopped. Freddy's eyes had started to flicker.

'He's alive!' I cried out, unnecessarily.

Freddy opened his eyes and tried to sit up. 'No!' Phil quickly stopped him with his hand. 'Stay there, Freddy. You're okay, you're fine, don't move.'

Freddy had fainted in the upright position and had stayed unconscious because all eight pints of his blood had fled inwards to maintain his vital organs. But when he fell sideways his head came to rest below the level of his feet, and so his displaced blood had an easier chance to return whence it had come. As if to confirm the diagnosis, Freddy's cheeks now had a splash of colour. He turned his head away and vomited.

Afterwards he said he felt better. We gave him a sip of water. 'I thought I was dying,' he said.

'You gave us one hell of a shock.' Phil looked at him with concern. 'I dunno, hypothermia, heat-stroke, what next?'

The next move. Could we manage to get him back to the car?

Or did we have to call for the paramedics? Before we allowed him to stand up we made him drink more water. I wet a handkerchief and wrapped it round his neck. Every two hundred yards or so he took a sip of water from our rapidly diminishing supply.

All the way back to the car Phil and I talked about anything and everything, just to keep Freddy's spirits up. He even took part in the game. 'If you'd been a bit more reasonable we'd have been standing on the platform of a steamroller now, eating ice-cream, instead of crossing the Sahara.'

Mercifully, we'd parked in the shade of a tree so the car interior was on the cooler side of hot. And, to Phil's immense relief, Freddy remained conscious all the way home and was not sick again.

That night Freddy rang to say – with apologies to Mark Twain – that reports of his death had been greatly exaggerated. He even sounded cheerful. 'Hah, bet it scared the Gruppenführer, that's the main thing. Keep him guessing.' Freddy chuckled at the thought. 'A good wheeze.' He sounded chipper.

'Just don't make a habit of it,' I said.

The drought continued into the following week but the temperature had dropped a few degrees, which made it bearable. Phil called Freddy and said he had a surprise in store.

'Why?' Freddy was immediately suspicious.

'To make up for last week.'

'What kind of pain will it be, exactly?' asked Freddy.

'No pain. I've been giving you a hard time so I thought a treat for the men might not come amiss.'

'So what are you going to serve me? A run up Thorpe Cloud in best boots and full pack or a nice easy fifteen-mile route march? I don't like your surprises, Gruppenführer.'

'All right, Buxton.'

'What for?'

'A day out,' said Phil. 'A walk round the town and then, if time –'

'A route march of ten miles.' Freddy cut in. 'Of course I'd expect no less.'

'No, you see you don't know me as well as you think you do …' Phil paused. '*And then, if time*, a look in Poole's Cavern which I've never been in and, Don tells me, neither have you – and, of course, an ice-cream.'

Freddy paused. 'Hmm, I see, but why?'

'Because you've had a lot to put up with this year. Don persuaded me. But the hike is suspended this one time only. I'll be back next week with the usual. So take it or leave it.'

'Hmm,' said Freddy again. It would take more than the offer of a day trip and an ice-cream to remove his deep suspicions that Phil had an underlying motive.

Buxton vies with Alston in Cumbria for the crown of being England's highest town, both places situated at around 1,000 feet above sea level. Let's dispose of the guide book by merely saying that the Romans discovered the warm springs and established a base there. It would not have been a welcome posting: 'Dear all, I'm here in Aquae Arnemetiae. It's cold up on these hills. My best mate, Caerelius, has got himself posted out of here down to Aqua Sulis! [Bath] Lucky devil.'

After that it reverted to being an ordinary town surrounded by moors and open countryside, with not much to recommend it except the bracing air.

Then along came an eighteenth-century Duke of Devonshire, the fifth, who was so stuffed with wealth from coal-, copper- and lead- mining that he went to Bath and came back singing 'Anything you can do I can do better' and so built the Crescent – a stylistic copy of the one in Bath – and the Royal Devonshire Hospital, instructing the architect to cap it with an unsupported dome which would have a diameter greater than any other in the world. This was more than a shade ostentatious but when we learn that the building was not designed as a hospital but as stables for horses, well …

We could not see any of these grand buildings as we entered the town from the south, not until we had parked the car in an ordinary- looking square and walked downhill past ordinary houses, with the kind of front doorsteps that proud housewives used to scrub.

And then – hey presto! – it could have been an eighteenth-century tapestry stretched out across our view. Great buildings, either Georgian, Victorian or Edwardian, presented themselves in such unabashed splendour that my spirits rose. There was the huge Palace Hotel, a 'vulgar' Victorian building some once thought, but today listed in the World Heritage list to rank alongside the Grand Canyon and the Statue of Liberty. Then came the Opera House, built in 1903, the centre of an annual arts festival of national importance. Next came the curved and elegant Crescent, representing the highest pinnacle of eigh-teenth- century Palladian architecture. The Pavilion Gardens, with its long and spacious Conservatory, completed a picture that has shouted out across the years: 'Aren't we British great? And isn't life wonderful?'

At least it did until the First World War, after which nothing seemed permanent, or certain, any more.

A man in colourful cycling gear rode up to the public well of St Anne, which stood in front of the Crescent. He paused long enough to top up his water bottle. After he'd gone I stopped at the well, took a deep breath and bent down to allow a few drops of water on to my tongue, ready to be appalled as I had been by the waters of Bath. But no, it tasted – well, like drinking water.

Freddy finally got his ice-cream and we wandered towards the Pavilion Gardens, bordering the river Wye and dominated by the Conservatory, deliciously Victorian in its glass and iron frame-work. All it required was nanny, patrolling with long skirt and sun parasol and pushing a large and ornate perambulator.

'CRAFT FAIR', the placard announced at the entrance to the Pavilion Gardens. A man and a woman, dressed all in black, juggled with sticks, kept dinner plates spinning, threw knives up in the air and caught them with their teeth. One man performed a self-gastroscopy with a sword. The fourth was a fire-eater, or rather fire ejector, who blew out a stream of paraffin and air from his mouth lit from a tarred flare. But what this had to do with a craft fair I failed to see. Perhaps it was simply a crafty way of luring people *into* the fair?

Stalls and pitches were stretched out along the pavilion promenade. They exhibited basket-making, pottery, doll-making, glassware, metal-ware, stuffed animals, paper craft, putting-big-ships-into-tiny-bottles, jewellery, clothing accessories and soap and candle figures. We walked along the lines, forced to admire the dedication as much as the craft. How many soap statues of Napoleon do you need to sell to make a living?

Then there was a face-painter, a woman, who had a queue of children with their parents in tow. What should they choose for their offspring: a red Indian, a Manchester United supporter or a Victorian chimney-sweep?

At the end of the first line of craftsmen, in between the gardens and the promenade, was a man who looked like Robin Hood's personal bow-maker. He was lean-built, about six feet tall, with strong muscular forearms. He sported a short grey beard and wore a frayed straw hat, a faded cherry-coloured waistcoat, a sleeveless brown shirt and threadbare trousers held aloft by white braces. He was anywhere between sixty-five and eighty.

On closer examination the 'long-bow' proved to be a bendy pole (greenwood). Attached to it was a cord operated by a foot treadle at one end, which drove a wooden lathe. When the pole bent it pulled at the lathe, spinning it round. Fixed into the lathe-jaws was a rough cylindrical piece of wood, about one and a half feet long. As the man pumped the treadle with his foot, he held a chisel to the spinning piece, lifting up neat curls of white shavings. Within the space of two minutes he had made a perfect chair leg, complete with ornamental central boss and ball foot. We watched in fascination. Freddy, especially, was entranced and asked the man what his craft was called.

'Bodging.' The man spoke abruptly and moved quickly to select another piece of wood, which he picked up and clamped into the lathe in one flowing sinewy movement. He had a long and sensitive face, cornflower blue eyes and a large red handkerchief around his neck which he used occasionally to wipe away the sweat on his forehead.

'I thought bodging was a bad job of repairing something,' Freddy dared to say.

The bodger made no response. His legs worked the treadle while the upper part of his body stayed in repose, all the fluid concentration flowing into his arms and hands. Another chair leg completed. He tossed it without a glance into a large basket. 'Bodging goes back at least five hundred years. The bodgers worked and lived in woodland. It was the industrialisation of the process that killed the craft. The new producers thought their work was better than a bodger's, so if someone showed them a chair leg they'd say "That's a bodged job". The bodger spoke with the cultured voice and confidence of a university-educated man.

'Oh, I see,' Freddy said with enthusiasm. 'This has to be one of the most ecological crafts there is. I mean, you don't use any fuel or power, you only use wood.'

'Wrong. It is *the* most ecological craft,' said the bodger. 'They lived in a hut in the woods and by felling selected trees gaps were left where seedlings grew, so it was self re-generating. Nothing was used up at all.'

'But you don't live in a wood, do you?'

'Yes, of course. I'm a bodger. It's my philosophy.'

'Sorry?' Freddy was intrigued. 'How do you mean – philosophy?

'There are two worlds of philosophy: firstly, the study of the universe in terms of language and, secondly, the study of the universe of nature.' The bodger put out his hand so quickly that Freddy stared at it for a split second before taking it. 'My name's

Bernard.' They shook hands briefly. Bernard withdrew to bend, lift, swivel and place another piece of wood in the lathe. Before he pumped the treadle Freddy nipped in with his name and introduced Phil and me. We shook hands.

Within a second the foot pumped, the lathe spun, shavings curled and another chair leg lay in the basket. 'A good bodger used to make 360 chairs a week – not put together, but all the parts needed.' Bernard slipped down a gear into human mode and studied Freddy's face. 'There's another explanation, the word botch – botch job – comes from Old English, meaning "to patch". Somewhere along the line it became the derogatory word "bodge".' He flashed a bungee jump of a smile from his pale blue eyes down to his thin lips and back again.

'You said it was your philosophy.' Freddy spoke a trifle nervously.

'Yes, I live in the universe of nature. Bodging is pure in mind as well. My goal is to realise the meaning of life through my interaction with nature.'

Freddy stared, transfixed. Bernard turned away. In Freddy's mind everything happened next in slow motion.

Bernard bent down to pick up another, larger, piece of wood from one of his two wicker baskets. He sat down, legs astride the 'shaving horse', and fixed the piece of wood in a clamp in front of his crotch. He took a large draw-knife with handles at either end, gripped it in both hands and drew it back towards him along the length of the piece, peeling back a substantial length of wood, including the bark. With the timber roughly in the shape he wanted, he removed it from the clamp, took it to the pole lathe, and fixed it in the turning grips. The lathe spun, the wood curled and chair production in the UK rose by another notch.

Freddy remained hypnotised. The phrase – the actual phrase – had been delivered with no trace of doubt – *the meaning of life*. Freddy's mind spun with the lathe – he had so many questions. And how could he detach Bernard from his work to discuss this world-shaking statement? 'I'm interested in philosophy,' he blurted out and then regretted it. He felt – and looked – awkward. 'Well, what you just said – the meaning of life.'

Bernard put down the lump of wood that was about to be held in the lathe and looked carefully at Freddy. It was an interrogative look accompanied by the faintest of smiles.

Freddy tried to smile back, but how long was Bernard going to stare at him? And then the bodger broke away, taking off his hat and red handkerchief, wiping his face as he did so. 'The best time for me to talk philosophy is over coffee,' he invited. 'I'm due for a break.'

Five minutes later Phil and I joined Freddy and Bernard in a café not far from the Pump Room. Over his cappuccino Bernard said he had read philosophy at Cambridge and had studied – albeit briefly – under that great and tortured philosopher, Ludwig Wittgenstein. Bernard had graduated in 1950, which made him well over seventy.

Freddy was initially hesitant. He didn't want to reveal his *Reader's Digest* level of expertise. But Bernard had seen through that. 'Listen,' he said. 'All men are simpletons when it comes to why we're here, doing what we do. But the question is not *why* we are here, but *what* we are? What is real? For you?' He tapped a pepper pot on the table to drive the point home.

A coach-driver blew out his cheeks and tried to read the *Sun*'s front page story about a pop-singer seducing a cabinet minister.

Two elderly ladies came in to sit two tables away. One carried a bundle of estate agents' sale leaflets.

'And what is reality for you?' Freddy was scared this might get too intellectual.

'Bodging.'

'Bodging.' Freddy repeated the word.

A bride of Dracula entered with her satanic escort, dressed all in black, the female with a white face and kohl-rimmed eyes.

'Yes, of course! Creation and simplicity. Philosophers use

language, but the world *wasn't created by language*, was it! Language was created by man!' He tapped the pepper pot again, louder this time.

Ms Dracula frowned in distaste at the noise. The coach-driver raised his eyebrows and turned to page three.

Bernard continued: 'Everyone should learn for themselves.'

'In the world of reality,' said Freddy.

'Yes. Experience the wholeness. Artists ask the same questions as philosophers but are more successful because they live the answer. The wholeness – the gestalt!'

'Gestalt?'

'Yes, it means an organised whole.'

So *that's* what he had to do – make an organised whole.

'Something *real*, Freddy?' said Phil as we got back in the car. 'That's what you have to do –' he grinned at me. 'Hike! That's real. That's something to do.'

On our way home, Freddy enthused. 'I've just remembered,' he said. 'Lab Sum said that's what mattered – reality, which is now, the present. And Kant said "live a life".'

'And Wordsworth?' I asked.

'Yes!' Freddy looked delighted. 'Wordsworth said exactly the same thing – the whole world was in a flower! We've substituted ideas for reality. Ideas are in language. I've got to *do* things. Oh.' His face fell.

'What's the matter,' I asked.

'I'm no good at woodwork.'

As we passed through Ashbourne I noted the MGB sports car with the number YAN 578G which had been parked in the same place ever since our first hike. Freddy had once suggested that if it ever disappeared from our view we should be as alarmed as Londoners would be if the ravens ever left the Tower of London. Today he hardly gave it a glance, preoccupied by his new-found knowledge.

When Freddy got home he asked Jean if she minded him taking up pottery as a hobby. 'Only if you do it in the shed,' she said as she put another shirt on the ironing-board. Her practical turn of mind was not going to allow Freddy to muck up *her* kitchen. She reminded Freddy of their friends in Repton. Janet had to put up with her splendidly crafty husband, Keith. His practical turn of mind often turned the house into a workshop in which he made ocean-going boats, or dismantled Porsche engines while watching rugby. Jean would not be a martyr to *that* cause, she said.

Freddy went outside to look in the shed. There was a lot inside it: lawnmower, bikes, garden tools and paint tins, none of which could be shifted to another location or thrown away. Then he remembered that pottery required sacks of clay and a wheel – as well as a kiln – for its proper function. Too expensive.

The three of us met later over a pint in the Plough and Rake. Freddy related his problem. The only practical experience he had was with glue. There was no meaning in that. 'I can just about clean out the MGB carburettor. I wish I could write books.'

'What about origami?' asked Phil.

Freddy stared gloomily at him. 'Look, paper-folding isn't going to illuminate the universe. I'm not going to find out anything with a paper rabbit.' Then he smiled at the thought. He kept on smiling. Then he started to laugh. He was still laughing as we broke up to go home.

He entered the house, chuckling. In response to Jean's raised eyebrow, Freddy said it was a man he had talked to, 'in a café'. Jean didn't press him for an explanation. She was used to his odd ways. It was the image of Bernard tapping a pepper pot on the table that kept him chuckling, he later told us. It was perfect. All this time he had tried to get to grips with the universal meaning of life – and now there it was, tidied up and with no strings attached, not in a nutshell but in a pepper pot.

9

SEPTEMBER

A few sprinklings of rain had done little to enliven the parched expanse of the Peak. It would be some time before the brown grass turned green and the Dove, Manifold and Wye became rivers in more than name. But the end of summer had arrived, signalled by subtle changes in the leaf colours of ash, sycamore and beech, by the gatherings of lapwings, starlings and swallows, by the acidic tang of farmyard manure and the smell of wood smoke and damp leaves. Autumn, in its faded beauty, reminds me of the passage of time more than any other season. As the eye follows the wheel of birds ready for the long flight to Africa, so it also turns inwards.

September has always been my month for reflection, tinged with sadness – but this is not true for Freddy. Keats may have asked: 'Where are the songs of spring?' as he stared into the dark days ahead – but not Freddy. He looks forward to autumn, surveying fields with an eager eye ready to explode into action, plastic bag at the ready, scurrying hither and thither, eyes bright and hands quick, gathering autumn's great treasure, mushrooms.

Phil's response to autumn, with its cooler weather, is normally to charge energetically up the nearest hill. However, this year his sixty-fifth birthday fell later in the month, the very pits. He would become an old-age pensioner or, more euphemistically, a 'senior citizen', both labels meaning 'knackered' and 'cast-off' in his view. He had almost got used to the humiliation of being called 'dear' or 'me old duck', but he was more sensitive to, and less forgiving of, the latest batch of insults. The first blow landed when he had to go by bus into Ashbourne to pick up his car after servicing. A man, no younger than forty, had *offered him his seat*. Phil thanked him and declined abruptly, glaring hard at the short-sighted twit.

It had taken him weeks to get over the shock. He wasn't even safe at his GP's surgery. When he went to pick up a repeat prescription for his little yellow pills the receptionist had called him 'darling'. This, on the steam-pressure scale, was near bursting point. 'Darling' – oddly enough, not 'dear' – in this locality is a term used by nurses or care-staff for infants or senile men. Phil, the tough power-house, still in his prime, stared at the silly woman. Hadn't he achieved a whole range of personal bests? His blood pressure, last checked a month ago on an expensive Boots machine, was 125 over 80 – good enough for a thirty-year-old but now rising to lift-off. Phil fled the surgery before he let rip.

Worse was to come when Phil received a letter offering him a place in a new sheltered housing complex in Morecambe. The final blow had been the insurance company mailshot that asked bluntly if he could cover the costs of his funeral. Phil was a haunted man.

Freddy was worried that this trauma would have serious repercussions on the hiking front. Each year the birthday boy entertains the other two for lunch at a pub of his choice. 'Oh Lord,' moaned Freddy to me. 'After what he's been through you know what he'll do? He'll choose a pub on top of a mountain that can only be reached by a dangerous glacier!' In the meantime Freddy did his best to calm Phil down, assuring him that he didn't look a day older than he had last year.

*

On the first hike of the month we sat on the village green at Parwich, next to the church, enjoying the autumnal sunshine. On one side stood examples of the fine seventeenth- and eighteenth-century houses that characterise the village. With its duck-pond and stream it is another candidate for our list of most-liked villages, and in fact is Freddy's favourite.

He swallowed the last mouthfuls of his Cornish pasty and fished out a magazine cutting, a horoscope for those born under Virgo – which included Phil. The Virgoan, it proclaimed, was 'industrious' and 'country-loving'. Phil nodded smugly. It was patently true. But why was Freddy laughing in derision?

'Because, Gruppenführer, it says here that you will put forward a proposition this week which might involve you in some duplicity – your middle name.'

Phil tried to snatch the cutting but Freddy was too quick. 'Get off!' he grinned, and held it away from Phil. He began – or pretended – to read: 'Be careful you don't jeopardise your relationships with friends by the adoption of duplicitous ideas. Huh!' he scoffed. 'You're full of duplicity. You've conned us since year dot!'

Freddy produced a bar of dark chocolate. Phil licked his lips as he watched Freddy snap off a chunk and hand it to me before sticking the rest back in his anorak pocket. Phil was open-mouthed. 'Don't I get a bit?'

'No.'

'I won't take you out for lunch on my birthday hike then.'

'You keep mentioning this. It worries me. Where is it?'

'It's a surprise. Has to be, rule 93c. You know that.'

'Sorry. No name, no chocolate.'

Phil salivated. It was rum chocolate, his favourite. 'Okay, I give in. Chocolate first.'

'No – pub first.'

'Okay, the Snake Inn. Chocolate.'

Freddy let out a whoop of victory, nearly choking as he ate.

'I knew it! I knew it! I fathomed you out, Gruppenführer. It's "kill two birds with one stone", isn't it? To get to the Snake Inn you have to cross Kinder. Fabulous.' He handed Phil a nugget of chocolate. 'You're not serious? You expect me to go up that trampoline-like, bog-ridden no-man's land again? Going up and down like a yo-yo hour after hour? Just for a free bangers and mash? '

'Not necessarily bangers and mash. You can have what you like.'

'I am not going up Kinder Scout again. I told you.'

Phil fell silent. But it was a tactical silence, I felt. Clearly, he was biding his time.

Before re-starting the hike, Freddy and I stopped to look around the graves in Parwich churchyard, a stone reference library of local history. Phil remained outside. It would be an admission of mortality for him to reflect on lives gone by.

As we stepped out of the churchyard a sudden gust of wind blew up. Dry leaves scurried across our path. Rain had been forecast but maybe we would escape the worst. We walked past the village pond and followed the stream that ran by the side of a cottage, then turned left to climb the steep grassy hillside towards Tissington.

We started to cross a field when Freddy let out a shout of joy. Out of his pocket came the plastic bag. The slow plodding hiker that had been Freddy was now transmuted into a robot switched on to fast mode. He ran around popping mushrooms into his bag with such rapidity that it gave the lie to his usual claim of fatigue, a fact which Phil drily noted.

Freddy had just about wiped out the complete show of overnight fungi when I noticed a man behind us. He was slightly built and wore khaki-coloured shorts down to his knobbly knees, a bright orange anorak and a green bobble-hat. He carried a small rucksack. On seeing me he seemed to quicken his pace. As he drew nearer I could see his expression, one of eagerness and impatience. His mouth was open and his tongue protruded over his lower teeth. He looked upwards and appeared to shout at a large formation of swallows which swooped and circled, before banking away out of sight behind a wood.

As soon as he was within earshot he called out in explanation: 'Do it every year at this time. I tell them to watch out for the French.' He saw our mystified expressions. 'Migration. I try and save the birds, the French slaughter them. La chasse!' he cried in a squeaky, cracked voice. 'Oh, it's terrible, terrible. What can we do?'

We knew what he meant. September is the time when every red-blooded Frenchman dresses up in hunter's camouflage and goes bravely out armed with a battalion's worth of ammo to bump off nightingales, song-thrushes, bullfinches and skylarks. There is a European Bird Directive, of course, but for the last twenty-four years the French have ignored it.

Our hiker was an ornithologist who wanted everybody else to share his knowledge. The trouble was that he wanted to impart it all in the space of one minute. His rubbery mouth flapped ten to the dozen. 'And look at the farmers poisoning crops – I know someone, well actually he's a second cousin once removed – well, not once removed, no, more like twice removed – anyway, he goes round fields in Norfolk testing pesticides for a German company and he says that some farmers are so ignorant they spray twice the dosage, thinking it will do twice as much good. Oh dear, what can you do, what can you do?'

He reminded me of a faithful spaniel in his eagerness to please. I began to wonder if the incident with the birds had just been an excuse to start up his vocal engine. At one point he talked about his aunt in Swansea who knew someone in Botswana who had been knocked down by a frightened hippo because she had stood between it and the river. He interrupted the flow with: 'Nice on a walk to have someone to talk to, isn't it?'

For the first ten minutes or so we tried to listen politely to what he said but the flow of his observations, opinions and life history accelerated the more he talked. After a while the language receptor part of my brain seized up, and I began to cast about for an excuse to get rid of him. Signals of this nature flashed between Phil, Freddy and myself. His endless chatter melded into a surreal stream of nonsense as it entered my ears. 'Working in a wine-vault as a student bringing casks out of bond' became 'Doing the high vault as a loser drinking tasks with James Bond' – or something like that. In the space of a quarter of a mile he had spewed out his entire childhood history. At half a mile he had filed his education, at three-quarters of a mile his work experience, and at one mile his medical history. All required a code-cracker as interpreter.

Somewhere, mixed up in this machine-gun chatter, I picked out his name, Clifford. From the subject of haemorrhoids he moved on to invalidity benefit, his bike, his mother's hearing-aid, the price of everything, budgerigar diseases, muddy mains-water in his taps, his cat, carpet- slippers, the price of wood, council tax, woodworm and hip replacements. Each of these topics was embroidered with tangential add-ons as his mercurial brain switched rapidly around the pre-Copernican world in which the planets swung around him alone, all conveyed in a voice like a cracked reed instrument. As a one-way conversationalist he had the sticking power of a limpet.

At one and a quarter miles I wanted to murder him. I thought I'd hire the deadly farmer with his shotgun, axe and lime-pit. From the looks on their faces, Freddy and Phil would be willing accessories to the crime. And so we arrived back at Tissington car park. To our horror, Clifford asked us to stay and eat lunch with him. We told him politely and through gritted teeth that we had eaten lunch in Parwich and were now going home.

Clifford hesitated – the first pause in his outpouring – and commented that he thought that our rucksacks looked full, as though we still had food in them. He laid a hand on my rucksack. His doleful face smiled at me. In that moment I said something silly: 'Got to go, emergency. Come on, fellers –' and piled Freddy and Phil into the car before they had taken off their hiking boots. I burnt rubber, big time, in our escape.

I caught my last glimpse of Clifford through the wing mirror. His baggy shorts were dangling even lower. His mouth was still open – and was that a look of sadness on his face? Not on our part. We celebrated our freedom with Classic FM. A soothing Mozart violin concerto had just started. Even Freddy was prepared to overlook the station's commercial backing on this occasion.

From time to time we stumble on bits and pieces of information that defy belief. One such titbit concerned a Naked Boys' Race which was staged annually throughout the seventeenth and eighteenth centuries. The tale was told to us by Bernard the bodger, who had it from an old man in Tideswell who died in 1960, the story having been handed down from generation to generation. This extraordinary competition involved a number of lads and only took place when there was snow on the ground, though why remains a mystery.

Freddy suggested that Phil should start a revival of the custom so that he could participate. 'Gruppenführer, you'd love it. Think of the exquisite pain!'

We started our next hike at Eyam village, a few miles north of Bakewell, which also celebrated some strange customs until about half a century ago. The most pleasing – and how lamentable it is that it is no longer practised – was 'clay-daubin'. This custom consisted in the neighbours and friends of a newly married couple assembling together and not separating until they had built them a cottage. As many people were involved, the habitation was generally completed in a day. The 'clay-daubin' concluded in rejoicing and merrymaking.

It is impossible to visit the village without being impressed by the story of the brave villagers who volunteered to isolate themselves from the world when the Bubonic Plague arrived in 1665. This was carried, according to general belief, by fleas in a bundle of cloth carted from London to the village tailor, George Vicars. No one realised the flea bites would be deadly. The traditional tale – there are dubious variants, one being that the disease may have been influenza – holds that George Vicars was the first to die of the plague, first having shown the telltale circular rashes around his swollen lymph nodes. That rash has been celebrated for centuries by unknowing children, though it is doubtful if the ditty was composed in Eyam, as they sing: 'Ring a ring a roses, a pocket full of posies, atishoo, atishoo, we all fall down.' (The posies, any collection of flowers or herbs that had a sweet scent, were carried in the vain hope that they would ward away the plague. The 'atishoo' was a sneeze – flu-like symptoms signalled the onset of the illness.)

The villagers' courage is laden with tragic irony as they were ignorant of the plague's cause. If they had fled the village and lived in makeshift huts on the hills they might well have survived, but at the end of their year-long quarantine between a quarter and a third of them had died.

Before we began our hike we stood and looked at the row of pretty dwellings on the left of the church. They are still lived in and known collectively as the Plague Cottages. This is where the tailor died, followed by most of the Cooper family. Plaques here and elsewhere in the village commemorate the names of the inhabitants and the dates of their deaths.

Inside the church we looked at the Book of Remembrance. Phil chose to enter the church for some reason, contrary to his habit. On leaving he lingered thoughtfully by the grave of the vicar's wife, Catherine, and was the last out of the churchyard.

September is the start of the countryman's year. The natural year over (spring to harvest-time), it is the traditional time to end a farm tenancy agreement and is the month in which sheep sales often take place. Biggin village, perched high above Wolfescote Dale, used to stage Derbyshire's biggest sheep sale, where as many as 14,000 sheep a day were sold. Now they are sold in the new market at Bakewell.

Sheep sales are fairly routine occasions, so it is the farm sales which provide the most interest. These often fall at Michaelmas, towards the end of September. Sometimes they are sad occasions as elderly farmers usually retire about this time. Tenant farming on these hills has been a way of life rather than a means of making money. Cattle, sheep, agricultural machinery and some household goods and vehicles are sold, signalling the end of one man's farming life. Hopefully, he then finds somewhere more economical in which to live with a pension in place.

It was Freddy who caught sight of the notice in the *Derby Evening Telegraph*. It read: 'Farm sale of property and dispersal of cattle', or words to that effect. It was a tenant's farm and so only his personal property, excluding land and buildings, was for sale. It listed cattle and sheep as well as a large number of items that included antique furniture, farm machinery and tools, as well as a number of undisclosed 'miscellaneous' items. A line in the advertisement caught Freddy's eye: 'Land Rover – Series Two'.

Freddy stared at the advert. He remembered that he had acquired a faded workshop manual for a Series Two Land Rover years ago, and had squirrelled the book away with no immediate use for it. Now, where had he put it? He searched the garage. And there it was, sure enough, in a box full of old *Motor* and *Autocar* magazines. He was lucky. Although a spilt tin of paint had defaced some of the magazines, the one he wanted was intact.

The advert made no mention of the Land Rover's condition, but a Series Two would not be as expensive as a Series One, which had the value of a prized first edition. That would have been outside Freddy's price range.

The real excitement came from the realisation that, in many ways, a Land Rover was even better than a Trabant. This was a workhorse: durable, agricultural – and British. It would cart anything around, from shopping bags to cement. It was built like a battering ram and unpretentious in the extreme. It was also a four-wheel drive. Jean was often worried about the hillside outside their house icing up in the winter. Four-wheel drives were made for it, weren't they?

Not only that – and here Freddy's heart almost skipped a beat – it would be a marvellous item with which to start his onedownmanship. Jean might have vetoed the Trabant, but this one would be hard to resist. The more he thought about it, the more excited he got.

He telephoned the auctioneer and a woman told him that the vehicle was not in good condition. She seemed surprised when he let slip: 'Oh good.' Freddy was delighted. The Land Rover would be in keeping with the image he liked to project of himself: plain, inexpensive, simple and honest and the nearest thing, in huggable terms, to the steam locomotive. Puritans are allowed Land Rovers.

Occasionally Phil will do Freddy a favour, the motive being to put Freddy in his debt and therefore make it easier to get him out in bad weather. In this diplomatic mood he volunteered to take Freddy to the auction. Freddy saw a bribe right away. 'It won't get me up Kinder,' he warned.

'It's not Kinder I'm after,' said Phil. 'There's an air-speed indicator from a Lancaster bomber in the sale.' He already had a collection of Lancaster instruments, an H2S radar display and switch unit, a pilot's aluminium seat and an engine control quadrant. Eventually he hoped to have a complete pilot's panel.

But Phil was not in the best of moods as he drove us towards the Peak. He had read another 'health' article in the press, yet again forecasting that fat people would eventually be able to slim by popping pills. Where was the personal obligation? Why should he have to inflict pain on himself to stay slim when any fat slob could manage it by pill-popping?

Phil braked to a standstill. We had passed Hartington and Sheen and were now heading in a northerly direction with the

Dove valley parallel on our right. He looked at his map and then at the note of the farm's address. 'I've just realised,' he said. 'Freddy, that Land Rover you're after – has it got dents all the way round, do you know?'

'SALE,' read the auctioneer's notice. It was pinned to a post at the junction of a road and a lane, into which a plastic arrow pointed. Phil turned into it – and stopped. It was impossible to go further with parked vans, cars and small lorries parked in every available space – gateways, verges – all the way to the farm. 'That's the way we went,' prompted Phil. 'Remember? The farmer down there with his ice-cream and his illiterate son?'

Having managed to park in the smallest of gaps between a Range Rover and a VW Beetle, we walked towards the farm. It all came back to me – the widening of the lane outside the farm and the gate that had been difficult to open. But the farmyard rubbish – the Metro wreck, black plastic binliners and rusting bits of machinery – had all gone, replaced by farm machinery in working order. Among the large number of agricultural lots parked around the yard were a baler, manure- spreader, drill-harrow, dump-trailer and fertiliser-dresser. It was more than likely that the auctioneers had brought in some arable farming machinery that had not met its reserve price elsewhere.

The animal sale had just started. Cows and sheep stood in their sheds or outside in portable pens. The punters here were all farmers, old and young. Some wore blue overalls and rubber boots, others tweed jackets or Barbours. The auctioneer stood at the table, a bucolic-looking man of about fifty, in a Harris tweed jacket, with a red handkerchief hanging out of the top pocket and a brown trilby-hat on his head. Seated at the table were his assistant and sale accountant. He called out to an old farmer, bent almost in half by arthritis hastened by many winters of cold and damp work on the hills: 'Have you got your bidding hat on today, Hubert?'

'No, it blew off last time from all that wind comin' out of yer.'

The animals were despatched with a non-stop monotone which rose half an octave before he paused for breath. 'Bid four five, out on my right at four five, four five – four six, four six anywhere?'

Phil found the open barn where the old stone-troughs vied with a host of household and farm utensils as well as antique items – harnesses, horse-brasses, a rocking-chair, the iron-work that goes with an inglenook fireplace (spit, tongs, poker, iron-grabs and speared fork), an oak corner-cupboard, a cream-separator, a scythe and several tool-boxes. An array of items was spread out over collapsible tables – yokes, an ornate chamber-pot, Victorian glassware, a de-activated rifle, porcelain, a pile of *Picture Post* magazines, a large pewter carver and a glass case holding what looked like a very old and tired Golden Eagle – *and,* of great interest to Phil, the Lancaster air-speed indicator.

There were no signs of the place having been turned into an ice-cream factory. The punters who inspected the items were generally a nondescript group of suburban people on the look-out for household goods, cheap antiques, maybe a ladder or tools – bargain-hunters most of them, dressed in worn sweaters and cheap jeans.

One or two dealers walked about, notebook and pen in hand. They glanced quickly at each item and noted down any that might interest them. There were a few retired couples inspired by the antiques programmes on television who browsed long and hard, and others, sharp-eyed folk and the unemployed, hoping they might find something to resell elsewhere at a profit.

Freddy and I searched for the Land Rover, and found it behind one of the barns. It stood next to a coarsely painted Riley Kestrel – a rakish aluminium-built car with a pre-selector gearbox – and a hard-used 35-year-old Massey-Ferguson 175 tractor. Freddy and I had a quick look round the Land Rover. Its skirt of hardened mud had been prised away, leaving a broad pale mark. It looked more tatty than ever. I heard a familiar voice: 'Hello there!' We turned round to find our farmer, the would-be ice-cream magnate. 'Jim Oldroyd. Remember me?'

'Of course!' Freddy and I shook his hand. 'I was just thinking about you,' I said. We walked back to the open barn. 'Those inglenook tools. They'd have been from your inglenook fireplace, wouldn't they?'

'That's right,' Jim said. He looked about, rather sad and bemused at the bustle of people pawing over his possessions. But then he turned back to show his uneven teeth as he grinned. The story emerged in dribs and drabs. The ice-cream idea, he confessed, had proved a non-starter. The loan had not been forthcoming. A bolshy bank manager had told him that his business plan was totally unviable – 'didn't stack up' was the phrase used. At the same time, for no reason that the farmer could give, the manager had withdrawn his overdraft. 'Pulled the rug from under me,' Jim said. 'I had no alternative but to sell up.'

But what had happened to his son? 'Ah,' Jim shook his head in disbelief. 'Had you not heard what he did?'

I confessed my ignorance.

'Oh heck, well, I s'pose for a better word he attacked the bank with the muck-spreader. Did you not hear? It was in all the news – telly and newspapers.' Then it dawned on me. I had not realised that the news story that had been given such prominence had involved his son. It was either hilarious or tragic, depending on your point of view.

Unknown to his father, Benjamin had driven the tractor into town (without a driving licence or any insurance) with a muck-spreader in tow. He'd backed up against the bank's large doors and then let rip with the pumping unit. The entire stone façade of the bank, including its grand doorway, had been plastered with a rapidly congealing, odious sticky mess.

Benjamin had got down from the tractor to survey his handi-work with a smile, joined by a growing crowd of shoppers, all of them transfixed. At one point the bank door had opened and the bank manager's head had appeared. As he cautiously looked out, a drop of slurry from the Grecian-style pediment had dropped on top of his bald head. This spectacular event was the sole talking point in most of the pubs, clubs, tea rooms and coffee shops. There was talk of Benjamin being given a medal by the local traders' association. Jokes abounded, with verbs like 'plastered' in popular use. An art teacher, remembering that a recent Turner artist had displayed a number of elephant droppings, had seriously wondered if the bank attack had anything to do with 'performance art'. The reply came: 'Yes, but it was the usual load of shit.'

For a time the locals saw it as a kind of popular insurrection. T-shirts were printed with a picture of the bank, together with the words: 'Get a load of this' or 'Here's mud in your eye'.

I was pleased that Freddy and Phil had joined me in time to hear the story. Freddy couldn't stop laughing. We learnt that no punitive action had been taken against Benjamin, other than by two doctors who had signed the relevant mental health declaration, thus 'sectioning' him into a psychiatric hospital. His father seemed not to be too stricken by what had happened and actually said he found it encouraging. After all, if, unprompted, his son had wreaked revenge on the offending bank, wasn't that a sign that he had known what was going on? And hadn't he felt a normal sense of grievance? On the basis of this action his dad had great hopes for him. It might even be construed as normal behaviour, given the level of provocation.

Jim Oldroyd was one of life's optimists. Most people in his situation would have been distraught after the events of the past two months. Farmers in any case feature high up in the league of suicides. But Jim seemed to cope with any adversity with a sunny disposition that was hard to deny.

Was he sad to be leaving? No, he said, he was not. He looked forward to living with his widowed sister in Scarborough. She was a studio- potter who sold her work through a number of Craft Council registered shops. He would help her build wood-burning kilns – piles of wood and bricks. Each one had to be rebuilt after a firing.

My curiosity got the better of my tact. 'What happened to the encyclopaedias?' I asked. 'Did you have any success teaching Benjamin to read with them?'

A flicker crossed Jim's normally open face. 'Yes, I gave it one go,' he said. 'Just to say I'd tried, like. But it was 'opeless, so I used 'em to prop a fence up out the back.' He laughed out loud.

Now it was his turn to pose the questions. What had brought us along to the sale? We told him about the Land Rover. 'You gentlemen don't want to buy that old thing!' He laughed in incredulity. 'Not worth a tanner, that.'

Freddy's face dropped. 'Why not?' he asked. 'Isn't the engine any good?'

'Oh, the engine's not bad. Silencer's gone, though. But it's tatty. You wouldn't want that to be seen at front of your house, would you?'

Freddy couldn't tell him that that was precisely what did attract him. 'How much do you think it will fetch?' he asked.

'Oh, I'd be happy if it fetched a hundred quid.' Jim had a second thought and looked about to see if he was overheard, and then beckoned us nearer. 'Tell you what. I'll let you have it for eighty.' He spoke surreptitiously, tapping the side of his nose.

'Eighty!' Freddy's startled cry brought a 'shushing' from Jim. The auctioneer would not be pleased to learn what was under consideration behind his back.

'Course! I owe you gentlemen a favour.' Our immediate denials met with a raised hand, Jim's bright shrewd eyes glinting at us in his characteristic smile. 'No. Listen to me. You were so kind not to tell me it was a bad idea, learning somebody to read, like that, with encyclopaedias. I could tell what you really thought, though. I could read your faces. That's all I wanted to know. If you really want that chariot, it's yours. I'll pull it out the auction. Eighty quid. How's that?'

Freddy was sorely tempted. Jim consulted his sale guide. 'Lot sixty. You've got a bit of time to think about it. I'll be inside the house.' And with that he made his way through the crowd.

Freddy looked at Phil and me. What should he do? We shrugged, bouncing the question back. It was Freddy's decision, and his alone. He made up his mind and set off to find Jim. The front door was open and Freddy stepped inside. There was no one in the living-room. Freddy's shoe stuck to a carpet-gripper and to free it he had to wrench it away. A cat mewed and sidled over to him, rubbing its back on his leg. He moved back through the hall into the kitchen. The cat followed, still mewing. No one there, either. He looked through the window into the second farmyard and saw Jim outside watching his cattle being loaded into trucks by men with sticks. One beast was determined not to leave and had to be pushed and encouraged up the ramp.

Freddy made a move towards the back door, and then stopped. Jim had turned towards him, tears running from his eyes. As he walked towards the kitchen door Freddy ducked out of sight and darted quickly back into the hallway and out through the front door. We met him with enquiring faces. He shook his head. 'Changed my mind,' he said.

We were forced to step out of the way of a reversing cattle truck. Phil heard the bidding start on the air-speed indicator. He got into a position where the auctioneer could see him, but he needn't have bothered. It went for a hundred pounds to a thirty-year-old man wearing a jacket sporting the golden coloured wings of a private pilot. Phil had dropped out of the bidding at fifty pounds.

It felt colder. An easterly breeze had sprung up. Freddy wanted to stay for the Land Rover sale. Phil suggested that Freddy call the auctioneer later in the day. This Freddy did. He was told that the Land Rover had fetched eight hundred pounds. I was with him when he called. He nodded and smiled gently. 'Disappointed?' I asked.

'No.' He said he was delighted.

*

Phil's birthday was only a breakfast away, coinciding with the hike. We sat over a pint in the Spread Eagle the evening before. I expected a melancholy Phil and was surprised to find him, if not exuberant, fairly cheerful.

The cause of this swift change of mood he put down to accepting the inevitable and then ignoring it. 'It's what people thought of me that got me down. I don't feel sixty-five, at least not measured by all the clapped-out guys we know. I'm just going to ignore it.'

Freddy was incredulous. 'Pardon me, Gruppenführer? Pardon me? Did my ears hear you say something that is so simplistic, so ingenuous and I am supposed to believe it? After all that fuss? You are just going to *ignore* it?'

Freddy had a point. Jean had spoken to Ruth, who had championed 'poor old Phil'. All he wanted for his birthday, she said, was a slog over Kinder. Jean, in turn, had expressed the same sentiment. 'Poor old Phil' would be so disappointed and Freddy should put up with a bit of discomfort to please him. 'Freddy, it *is* his sixty-fifth and you know how he hates getting old. Surely you can go over Kinder Scout just this one more time?'

Freddy said he felt like a man about to be beheaded but instructed to be considerate to his executioner by keeping still. No wonder he looked so gloomy. With all that pressure he had been forced to give way. The 'death march', as he called it, was on.

Phil could see that Freddy was less than charmed by the arrangement and tried to be kind. 'Freddy, we'll have a superb meal at the Snake. And it's only a fifteen-mile hike.'

Freddy stared at Phil in the way that a sixty-year-old prisoner might look at a kindly judge when told that his age has been taken into account and he'll only have to do thirty years instead of sixty.

The hike over Kinder was, as usual, exhausting. Phil was on top form and said the side-effects of his sleeping pills had faded. He was at his most juvenile, viewing with contempt the label of old age placed upon him by the ancient Romans.

'Think of this,' he said, hurling himself into a grough. 'We measure out our lives by a two-thousand-year-old calendar —' he paused to scramble to the top of the next bank. 'The moon and the sun. That's our problem. I reject it. Julius Caesar' — pause for a sliding descent — 'can take his days and years and stuff it. I now live in my time. I am not sixty-five by my reckoning.'

In this mood of feisty independence Phil rock-and-rolled over Kinder top. Every now and then he would slow down to allow his poor subordinates time to catch up. Freddy was determined to be nice about it, gritting his teeth and counting up to ten to avoid exploding in the face of continuing torture.

'After all,' he solemnly whispered, 'he is sixty-five and we have to be kind to old men.'

Freddy had brought a map in case we were split up by fog. He wanted no more of that kind of experience, thank you very much. As we approached a fir forest lying below the edge of the high moor he stopped. 'Ah hah! I thought so.' He stopped Phil with a shout. 'Gruppenführer! Back here, please!'

Phil stopped just as he was about to leap into a grough. He turned with a frown. 'What's wrong?'

'Here please!'

Phil reluctantly ploughed his way back over five groughs. 'We've got to keep going that way,' he said testily, and then fell silent as Freddy showed him his opened map.

'That's where we are,' Freddy pointed. 'About to drop down to the Ladybower reservoir. And there's the Snake Inn.' He pointed towards the north-west. 'We're miles off course.'

Then he pulled up his anorak to show a pedometer clipped to his belt. 'I bought that as insurance. It tells me we have already done five miles. The distance to the Snake Inn from here is seven miles as the crow flies. As we walk — turning, diversions — you can almost double it. All right, say eleven miles. That's sixteen. If we go directly back to Edale it's about six. Altogether we shall have done over twenty miles.' Freddy looked into Phil's face for a response.

Phil took the map and studied it, buying time. 'Hmm, you're right,' he said. 'I'm off track.'

'Precisely.' Freddy waited.

'You know, I can't believe this.'

'Oh, I can, Stevens. I can believe it. You are an ex air-traffic controller. And you know about headings and distances. You planned this. And I've found you out.'

Phil took a deep breath and grinned. 'Well done. It was a test. I was trying you out. Well done.'

Freddy folded his arms and did his very – *very* – best Oliver Hardy. He took back his map. 'Now, *this* is where we're going. Down to Ladybower and back *this* way.' He traced a route with his finger along the road that leads from Edale End, at the eastern side of the vale, back to Edale. 'That, as near as damn it, is fifteen miles.'

We started a turning circle, returning to Edale via the Ladybower reservoir, Win Hill and Thornhill Brink. Phil kept apologising, but never admitting any duplicity.

Freddy was top dog, not bothering to argue, knowing he had struck a blow for sanity and the ethics of hiking. The Snake Inn was now out of the reckoning with our new, southerly, heading. We joined the Hope– Edale road to walk westerly towards Edale and the Olde Nag's Head.

Phil went overboard. He said we had been so good as to accompany him up Kinder on his birthday, it was the least he could do to buy the meals. He seemed to have forgotten that we had set off with that as the expectation and the intention.

We feasted as we had never feasted before. I ordered guinea fowl in red wine with belly pork, parsley sprigs and a salad. Freddy went for partridge pudding, an old Saxon delight. Rump steak accompanied the partridge, with locally collected mushrooms (oh, those mushrooms!), cooked in a glass of claret and chicken stock and all contained in a suet crust. Phil had a saddle of venison cooked in port and served with redcurrant jelly and chips.

Rhubarb tart with ice-cream was to follow. And all washed down with a bottle of Pinot Noir.

We were soon in such good spirits that Phil was moved to admit his guilt – it was a test, he said, a wheeze like one of Freddy's many. Freddy was mellow enough to forgive him. 'After all,' he said, 'it's the last time we shall ever do Kinder again.'

Despite his good mood Phil caught Freddy's words like a smart tap on his nose and sat back to consider the statement. 'Don't let's write it off. There are a number of ways to lead a horse to water.'

'Yes,' said Freddy. 'But you can't make it drink.'

'That's what I was about to say,' Phil replied. 'But you can make it drink if it's *thirsty*, can't you?'

Freddy shook his head. 'I shall never, ever, get so desperate as to want to go over Kinder again.'

'Okay,' said Phil. 'I'll have a bet with you. Some time you'll do it again. You did enjoy today, didn't you?' Phil clinked his glass against Freddy's glass.

'Yes,' Freddy nodded. It was true. He had enjoyed it. But – and here Freddy savoured the moment, taking a sip from his glass – the meal and wine were all the sweeter for the Gruppenführer having been caught out, game set and match.

10

OCTOBER

We climbed the stony path away from the car park en route to Chatsworth Park, side-stepping places where the recent rains had deeply scoured out the surface. Elsewhere, more damage had been caused by swollen water courses washing down peat from the moors, thereby turning the water into a shade of orange.

As we picked our way uphill I noticed that the sky on our left – towards Bakewell – was pale blue, while black cumulo-nimbus clouds had gathered overhead. The first spots fell within minutes, followed by a downpour. All three of us wore anoraks and it was a simple matter of pulling the attached hoods over our heads. Freddy, however, brought out a small pink umbrella from his rucksack. It was up and over his head in a flash. He smirked at Phil, who did a classic double-take, mouth gaping.

Freddy looked blank. 'What's wrong, have you never seen an umbrella before?'

'What are you *doing*?' shouted Phil. 'Freddy, for God's sake!'

'Sorry, Gruppenführer, could you speak up?' Freddy looked at Phil innocently from beneath his fetching pink canopy.

'What do you think you're *doing*?'

Freddy raised his eyebrows in surprise. 'Oh, the umbrella? It does the job, you have to admit.' He lowered the umbrella to lie flat on his head like a coolie hat. 'Is that better?'

Phil sighed, put his hands on his hips and nodded patiently. 'Okay, Freddy, very funny. But hikers do not carry umbrellas, especially ladies' umbrellas! And you're wearing full waterproofs!'

'I know, but somehow heavy rain gets down my neck. A gypsy told my mother I'd be all right if I kept dry!'

Phil shot a piercing look at Freddy and spoke calmly. 'Are you setting me up?'

'Gruppenführer, would I do that?'

'Yes. What if somebody saw you like that?'

'Well, if anybody saw me they would have a bad opinion of me. They'd say, "This man is a backslider, a no-good hiking moron."'

'Exactly!' Phil looked at me for guidance. 'Don, what's he up to?'

'I think he's practising onedownmanship.' I grinned.

Phil moaned. 'Not on the hike, Freddy. Do your mad things at home, not on the hike. Please, not on the hike?'

Wearing a look of injured dignity, Freddy packed away the umbrella. I waited until Phil had resumed his descent. 'Was it on?' I mouthed, pointing to his anorak. Freddy nodded. His cousin, an industrial security man, had loaned Freddy a miniature water-proof tape-recorder – similar to that used by special forces. It had a directional microphone with an extraordinary range and frequency response – it could even pick up a whisper a number of yards away.

This was the first time Freddy had used it. The plan was to present Phil with an edited version for Christmas, in front of our wives.

We reached New Piece Wood on the south-west side of Chatsworth Park, where Freddy stopped as though he had remembered something. 'Oh, Stevens, I've brought my camera. You know we haven't got a picture of the three of us hiking? Were you aware of that, mein Leader?'

Freddy went to a small ash tree and tucked the camera in the fork formed by two branches. He set the shutter on 'timer' and moved quickly to join in the shot. He stretched out his arms and pulled the ugliest face imaginable.

Phil sighed. 'Just a minute. Freddy, could we take a photograph of three *hikers*, not three idiots?'

'I thought it would look funny.' Freddy pouted.

'Well, yes, but I thought you meant *real* hikers, not ponces or clowns, just guys who like hiking?'

Freddy raised his eyebrows in a Stan Laurel lookalike expression. 'Another fine mess I've got him in,' he squeaked.

Phil waved a hand in despair and turned away to continue the hike. Freddy switched off the tape-recorder.

We entered the western side of the estate, a mile and a half to the east of Bakewell, by climbing over a ladder-stile. A mile away, across a vast expanse of sheep-cropped parkland, stood Chatsworth House, its west-facing windows caught in a dazzle of sunshine. The hundreds of gold-leafed glazing bars were lit up so that even the stonework seemed to glisten.

Chatsworth, situated approximately three miles north-east of Bakewell, is the residence of the Duke and Duchess of Devonshire and recently voted Britain's finest stately home. On our hikes there we usually 'beat the bounds', a circular walk encompassing most of the 1,000 acres of park and woodland which has been open to public access for nearly two centuries. Chatsworth, the park, gardens and working farm make up the main leisure facility in the area.

Surrounded by placid sheep (they are used to walkers), we headed north towards Edensor village. Prior to 1839 the village was in a completely different place from where it is today, straggling out along the road that leads through the estate. It was the 6th Duke who had rebuilt it as a compact unit. There was no planning authority then. Which builder or architect today would get away with mock-Tudor houses side by side with Italian villas and Swiss chalets? It sounds a terrible mismatch, but the result is a village that looks harmonious, and each building is worth looking at.

Freddy headed towards Edensor's small churchyard.

'This is not part of the hike, Freddy.' Phil looked uncomfortable, as always at such an overt reminder of his mortality. But we followed Freddy through the gateway and walked towards the top side of the churchyard. He had stopped to read the wording on one of the plain headstones: 'Kathleen, 1920-1948, widow of Major the Marquess of Hartington killed in action, and daughter of the Hon. Joseph Kennedy, sometime Ambassador of the United States to Great Britain.' Fixed in the ground by the side of the grave was a simple plaque which read: 'In memory of John Kennedy, President of the United States of America, who visited this grave, 29th June, 1963.'

Freddy took out his camera and photographed the plaque and headstone. John Kennedy had stood on this very spot and meditated at his sister's grave. The tragic irony was that within twenty-one weeks he'd be dead too. Predictably, Phil was the first to break away.

We sat on the circular tree seat facing the village and had our coffee break. Freddy and I ate slices of walnut flapjack made by Liz that morning, but Phil waved them away impatiently and was on his feet the minute we'd finished. Then we left Edensor and re-entered the grassy parkland, walking on a gold and copper carpet, the musty, sweet odour of its rotten leaves all around.

Capability Brown had laid out the entire park as well as the 105 acres of garden. To the right of the house, within the garden, is the small stone-base of a fountain set in a lake. As we drew nearer, it shot a plume of water to a height of 290 feet. Known as the 'Emperor Fountain', the 6th Duke had built it ready to welcome Czar Nicholas of Russia on his proposed visit to Chatsworth in 1843. He never came, which was a pity as the Duke had built a fountain that would beat, for height, the Czar's own fountain jet – at the time the world record-holder. The Duke was a very disappointed oneupman when the Czar cancelled his visit. But Chatsworth's fountain still holds the world record as the highest gravity-fed jet.

Our route took us over the Derwent river by a stone bridge, then north for about a mile. We then turned up through the woods that tower over Chatsworth. Set amidst the deciduous mixed trees, six hundred feet above the house, is an Elizabethan hunting-tower. It was built in 1582 for Bess of Hardwick, ancestress of the Duke, and was primarily used as a viewpoint by ladies observing the hunting dogs as they worked the woods and fields around the tower.

We sat on a bench in front of three cannon, all of which had taken part in the battle of Trafalgar. I gazed down at Chatsworth, on its half-acre of lead-covered roofs, at the stables, the surrounding gardens and working farm, host to numerous school trips.

'I wonder what the early Dukes would have made of Chatsworth today,' I mused.

'They built to show off their wealth,' Phil said. 'They'd probably have had a heart attack at the thought of a present-day Chatsworth open to the public.'

'The old Duke wouldn't have,' Freddy said. 'He was the sort of bloke who wouldn't have worried if he had to live in a two-up.' Someone who didn't know Freddy very well might expect his Puritanical, onedownman nature to abhor the aristocracy – but he had met the late Duke on two charity occasions and found him without pretension. Freddy takes people as he finds them.

Our next hike was to be the figure-of-eight from Hartington. We set off from the duck pond past the cheese factory and out into open country. We would stop for coffee at Pilsbury Castle – nothing to get too excited about. It is a mound of earth and rock, the remains of a Norman motte and bailey earthwork. From there it would be a two- or three-mile hike back into Hartington. After lunch by the duck-pond we would hike the southern loop.

Shortly after we had left the village we climbed the grassy hillside out of the valley, so steep and muddy after a deluge of rain that it was a struggle to remain upright. Once on the hilltop the footpath narrowed and became a parapet overlooking the hollow in which we had seen the predatory fox. We were about to enter the topside of the wood when I happened to glance backwards, whether from instinct, intuition or pure chance, I have no idea. What I saw sent a chill of terror through my gut. 'Move on, move on, for God's sake!'

Phil and Freddy turned round to look. 'Oh my God,' said Phil. 'Oh hell,' said Freddy. 'I don't believe it. Is it … is it …?'

'It is,' I said.

There was no doubting the green bobble-hat, khaki shorts and orange anorak, the eager gait, head on one side, mouth open. It was the human predator, the monster of the hiking world – Clifford.

He was about a hundred and fifty yards behind, trying to close the gap. Had he recognised us? Did it even matter if he knew us or not? He was obviously bent on catching up with us to deliver his non-stop verbal attack. We had approximately an hour and a half of hiking back to Hartington. I could not face ninety minutes of Clifford. Phil moved quickly through the trees. Then he broke into a jog, his rucksack bumping against his back in rhythm.

'Gruppenführer!' Freddy panted from behind. 'We know your father had to leave the wounded behind in the jungle to the enemy – but don't leave me behind!'

'You see! Now who wishes he'd exercised? Who wishes he could race up hills?' Phil was right. His fitness would keep him out of the clutches of Clifford, but would he desert his troops?

Fear of Clifford prompted the kind of adrenalin rush that Phil would have felt climbing Shutlingsloe. I was fitter than Freddy and could keep up the pace. There was no possibility of hiding. We were in open country. It was a race to see who would reach Hartington first. I had a mental image of the three of us leaping into the car and burning rubber. The delights of lunch by the duck-pond would be easily forsaken in the interests of our mental health.

Phil, in sadistic mode, was enjoying Freddy's distress. 'Now you guys know why it's important to keep fit!' he shouted back at us.

No doubt Phil would live on this tale for years to come. We stumbled and struggled through fields and over stiles, then along the Sheen hillside – all the time glancing behind us to monitor Clifford's progress. There was no doubt that we were outpacing him. As we reached the steep slope, at the bottom of which was the short bridge over the river Dove, Clifford was at least four hundred yards adrift. Phil wasted no time and bounded downhill, keeping his balance.

Freddy and I had greater difficulty, taking quick short steps. Phil reached the bridge fifty yards ahead of us, but something was wrong. He was standing and looking, not crossing the bridge. Then we saw why – the bridge was no longer there. The stile-access remained, but not much more. No doubt the recent deluge had swollen the river to such an extent that the twelve-foot width at that point had become a bottle-neck, the pressure creating a force that had been irresistible.

I swivelled round and spotted Clifford on the skyline. We had a minute – maybe two – in which to formulate a plan. We joined Phil, desperately searching along the bank for a plank long enough to bridge the river. Finally we found one, caught by undergrowth and wedged between a hollow in the bank and the roots of a tree overhanging the water.

Phil and Freddy quickly lay on their stomachs and managed to drag the plank free. I found a place where it would span the river, and looked up at the hillside – Clifford was a quarter of the way down.

'Hurry!' I shouted.

We carried the thick plank to the bridging-point, raised it to the perpendicular and then let it drop, praying that it would land on the other side. It did – just. Remarkably, it stayed firm and flat. Phil lost no time in stepping across. Freddy was next. But he stopped mid-way, staring at the water.

'Freddy! Come on!' Phil should. 'Don't look at it! Come on!'

We had lost vital seconds. Clifford was halfway down the hill-side. Phil made 'come on' signs with his two hands. 'You're okay, come on. Look at me. Look at me! That's it. Keep going.'

Freddy made it to the other side. I started to walk the wooden tightrope – as you age your sense of balance is one of the first skills that is affected – and struggled to keep my panic under control. Phil hissed at me to hurry. I crossed safely.

'Come on, lift it!' Phil began to lift the plank. We joined in, ready to pull the plank away, and then I stopped – motionless. We looked up to see, walking towards us on the other side of the river, Clifford. He was out of breath and stared open-mouthed at the realisation of what we were about to do. His spaniel-like look, a mixture of mournfulness and anxiety, caught my conscience. 'Oh hello!' I said awkwardly, feeling the worst hypocrite in the world. 'We didn't see you!'

Clifford stared at the end of the plank, which broke the surface of the water, and then looked at us, his mournful face registering great sadness of childlike proportions, touching in its trans-parency. In our panic we had forgotten our better natures and what we stood for. It would have been an act of selfish cruelty to have left him stranded. Slowly we stood up and pushed the plank towards him.

Clifford bent down, and with some difficulty managed to lift the plank and manoeuvre it to the spot where it had previously rested.

'Just step on it,' I said. 'It's quite easy.'

Clifford stepped on to the plank and waddled across, arms spread out, panting heavily, his tongue lolling out of his mouth. As soon as he reached dry land he began his litany of thanks, followed by a plethora of fact and information. He gabbled all the way to Pilsbury Castle and through our coffee break. We heard more than we ever wanted to know about sun-dials, bird-seed, oriental fish, rocking- horses, acid indigestion, digital cameras, carpet-fitting and weather-forecasting. It seemed that each topic triggered a cluster of rusty springs in his hyperactive brain and threw a new subject into his non-stop verbal machine.

We had intended that the second half of the hike would start back at Hartington, but none of us could withstand further mental savaging from Clifford. As soon as we arrived by the duck-pond we made the same excuses as before, but this time muddy boots came off before they dirtied the car, during which agonising minute we learnt all about pregnant fish.

Rucksacks stowed, apologies, quick entry to the car, doors slammed, arms waving our goodbyes – we were free! And once again, there was the sad and forlorn figure of Clifford getting smaller in the mirror and watching us out of sight.

'Right!' Phil drove happily back up the steep hill towards the A515. 'Where shall we go for the second leg?'

Freddy looked at him in concern. 'Gruppenführer, the hike is ended once hiking boots are removed, rule 17B!'

'No, Freddy, rule 21A, no hike shall be deemed to have ended unless the navigator declares it.'

Phil drove us to Parwich for a short circular route that would turn halfway at Bradbourne, Freddy muttering most of the way about unfairness and cruelty and stating that Phil, in his own way, was every bit as maddening as Clifford.

'Funny that,' said Phil, nodding towards the fields leading to Tissington. 'Over there's where Clifford first found us.' A chill of horror ran through me. 'What if he's followed us!' I heard the sound of a car and turned quickly in shock. It was not Clifford, but a local resident turning to park outside one of the fine stone houses facing the green.

'If you two had been fit,' Phil said forcibly, setting off towards the bus shelter where we would have lunch, 'we'd have given him the slip.'

'But we're human,' Freddy said. 'You're not. We can't all be superman.'

Phil tried to put it in perspective. If we had been captured by the Vietcong and subjected to water torture, we would have suffered more, he said.

Freddy interrupted him again. 'Three men who endured mental torture for their act of charity with Clifford should have been awarded a Nobel Prize for restraint. We didn't murder him.'

And then it became funny. First it was Freddy who started to chuckle, then Phil and finally I joined in. 'Three blokes running away from an idiot like him!' Phil guffawed.

'It just shows the menace he is! The power he had over us!' Freddy marvelled, and then imagined Clifford as a weapon of war. 'Just let him loose on the enemy and he'd talk them to death!'

We broke off as we approached the bus shelter, aware that a man was sitting inside. It didn't matter if he were waiting for a bus – the shelter was ours, by dint of usage. I felt a surge of indignation that the man, a bus passenger (a hiker would have been acceptable) had hi-jacked our lunch stop.

The man wore a blue anorak, a brown turtle-necked sweater and grey trousers. He looked about fifty and had rimless glasses, a professional type. His shoes were made of good-quality leather and the briefcase at his side had the initials A.W. in gold lettering. But there was something odd about him. He was sitting bolt upright, his head resting against the back wall of the shelter, his eyes closed and his mouth open. He did not look as though he were sleeping. Then, as if to answer our unspoken question, he came abruptly to life with all the motion and momentum of a robot. Clenching both fists, he rammed them into his chest, then pushed both arms straight above his head – reminiscent of Phil claiming victory. At the same time he inhaled deeply.

We watched this weird piece of sedentary gymnastics in amazement. The arms slowly descended in parallel with a hiss of exhaled air, sounding like hydraulic pistons, and ended with both hands resting gently on his thighs. His eyes remained closed, his body motionless – then both eyelids flickered before opening wide to stare blankly at three men peering into his face. Out of his trance he jerked forward, flustered and embarrassed.

'Oh, sorry about that,' he said and took a deep breath. 'I was doing my autogenics. Takes a bit of time to come fully out of it. It's a form of self-hypnosis.'

The bus arrived. He got up to board it. 'It's a wonderful way to restore energy or get to sleep. I just took the opportunity – didn't realise anyone was about.' He chuckled in an embarrassed way and made to step on the bus.

Phil was galvanised into action, scrabbling in his pockets for pen and paper. 'Autogenics, have you got a phone number for it?'

The man hesitated and then said rapidly, 'British Autogenic Society – write it down – find it at the Royal London Homeopathic Hospital.'

'Thanks!' Phil hurriedly scribbled the information on a scrap of paper as the man disappeared behind the closing doors, and the bus moved away.

Phil looked at us. 'Autogenics, don't forget. Autogenics.'

We sat down for lunch in our rightful place, and ate happily. Phil took his scrap of paper out and stared at the words he had written. 'Homeopathic Hospital, I didn't know there was one.'

Freddy threw me a grin, which I returned. There was one thing you could not fault Phil over, and that was his willingness to try anything and everything until he had achieved his goal, whatever it was.

The third hike of the month took place in the middle of 'St Luke's Little Summer', his Saint's day being 18 October, traditionally a time of good weather when poor people hunted for nuts and acorns, cheating the squirrels. Acorn coffee was made and the squirrels would be trapped and baked for supper. Nothing was wasted.

'Unless you happened to be a squirrel,' said Freddy.

We were walking the southern edge of Macclesfield Forest, our most westerly hike, climbing towards the low sun and the base of Shutlingsloe, a steep conically shaped hill, half a mile north of Wildboarclough. It was 1,659 feet high. The last time that Phil had raced up it was three years before. He aimed to beat that time and record another personal best.

Freddy tried to slow Phil down by annoying him. 'Gruppenführer, you will die regardless of what you do or say. You will get more and more scared the more you try to resist facts. I've told you before, the secret is just to accept that you're going to die.'

Phil turned to climb and then came back, making jerky movements, wanting to argue with Freddy. His adrenalin-rush, born of frustration, was such that he dithered angrily, caught between two impulses. Finally, like an aircraft, braked against full power, he released the brakes and shot off – whoosh! – up the hillside. His momentum carried him some way, but then he had to slow down, thereafter reduced to digging his boots into the hillside with fast little steps. We could see him tiring and labouring hard.

Finally, on all fours, a combination of scramble and scrabble, he gasped and heaved his way to the summit. As soon as one hand touched the concrete triangulation pillar (used by the Ordnance Survey in mapping) he clicked his stopwatch with the other. He lay on the ground, chest heaving, staring at his time.

We knew that something momentous had occurred because he came to the edge to grin down at us and then punched the sky three times in victory. Then he went from edge to edge of the summit, arms aloft, in a state of euphoria. What more proof did he need that ageing can be reversed? He addressed Freddy as he arrived panting at the top: 'Freddy, I knocked off two seconds. You carry on saying stupid things and getting me worked up –

but wait until we reach a hill. I reckon I could break no end of personal bests.'

'Gruppenführer, the time has come to ask – where would you like your ashes scattered? Here or on the top of Thorpe Cloud?' Freddy spoke sincerely.

It had little effect on our leader. He bubbled with joy as we struck north towards Cuckoo Rocks, and told us of another trick that had caught his fancy. He said he had read that mature men – he did not say 'elderly' as per the announcement – might soon be required for the flight to Mars. (He didn't give the reason, but I knew that it was because the long-term radiation risk was so great that elderly people would suffer least as their life expectancy would not be substantially reduced on returning to earth.) Phil saw it as the ultimate time-stretching exercise.

'What a perfect way to get rid of you, Stevens. Do that.' Freddy said he would put Phil's name forward. Then, still in mischievous mode, he spoke carefully. 'Phil,' he said – rarely does he use his first name. 'How come aircraft were in your care landing and taking off? If those pilots had known how crazy you were they'd have gone somewhere else, wouldn't they?'

If Freddy had thought that Phil would be stung into some crazy remark to be preserved on tape he was disappointed. Phil was in his smuggest, most self-satisfied mood. In his estimation his new personal best meant that he was now younger in body and spirit than he had been three years ago. Freddy's comment simply washed over him.

'Not so, Freddy,' he said. 'I was a top-notch controller, you know why? Because having those aircraft in my hands gave me a buzz. I loved SRAs – surveillance radar approaches to you – because I was the boss, not the captain, of a 747. *I* told the pilot what to do. And I had over 300 lives in my hands.' Phil paused, and his voice dropped to a matter-of-fact tone. 'I'm watching the screen and he's there. "Air Canada five miles from touch-down. Height should be 1,550 feet. Heading two eight zero is good."

I keep watching. He's good. "Four and a half miles from touch-down, height should be 1,400 feet, slightly right of track, turn left three degrees heading two seven seven." He does that, and you go again: "Four miles from touchdown. Height should be 1,250 feet. Do not reply to further instructions." Why? Because I've got him there. He's ready to land.'

I was impressed but Freddy nodded to himself as if in recognition of some grim fact. 'It all adds up, doesn't it? You were god the navigator, the ultimate control freak. We're the poor pilots now. Nothing's changed.'

He kept his tape-recorder switched on – just in case.

On the way home Phil's mood had changed from one of ebullience to one of grim determination. 'If I can beat a three-year-old record I can get rid of those sleeping pills.' He said no more on the subject but it was clear that the mere fact of knowing he relied on medication depressed him. I knew also that it weakened his image as a tough guy. He was determined to find an alternative solution to his sleep problems.

The next day Phil took a cheap day-return to London to poke around the new-age shops in Islington and try to improve on the sleep tapes he had bought a few months ago. He brought back a couple but decided they were useless when the tinkling sound of water forced him out of bed to visit the loo.

So he had himself hypnotised – again – and ran himself silly at ten o'clock at night in the hope that sheer exhaustion would lead to blessed sleep. Ironically, violent exercise kept him awake even longer. Friends and relatives, who had previously termed him 'peculiar', revised upwards their estimation of his madness. They now referred to him as 'batty'.

It was Halloween.

'Bernard the bodger is making a besom. Bernard the bodger is making a besom.' Freddy murmured the rhythmic phrase as we watched an ash-branch, cut and roughly fashioned by a draw-knife, placed in the grip of the pole-lathe. We were at Bernard's place in the woods, somewhere in the north of the Peak, taking a break during the last hike of the month. Bernard soon had the besom handle rounded, smooth and ready for use. Hypnotised, we watched the next stage, a bundle of silver birch twigs placed in the grip, a binder of witch-hazel tied round it and a bond-poker – a curved, spiked tool – used to draw the binding tight into a knot. The bundle was then tied to the ash-pole. A spot of trimming and, hey presto, the besom was complete and handed to Freddy in exchange for ten pounds.

His tiny cottage, built on one level only, stood in a clearing measuring a hundred by fifty feet. It was a simple construction of old bricks that had been cleaned and dressed by Bernard and painted white. The wavy roof tiles were also second-hand, in a shade of terracotta. There was a loo and kitchenette. A chimney pipe stuck out through the roof, connected to a small wood-burning stove in the living-room. There were no curtains around the small windows since, as there was no artificial light pollution in the area, Bernard liked to lie in bed and stare at the stars.

Every inch of the clearing was devoted to self-sufficiency. Cabbages, potatoes, leeks, peas and beans were grown in one half of the patch, while on the other was the work area: the pole-lathe, wicker baskets, shaving-horse and piles of timber. At the edge of the clearing, a beech tree had been felled and half used. The remaining tree-stump was used as a block on which sections of the trunk were split into 'billets', lengths of wood ready for the lathe. Bernard only used 'green' wood, or freshly felled timber.

Inside the cottage, heating and cooking were powered by portable gas-cylinders and an electricity generator. Water came gravity-fed from a main in the nearby road. It had been the water-supply that had saved Bernard from being evicted on health grounds by the local authority. They will allow you to live without electricity or gas, but not water – and not without a recognised sewage system. So Bernard had constructed his own.

Sewage left the cottage by a pipe leading down a gradient into a 500-gallon septic tank. Through the natural function of enzymes the sludge stayed at the bottom and the liquid rose to emerge at overflow level and percolate downhill through a series of sand and gravel beds, after which the relatively pure water ran off into a stream. We congratulated Bernard on being able to live without much technology.

'Well, not quite,' he said, and produced a mobile phone. 'I couldn't do without it. I travel to all the fairs, and there's a lot of people to communicate with.'

Freddy picked up the besom and stuck it between his legs. 'I'm killing two birds,' he said. 'This will sweep up the leaves but also do for my neighbour's Halloween party tonight. I'll give it a test flight.' And with that he sped off downhill into the trees.

'I sell a lot of those at fairs,' commented Bernard, heroically unfazed by the sight of a sixty-something man in waterproofs zooming to and fro between the trees, making 'wheee' noises. 'Women still use them on tiled floors. Guess what the other use was,' Bernard challenged us suddenly. Phil and I shook our heads, foxed. Bernard flashed us a smile. 'They were used in Sheffield steelworks – for sweeping up hot metal shavings.'

'Off to the rooftops!' cackled Freddy as he emerged from the trees, the besom still stuck between his legs. Buying the besom had just been an excuse. Freddy really wanted to talk philosophy – or, more accurately, sit at the feet of the master. He had told Bernard by phone that he was having problems.

Bernard selected a piece of tree-trunk for splitting. 'So,' he said wisely, 'you're up against a blank wall again. Hmm. Are you good at music?'

Freddy shook his head. 'I can play Chopsticks, that's about all. What you're doing now.'

Bernard roared with laughter. Here in his own world he seemed a different man from the impatient guru in the café. He placed the circular log on the stump, picked up a lump-hammer, placed a splitter (an iron bar) into a crack in the centre of the wood and brought down the lump-hammer with a clang. The log split neatly into two parts. 'We're talking about living. Not about the meaning of life. There may be no meaning as such. I think what you want is a fulfilling existence.'

'No.' Freddy surprised himself at his reply. 'I want to know what we're doing, why we're here. I think about it every day – do other people?' Freddy tailed off.

'Hmm,' Bernard tugged at his beard, picked up one of the two halves of wood, and placed it on the tree-stump. 'I don't need the language of words to tell me anything, as you do, because I'm intuitively – keep clear –' He raised his lump hammer. 'I'm part of my world, not an outsider as you are.' Clang. He now had three billets.

Freddy suddenly said, 'When people search for a meaning is it because they're afraid in some way? I've never felt that, but it may be subconscious, who knows?'

Bernard shrugged his shoulders. 'But of course! Of course! The fear of dying drives humanity. If we were to live forever we wouldn't be bothered, would we? We wouldn't be asking questions, because *we'd* be the answer. We'd be God. We do what we do because we know we only have a limited time here. Existence wouldn't be existence if it was permanent, would it? It only becomes questionable and worrying if we know it's coming to an end.'

Sunlight struck down through the trees and lit up Bernard's cherry waistcoat, his white braces and red handkerchief. With his lump hammer and iron splitter, he looked like a figure out of an old wood-cut come to life. In that sunlit moment I thought I understood what he meant about being at home in his 'universe of nature'.

We said goodbye to Bernard and walked through the wood to our car. Freddy held the besom over his shoulder. Autumn's scent of damp and rotting leaves was rich and powerful. Red strobes of the dying sun flickered through the trees. Freddy put out a hand for us to stop. 'Is that magic, or isn't it,' he said quietly. The heavy stillness was broken only by the soft fall of leaves.

We drove home through Bakewell, home of the County Show and several antique shops, but Freddy's broom was a reminder of the darker history of the place. It was in October 1607 that two ladies of the town, Mrs Stafford and her sister, were branded as witches. They were denounced as such by a Scotsman whom they had ejected from their lodging house. He claimed that they had 'flown' him on a besom, against his will, to London.

It seems staggering that such a biased witness would even be given a hearing, but the magistrate wanted to curry favour with the friends of the superstitious King James, so he took no time in declaring them to be witches and had them hanged in Derby. After the hangings the bodies were displayed on a gibbet as a warning to others.

It was dark by the time we arrived home to find the village already patrolled by groups of children with blackened faces, or wearing masks, carrying collection bags.

Halloween began with the commemoration of the Festival of the Dead, originally a Celtic festival called Samhain. In the belief that dead relatives would pop in during the night, cottagers would go to bed having left food and drink on the table and the door unlocked. Personally, I would have locked it.

Another tradition was practised at the stroke of midnight on 31 October. Local girls would get out of bed and sit in front of a mirror. No explanation has been given for what they did next – brush their hair and eat an apple – after which they would stare in the mirror in the expectation that the image of their future husband would appear. For insurance they would place a twig of rosemary beneath their pillow.

It is often assumed that the Halloween customs of children wearing grotesque masks, and the naughty pranks of 'trick or treat', come from an American rather than British tradition. Not so. They go back centuries in Peak villages, with children 'guisering', or play- acting, their blackened faces lit ominously by the candlelight from a turnip-lantern. Around the middle of the eighteenth century they began to play tricks on cottagers, tying door-handles together, or banging on doors and fleeing. Their adult victims gave Halloween a new name, 'Mischief Night', and it wasn't long before people began handing out money to children in return for protection from molestation.

The American godfathers owe a bit to the lads with the turnip-lanterns.

11
NOVEMBER

'The lonely season in lonely lands when fled are half the birds
And mists lie low, and the sun is rarely seen,
Nor strayeth far from his bed,
The short days pass unwelcomed one by one.'

At some point in November Freddy always recites this poem by Robert Bridges as a kind of communion with nature. November is, indeed, a lonely month. Life seems to stand still, the mournful quietness occasionally broken by the bark of a distant dog-fox or the caw-caw of rooks from the highest branches of the bare trees.

As nature continued to preserve life by hiding it, the visual joys of the hike were few, but spectacular. At midday on the first hike of the month we walked through a wood near Youlgreave, three miles south of Bakewell. The sun, which had lurked all morning behind a layer of thin cloud, burst against the overhead canopy of branches like a diamond under spotlights, dazzling with its glittering splinters.

The afternoon darkened. Broad multicoloured bands – red, yellow, orange, gold – that had stretched across the western sky gradually gave way to a deep crimson tinged with black. In this rich twilight a white apparition drifted beneath us along the course of a rock-strewn stream. It had the shape of a human figure but quickly vanished into curls and wreaths of rising mist. 'Did you see that!' said Freddy, blinking hard. 'What was it!'

'What was what?' asked Phil. 'Oh, that ghost, you mean. Oh yeah, I saw that.' He grinned at Freddy. 'You don't know your Peak traditions, do you?'

I confessed to sharing Freddy's ignorance. Phil enjoyed our bafflement. 'Look, this time of the year – rocks and timber near water, what happens to them?' He received blank looks. 'They get moss on them, right? That was a woman, I reckon, dressed in a white headscarf and white coat. She was gathering moss.'

And all the time I thought Phil only looked at the hilltop his nose was pointed at.

The following week, Freddy sat at the kitchen table and scooped out the last bit of egg-white from the shell. He had tried to revert to a low- carbohydrate diet in order to reduce his cholesterol, but Jean had ordered him to eat an egg. 'You need some fat, Freddy, to keep the liver working. Eggs are good for you!'

Once he'd finished he picked up the phone and dialled Phil's number.

'Freddy,' said Phil, anticipating who it was. It was 8 am, his usual time to take Freddy's call if the weather was in doubt – or not in doubt, as today in Phil's estimation. 'It's only light snow. Look outside. No need to panic.'

'Have you seen the forecast? Heavy snow expected in the Peak – with an increasing cold easterly?'

'When did we last have snow that bothered us?' Phil sat in his conservatory shovelling in calories ready for the day's exertions in the deep freeze. After three rashers and a couple of eggs he had devoured toast dripping with butter and honey, and was now drinking a mugful of Ruth's killer coffee. He was eagerly looking forward to a day out in snow. It had been lacking in recent years and he wanted another challenge.

'Freddy, you keep banging on about global warming. This snow won't get any worse.' He glanced at *The Times* in front of him, open at an article about cryogenics – the process by which a life-form is suspended in ice until required for re-animation. The last six letters of the word – genics – could act as a memory trigger for 'autogenics', he decided. He had forgotten to start these relaxation exercises so many times.

'Stevens, listen.' Freddy sounded peeved. 'I have in my possession evidence of your statement of February last, let me quote ...' Freddy rustled the newspaper close to the phone. 'Here we are, papers dated 5 February last. Your words – we only cancel for snow and fog. Your words, not mine.'

'Let me quote you, Freddy. Your words – the weather in the Peak is a fickle Lothario, not deciding which liberty he will take.'

'Who's Lothario? What liberty? By the way Jean's trying to book a flight to Malaga tonight. I thought I should warn you.'

'You're leaving the country to escape the hike – that's contrary to rule 6B.'

'Three lawful reasons for cancellation and you've ignored all of them – snow, fog and holidays. I think you should study your rule book, Gruppenführer.'

'Freddy, I am ordering you out on this hike. You have signed up and sworn your oath of allegiance to the navigator. Rule 43.'

'Charming words, Gruppenführer, charming words. I have another call coming in on the mobile. Can I call you back?' Freddy switched off his phone and went to the kettle to make another mug of tea. By the time the tea-bag had been tossed into the bin he was ready once more for the attack. 'Ah, Gruppenführer. That call was from my aunt Mabel, who lives in Buxton. She told me not even to think about it. The drifts are six foot deep. What do you say to that?'

'You haven't got an aunt Mabel.'

'Don't you remember her? She had her garden gnomes pinched and they came back three months later with "I've been to Hollywood" plastered all over them. She flew Lancaster bombers from the factory to the airfields during the war.'

'Get out of it.'

'Oh yes, and she high-jumped for England at the Rome Olympics in 1960. She left me her collection of beer mats.'

Phil spoke drily: 'And saw the first leprechauns down the garden. Very entertaining, Freddy, but it won't wash. We are going. Don just called. I'll pick you up, usual time.' He switched off the phone and stared at the wall, annoyed with himself. A thought, which had been in his mind at the exact moment of Freddy's call and which required acting upon, had vanished from his memory bank. It wasn't as funny as it had been in the summer, when all three of us had confessed to a few million brain cells going absent without leave. No, his pang of annoyance was accompanied by a stab of fear. If things were going awry up top it would sabotage all his hard physical efforts.

He walked out of the conservatory, newspaper in hand. This was painful. Not only had he forgotten something important, but he had also forgotten the trigger-thought which was supposed to remind him of it. If he needed a memory jog while hiking he would put a small twig in his lunch box, but a house has so many objects in it. He walked around looking at them: imitation cottage spinning-wheel, painting of a Derbyshire water-mill by Harold Gresley, hiking gear, phone, television, Tom the cat.

He sat down at the kitchen table opposite Ruth, who was engrossed in the crossword. He put both hands to his head and made a growling sound. Ruth paid no attention. Phil often growled.

'Something Cooper, English actress,' she said.

'What?' Phil stared at her. 'Gladys,' he said, from some distant past.

'It fits,' she said and wrote it down. She accepted Phil's oddities. There was a history of peculiar behaviour in his family. One cousin had surrounded his house with a length of wire 'to keep in the essential energy which would prevent him from becoming impotent'. And his uncle Reuben used to make sure that all the power sockets in the house had plugs in them in case any electricity leaked out from them during the night.

'What matters most in my life?' thought Phil. Ah! 'Life' – that was to do with it. He saw Ruth opening the fridge door. That was it – something to do with the fridge. Got it: 'Cryogenics!' That was the trigger – but to *what*? He stared at the word 'cryogenics' – and then let out a huge sigh. At last he remembered. The last six letters were 'genics', which prompted the thought of autogenics. Cursing himself for his forgetfulness, he dodged quickly into his study and breathlessly wrote a message in his diary – 'start autogenics NOW.' Then he stopped. It was already there. He had written it down the previous night.

The next day he rang the Homeopathic Hospital for more information and learnt that autogenics was a mental exercise involving self- hypnosis. The strange physical exercise demonstrated by the man at the bus shelter was the way in which the hypnotic state was cancelled so you could return to normality without ill effect. He decided, there and then, that the practice of autogenics would keep him mentally sound until his body was about to expire, and then he would slip into hibernation via cryogenics.

Freddy had been commissioned by Jean to deliver a recipe for Bakewell tart, known by some people as 'pudding', to her niece in Kirk Ireton. It had to be delivered privately as it was a secret, she claimed, literally handed down in the family, generation to generation. Freddy couldn't understand what the fuss was all about. It didn't taste very special to him, but then what did he know? Intrigued, he made an effort to get to the bottom of the Great Tart Mystery and this yielded unexpected results. He found out that the tart was created as the result of a mistake.

In 1865 a Mrs Greaves, stout landlady of the Rutland Arms, made the error of allowing an inexperienced kitchen maid to make a strawberry tart. She, in turn, made the error of omitting the egg and sugar while making the pastry. She spread the jam over this base, and put the egg and sugar mixture on top. And then fate guided her hand to pick up an ingredient that has remained a secret to this day. A paean of ecstatic praise came from the dining-room, and Bakewell became famous.

Three bakeries in the town lay claim to being sole owners of the recipe, but how on earth did Jean's family come to possess it? Freddy reckons Jean's great-grandfather had a dalliance with the serving girl and learned the secret from pillow talk.

After delivering the recipe we drove northwards to the deserted car park at Middleton Top. Freddy stared at the wind-screen-wipers clearing the glass of small snowflakes. The road was clear and there was no sign of the snow settling – yet. 'No good will come of this,' said Freddy. As he got out of the car he looked upwards at the heavy gun-metal sky. 'Gruppenführer, be it on your head.'

Phil grinned and blinked hard as a snowflake hit his eye. 'Freddy, this is –'

'What it's all about,' Freddy cut in. 'We know. It's about pain.'

We set off down the trail, following the path of the old Cromford and High Peak railway line. All the way down there were reminders of the great age of steam: bits of cable, wooden sleepers, rack and pinion systems and side markers. The incline and its 1825 steam engine worked till as late as 1963 but, oddly enough, the cargo it carried had nothing to do with the great age of steam and industry. Mostly it carried milk churns gathered from the farms.

At the bottom of the incline we passed the old rolling-stock exhibits and turned left around the former railway office, now a shop, to walk along the canal towpath. The snowfall was still constant, if light.

I never pass a canal without thinking of a book published in 1944. *Narrow Boat* by L.T.C. Rolt was the inspiration behind the waterways preservation movement. I have read this classic book a number of times, and anyone who has an affection for the British countryside should read it.

Half an hour later we arrived at Cromford Wharf, which still has its original railway buildings at the side of the canal. Phil called our usual coffee break and we sat at one of the bench tables provided for picnickers. A monster mutant snowflake drifted across the table. I held out a hand to capture it and failed. Then several more large flakes fell. When we resumed the hike it was snowing steadily.

We entered the nearby churchyard, the short route into Cromford village. Near the church stands the stone mill built by Sir Richard Arkwright and Jedediah Strutt in 1771, the first ever water-powered cotton-spinning mill, dispatching its textiles to all parts of the world. We left the churchyard and crossed the road into Cromford village, the wind now stronger, the snow heavier. 'This is our last outpost of civilisation, Gruppenführer.' Freddy pulled the hood of his anorak tighter around his face and looked up at the steep wooded hillside. 'You are not seriously suggesting we follow you up there, in this? There is a limit to loyalty, Stevens, it's called sanity.'

But Phil paid no attention. He was looking in the window of a bookshop, one that deals partly in old and rare books. It is usually Freddy who is drawn, as if by a magnet, into the narrow passage-ways inside, a warm warren crammed with books on all subjects. He harbours the notion that somewhere inside he will find the 'meaning'. Phil's job, of course, is to keep him walking.

'I didn't know you read books, Gruppenführer,' Freddy declared. 'Apart from *Mein Kampf* or *How to Grow Old Without Dying*, of course.' He followed Phil's eyeline. The book he was looking at was called *Vitamin Wisdom*.

Phil made a move to enter the shop. Freddy stepped into his

path. 'Oh no, Gruppenführer.' Freddy spoke patiently. 'Before you read that you should start with your own wisdom. Like not venturing forth into conditions that put us into grave danger.'

'I only want to look at the book. I'll just be a minute.'

'Gruppenführer, there is not one rule for you and one for the poor bloody infantry. Sorry, you'll have to come back in your own time.'

Phil peered into Freddy's face as if deciding what kind of challenge he presented. He made up his mind. 'No, you're right. Absolutely right. Good man. Just testing to see if you're on the ball.' Phil grinned. 'Come on, let's go.'

The snow had started to settle as we struck off the road through the woods in the long climb up to the Heights of Abraham, so-called because they are said to resemble the Heights of the same name scaled by General Wolfe and his men in the 1759 capture of Quebec. Reaching the top we took a left turn to walk up Masson Hill, 1,132 feet at the summit. The snow-driven easterly which had been strong in the dale now blew at blizzard speed, fortunately for the moment striking our backs, the snow whipping past horizontally. 'So this is it, Gruppenführer! I believe this is what they call a blizzard,' Freddy called out to Phil trudging in front of him. 'I do believe I even mentioned it this morning.'

Phil looked at him in delight, narrowing his eyes against the lashing snow. 'Now, this is really what it's all about!' he bellowed.

'Oh, God,' Freddy groaned, then shouted so Phil could hear: 'I can see the headlines: "Hikers praise mountain rescue, mad Gruppenführer blamed. Pensioner loses toes, says he'll be back!"'

Phil cackled. 'No pain, no gain! Remember?'

'"Two survive by eating friend,"' called Freddy.

'Which friend?' I yelled.

'Not me,' shouted Phil. 'You need a navigator. Anyway, without my survival skills you wouldn't last ten minutes. And which one of us can use a compass except me?'

'What, after getting us lost on Kinder Scout?' Freddy showed mock outrage. 'You're prime candidate for the pot. In fact, I vote for you because I'll be free – FREE! Think of it. No more pain!'

The snow fell faster and thicker. I pulled my hood-drawstrings tighter to prevent the snow getting in. No doubt at some point it would penetrate, given the strength of the wind. It always does. In severe weather the best of waterproofs are only as good as the wearer's ability to tighten the seal between neck and face. Cold water running down the neck and shoulders is not just unpleasant but can lead to a chill and, of course, hypothermia.

Freddy pointed out, with relish, that we had reached the point of no return. It was now as quick to go on as to go back. Our fate was sealed. 'If I don't survive, Gruppenführer, there is a letter at home on the mantelpiece referring to your endangerment of our lives. The lawsuit will be for five million!'

After another twenty minutes of grumbling from his troops, Phil finally called the lunch break. We sat behind a wall facing west, cheating the blizzard. With our sandwiches we had brought some flasks of hot soup, and we clasped our cups as we drank, warming hands and faces. We didn't linger over lunch, but quickly packed up and were on our way again.

Back on the hike we passed snowdrifts banked up against walls, and across the open ground ahead we could see long sculptured shapes with fine particles of snow whipping off their sharp ridges to form other drifts further on. We now plodded rather than walked, taking one energy-sapping step after the other through a world that had shrunk to white powder.

'By the way, how do we get home?' Freddy shouted at Phil. 'Do we hire a four-wheel drive? No doubt you will have organised that, having seen the weather forecast? Or do we hire a toboggan?'

Phil cackled. 'I'll get you home, don't worry! We'll go the main road way.'

'That's good. And of course you've left word with mountain rescue of our estimated time of arrival back at base?'

Phil peered at Freddy through the blizzard, the left side of his hood and face caked in snow. 'What do you mean?' His voice came out mangled through clenched teeth.

Freddy, pushed by the wind, leant into Phil: 'Say again, Gruppenführer, say again?'

Phil pointed at his chin. 'Mmm jaw's ozen!'

'Sorry, was that code? What did he say, Don?'

'I think he said his jaw's frozen!' I called out.

'Oh dear. Where's the nearest rescue post?"

Phil shrugged. 'Ot do you ont ith ountain rescue?'

'I think he's talking Japanese, Don.'

'Ee ha only two iles to go!'

'Have you an Enigma machine for decoding? Or is it still Japanese?'

I called out. 'He said we've got two miles to go!'

'Oh, I see! Is that what you said, Gruppenführer?'

'Yes!'

'Hah, two miles. Now, survival – have you got any instant energy food – Kendal mint cake perhaps?'

'No!'

'Was that "no"?'

Phil nodded, grimacing at Freddy. 'You 'ont need it.'

'Why not? Scott was only eleven miles from base when he perished. These are important questions that need answers.' Freddy could hardly keep the smile off his face as he glanced at me. 'Oh yes, and of course you have the three plastic bivvy bags in case we have to dig into the snow for the night?'

'No need! You ill slee at own tonight.'

'Now then. I think you said we will sleep at home tonight. Nod your head, good Gruppenführer, to confirm or deny.'

Phil nodded.

'Have you brought your mobile?'

'Yes! Not erking!'

'Was that "not working" or "stop talking"?'

'Oh, od's sake, eddy.'

'Oh, God's sake, Eddie? Who's Eddie? You do realise you will be charged with a reckless pursuit of ego trips whilst putting in danger the lives of those in your care. You would agree? What if we're marooned up here?'

'Irksworth is close. Ee can ork it.'

'Walk to Wirksworth? Then what? What if the buses aren't running? I told you this morning about the forecast. And what is worse now is that you show no remorse!'

Phil grunted. We struggled uphill towards Middleton village – not to be confused with Middleton-by-Youlgreave. The only traffic in sight was a large white Rentavan, slipping and sliding as the driver tried to climb a slope.

The last leg of the journey was across moorland, at a height of nearly twelve hundred feet. With no trees or hillside as a barrier the blizzard never faltered. The force of the blast meant that we now had to move forward disjointedly, pointing the top of our bodies to the right while our legs went straight on. In this curious crab-like mode, plastered from head to foot in snow, we staggered across the moor.

Phil at one point found himself up to his thighs in a hole. He sighed and put out a hand, expecting an immediate pull-out. Freddy paused long enough for Phil to register his look of infinite patience. As he struggled free, Phil tried to laugh through a tight mouth to show his insouciance. It came out as a cross between a croak and a gargle.

We eventually arrived back at Middleton Top. The Visitors' Centre was unrecognisable, the signs and markings obliterated. It could have been a polar base. Our car, a snowbound heap, was the only one in the small car park. Against the driver's door was a snowdrift that reached up to the middle of the window. Freddy folded his arms. 'So, Gruppenführer. Where's the spade?'

Phil took off his rucksack and drew out his thermos flask. He poured out the last of his soup into the tumbler and held it against his jaw for warmth.

I pulled at the other, unencumbered front door. It required a sharp tug and made a cracking sound as it broke free from its icy seal. Phil climbed inside and clambered across the gear stick to sit in the driver's seat, still keeping the tumbler to his face. He slowly turned his head to see a gap appear in the snow that covered his side window. Freddy's face appeared up against the glass, staring at Phil with a gentle smile as if in sympathy.

Phil took a deep breath and turned the ignition key. In the low temperature it took a few turns of the engine to make it start. It ran noisily at first. I used the edge of my lunchbox lid to scrape the windscreen and finished off by spraying de-icer fluid over the granules that obstinately remained stuck to the glass. Meanwhile Freddy scooped, kicked and pushed the snowdrift until there was enough clearance for the doors to open.

After ten minutes the car looked more like a vehicle and less like a snowdrift with windows. Phil gunned the engine in neutral and lowered his side window. 'Stand back!' he called, slipping into first gear. At the same time he slowly let in the clutch. The car juddered and shuddered, spun its wheels and slithered forward and sideways for about three feet and stopped. Phil tried again, this time applying the lightest of throttle. The car swung left and then right, but had moved no distance.

'Give it a shove!' Phil shouted.

Freddy and I applied our shoulders to the rear of the car. The wheels spun again, but remained more or less in the same position. Phil lost patience. Brutally, he put down the power, trying to blast away the snow from under the wheels in order to get them to bite. The result was spectacular.

Freddy and I leapt for safety as the car first veered sideways and then turned through 180 degrees. Phil must have forgotten his foot was on the accelerator – or he was in do-or-die mode (perhaps the cavalry leader charging at the guns) – as, braking hard, he spun the car round yet again. Still he wrenched at the steering wheel. The car lurched forward, then swung half-round to career backwards through the exit. Phil fought the wheel and braked hard, a mistake. The car hurtled straight for the biggest snowdrift in the lane – 'Whumf!'

It was buried up to its windows on both sides, more snow-bound than it had been when parked. Phil sat for a moment and then switched off the engine. Silence, except for the ticking of hot metal and the sizzle of melting snow on the exhaust.

Freddy strode out of the car park, forced to high-step his legs into the drift. He leaned on the car roof and looked inside at Phil. 'Quite stunning. How did you manage to exchange one snowdrift for another? Absolutely brilliant, Gruppenführer. Bet you couldn't do that again.'

Phil gave him a resigned look and pushed against the car door. But the compression of snow built up the more he pushed. It would only open by about a foot. He tried to escape by the other door. The same thing happened. He was forced to wait while Freddy and I performed yet more sterling service with combined sandwich boxes and tired legs.

Ten minutes later, the driver's door was open wide enough for Phil to slip out, literally, on to his face in the snow. After a moment, he turned over and slowly cleared it away from his eyes and mouth – to find Freddy smiling down at him. 'Sorry, Gruppenführer, what did you say the weather forecast was?'

Phil rose to his feet, a look of stoicism on his face, and got back inside the car. His efforts to free the car from the snow-drift by driving it again, despite taking more care this time, failed. We had no idea where there was a garage that could tow the car – and how many other calls for help would precede ours, even if we did find one? And Phil was not a member of a car rescue service.

We stowed our rucksacks away in the boot and set off on foot for Wirksworth and inspiration. Phil blew out his cheeks, shook his head and said, 'What a balls-up.'

'You said it and you caused it.' From then on, ploughing down the hillside, Freddy kept his silence. The Gruppenführer had taken enough – for the moment.

We reached Wirksworth after about half a mile. As we entered the town Phil surprised us by suggesting a drink in the pub. 'We'll get ourselves warmed up, and we can phone home.'

'Who are you going to phone?' asked Freddy as we ordered the drinks. 'You won't be able to get the car from Middleton Top till this snow's gone, and who's going to turn out to pick us up? Jean, Liz, Ruth? No chance. They might get stuck.'

'Then I'll walk home – it's only about twelve to fourteen miles. I can go and get Ruth's car. If the roads are passable I'll come and pick you up.'

'Why can't I be the one to go?' asked Freddy.

'Eh?' Phil was open-mouthed. 'Why do you want to do that?'

'Because I want a Land Rover.' Freddy nodded, with a smug grin as if to say 'sort that one out'.

'Freddy, how do you get a Land Rover by walking home?' Phil turned to me. 'I knew it. He's lost his marbles.'

I had to admit that I could see no connection between the two.

Freddy looked pleased that we had failed to grasp the link. 'Well, just think. I arrive home knackered – as I will be – and Jean says, "You can't do that again." And I say –'

Phil butted in: 'I need a four-wheel-drive Land Rover. No, it's my job to go, Freddy, not yours.'

Freddy reached into his pocket and produced a coin. 'Toss you for it.'

'No vote. Navigator decides – rule 9c.' We went into the lounge and sat down by the fire.

Freddy had an idea. 'If we killed you now, Stevens, and packed you in ice a millisecond before you were dead, would that be murder?'

Phil looked at him. 'It's all been running around in your brain, hasn't it – how to get rid of the Gruppenführer?'

'No, not exactly. We'll just send you away for a year or two.

When we've done all the known hikes we'll defrost you to come back and navigate some new ones – and then pop you back in the freezer until we need you the next time.'

'You may joke, Freddy, but it's going to happen. There's now an updated version of cryogenics which actually works.'

'You mean they pack you in colder ice?' Freddy looked seriously at Phil.

Undeterred, Phil said that a leading professor of neurosurgery was convinced that he could cool the human body down to a level that cuts off signs of life for at least an hour. This technique could be harnessed to put patients into a state of hibernation.

'So, Gruppenführer, do you think that Adolf, your leader, is in some cold room in the Austrian Alps just waiting for you to give the sign, at which he'll burst forth with a rendition of the Horst Wessel?'

'No, Freddy. That original cryogenic stuff was a con,' Phil said. 'As you thawed out all that happened was you cracked and fell into little bits.'

'But you are already, aren't you?'

'What?'

'Cracked.'

Phil smiled and nodded. Yes, he'd have to allow Freddy that one. He wasn't entirely humourless.

'All those in favour of me going?' Freddy looked at me, confident I would give him my vote.

I shook my head. 'No,' I said. 'Neither of you – look.' I pointed through the window at a single-decker bus standing at a stop facing south, its wheel arches packed with ice and snow, proof that public transport had not come to a halt. 'Drink up – that's the Derby bus.' We left the pub quickly.

The bus driver stood outside his cab smoking a cigarette. Yes, he said, the service was running. The roads were pretty bad but snowploughs were in use and with any luck we should reach our destination.

Freddy shrugged and said, 'Bang goes the Land Rover.'

Phil looked peeved. It had been the perfect situation for showing his mettle as a leader. It was almost fourteen miles to reach home, and that was only the mileage as the crow flies. It would have taken him at least five hours in this snow, and by the end of the day he would have hiked at least thirty miles in conditions more suited to SAS training. The Kinder Scout expedition was small beer compared with this. He doubted if he would ever have a better chance of glory.

The journey home seemed to take for ever, a slow crawl along a narrow white track the width of a single vehicle. We spent half an hour trying to get round an articulated lorry that had jack-knifed. It was freezing inside the bus and condensation on the inside windows added to the general gloom. It was just like travelling in the cold austerity of the post-war years.

Encouraged by this experience, Freddy decided to draw Jean's attention once again to the benefits of owning a four-wheel-drive vehicle – and, specifically, a Land Rover. It would save him from being snow-bound in the Peak and it was ideal for her shopping adventures or for carrying that old sofa in the garage to the municipal rubbish dump. And it would deal with the problem of ice on the hill outside. The other advantage – an excellent onedownmanship ploy – he was careful not to mention.

'Frederick, they're diesel – all those fumes – and they're terrible to be in. We were given a lift once, remember? And the suspension – well, they don't have any, do they?'

'The Queen loves them. She drives round Sandringham in one.'

Jean shook her head in pity. 'You are very peculiar, you know. Why can't it be an ordinary car?'

'We've got the Polo. I'll sell the MGB.'

'Oh, for goodness sake, Freddy, get the blessed thing,' she snapped. 'I've got all this washing to do.'

Freddy could hardly believe his ears. He hugged close his joy and tried to sound reasonable. 'I won't get it, though, if you don't want it.' He hoped he sounded pathetic. He often found this technique worked, as Jean never liked being shown to have hurt his feelings – or so he liked to think. On this occasion she ignored him, but he'd made the gesture and eagerly scrutinised the *Derby Evening Telegraph*. The Land Rover had to be really cheap and grotty-looking but with a decent engine.

Soon he found what he was looking for, a Series 2A Land Rover, 'offers invited' – code for its condition not being good. Freddy rang the owner to arrange an immediate viewing. Within an hour of having seen the advert he had clinched the deal. He mentioned nothing of the business to Phil or me, as he wanted it to be a surprise.

The next hike morning dawned, with Freddy's turn to be hike driver. Phil stared at the Land Rover outside his house. Eventually he mustered a: 'Well, yes, Freddy. It – er – certainly is impressive.'

'Tatty – go on, say it!' Freddy was delighted with Phil's reaction.

A few minutes later it was parked outside my house, and my turn to view for the first time his pride and joy. 'It's certainly tatty,' I said. 'But is it tatty enough for your purposes?'

It looked as thought it had done service in nothing but quarries and ploughed fields. Jim Oldroyd's Land Rover had been in better condition, though the engine sounded healthier than Jim's. The gears worked and the brakes performed a reasonable job. It was very noisy at speed, and draughty. The suspension was either non-existent or set in concrete. The lights and windscreen wiper worked. It was uncomfortable. And that was about all you could say about it.

Freddy said he would show us 'what it could do'. En route to Longnor he turned off the road without warning on to a cart track. Alongside it was a steep bank rising to about eight feet. 'Hold tight,' Freddy shouted and turned into the bank in low gear. We were halfway up when he slowed down and, defying gravity, made a left turn to travel along the length of the bank. We tilted over to an alarming degree. Phil looked petrified, but he dared not make a sound. How could he? He was the brave leader. I screamed out for both of us: 'Freddy, we're going to turn over!'

Freddy pooh-poohed the idea. 'Land Rovers don't turn over,' he said. Just then I felt the offside wheels lifting. Freddy braked to a full stop. We were poised on a knife-edge, teetering gently.

Freddy was frozen at the wheel.

'Move as far as you can to the right!' Phil said crisply. I eased myself over, as ordered. Phil, in the front passenger seat, leant in towards Freddy. The Land Rover settled with a creak and a bump back on to all four wheels.

Little by little, Freddy turned down the incline, easing the load and also our terror. Creaking and groaning, the machine lumbered down the bank and plonked back on to the track. 'Wasn't it brilliant?' Freddy turned to grin at us, in relief.

Our looks did the speaking. 'Oh,' said Freddy, disappointed. 'I thought you'd like a bit of adventure – especially you, Gruppenführer.'

Later that day, Freddy took up his vantage point in his bedroom, hidden by the curtains. At four o'clock it was still light. Freddy had parked his muddy Land Rover on the drive in a prominent position. He was waiting for his Porsche-owning neighbour to arrive home, as he always did, just after four.

Soon Freddy heard the rasp of the Porsche 911, the driver giving it a bit of gun in low gear for effect. It turned into the adjacent driveway and, with a final blip on the throttle, stopped. The driver got out, a small neat man wearing a charcoal grey suit. He pulled out his briefcase from the passenger seat, pointed his zapper at the car and, with a glance towards Freddy's drive, set off for his front door.

Then he stopped dead in his tracks. Slowly, his head swivelled round to look at the monstrosity parked on Freddy's driveway. He took two steps towards it, staring in disbelief. His status and authority, symbolised by the Porsche, was undermined by this 'thing' on Freddy's drive, which didn't challenge it but simply ignored it. It was like being the Premier Division champion of the Football League with no other team in existence. How could you lord it over something which had bypassed all the rules? His Porsche demanded that next door should be at least a Peugeot 306 or Ford Mondeo, better still a BMW or one of the cheaper Mercedes. It was like being Prime Minister of a desert island. He shook his head in anguish and fled indoors.

Just before darkness fell Freddy went outside and pretended to check the Land Rover. He walked round it with an air of pride, kicking each tyre and gently caressing its battered bodywork. Out of the corner of his eye he saw the neighbour's curtains twitch. Freddy was in high good humour for the rest of the evening.

The next day he relented slightly. He had enjoyed his wheeze with the neighbour, but now decided that enough was enough. He took the Land Rover to an automatic car wash. It took two washes to rid it of the mud of years and, like a chameleon, it changed colour in the process. Freddy had thought it was grey. It wasn't, it was green.

It still looked tatty after the clean-up but with that acceptable and comfortable 'old slippers' look. Freddy drove it home with pride.

12

DECEMBER

The snow had disappeared by the start of the month, for a time bringing days of fog and darkness. But on the eve of our first hike a high-pressure zone had moved in, heralding blue skies and a white frosty landscape, a joyous prospect for hikers.

Phil took us to Castleton, on the borders of the Dark and the White Peak, lying in the Hope Valley a few miles south of the Ladybower reservoir. 'Castleton's cosy cluster of cottages,' Freddy said, looking round. He has a yen for alliteration. 'Now, what about next week, Gruppenführer? What's the treat going to be?'

Last year we had decided that we would take it in turns to provide a 'treat' at Christmas, which could be anything so long as it was a surprise and entertaining. I had provided the first with a hike that passed close to Castleton, taking Phil and Freddy to a 'bottomless pit', a truly awe- inspiring chasm deep underground full of water and reachable only by rowing-boat. This was the Speedwell Cavern, a trip not for the timid. Freddy and Phil claimed to have enjoyed it.

Phil shook his head. He was not to be drawn. 'No, Freddy. You insisted it had to be a surprise, so that's what you're getting.'

Freddy groaned. He knew that Phil's idea of entertainment was of the 'isn't it nice when the pain stops' variety.

Today we left Castleton to walk towards Winnat's Pass. This is big country which has little of the 'domestic' atmosphere of the White Peak, and is not a typical dale, with white overgrown cliffs on either side, but a wide valley. At its head on the western side was Mam Tor, or the 'shivering mountain' as it is known.

Winnat's Pass to the south of Mam Tor offers a way out of the valley, a craggy narrow ravine, a defile some might say – between steep rising hillsides, a miniature version of the kind of wild mountain pass that used to harbour bandits. In 1758 two rich eloping lovers were waylaid by five lead-miners, who murdered them for their money bag as they rode through the Pass on horseback.

High on the side of Mam Tor is the 'Blue John' cavern set back from the roadside. Blue John gave Castleton its nickname, 'Gem of the Peaks', the only place in the world where it is found. It was discovered by lead-miners as they explored the cave systems. The mineral is a deep blue, its brittle nature making it notoriously difficult to fashion, so craftsmanship of the highest quality is called for. You can get some idea of the depth of the veins by walking down 250 steps, which allows visitors into half the cave-system.

Freddy walked by the Blue John cavern with hardly a glance, his mind on matters equally low. 'I know what your treat's going to be, Gruppenführer. We'll all be shackled together with ball and chain following you on a quick sprint up Kinder Scout, after which we'll give each other a sound thrashing with spiked whips.'

Phil sniggered but said nothing. He would let Freddy wriggle on the hook in revenge for his merciless teasing during our frolic in the blizzard last month.

We walked around Mam Tor at 1,695 feet high, a rarity of a hill in its constant movement. The former main road from Stockport to Sheffield used to pass around the Tor but was swept away by a landslide in 1974. 'Not attempting your personal best, Gruppenführer?' Freddy nodded towards the summit.

'No,' Phil frowned and kicked a loose stone, sending it skittering into some loose shale. I felt that something else was bothering him and was very surprised when he confessed what it was. 'No, I had another memory loss. I even forgot the thing that was supposed to remind me what it was I was supposed to be remembering.'

I laughed. 'Phil, how many times have we talked about this? I do it all the time, but I go back to where I had the thought and stage a reconstruction. It usually works.'

'Hmm,' Phil was not convinced. He said he worried that he might even forget what he was worrying about.

This brought a loud guffaw from Freddy.

'You may laugh,' Phil said, 'but I reckon a dodgy brain won't do much for my physical fitness.' His admission stemmed from frustration. He could hardly take his brain on a Dove Dale Dash or give it a stint of rock-lifting.

'Gruppenführer, your idea of being fit is to climb Everest before breakfast. Mine is to wake up and not look like my passport photo.'

When Freddy and I next met in the pub it was the eve of Phil's treat day. Freddy said it was more like the eve of D-Day. 'I shan't sleep,' he warned.

At that moment Phil walked in. He spotted us in the corner by the juke box and strolled over. Freddy decided attack was the best form of defence. 'Gruppenführer, I tell you now that I am not walking twenty miles for bangers and mash at the end of it. Tell us what it's going to be.'

'No.' Phil sat down beside us. 'Mine's a Pedigree.'

'You know I'm seeing a chiropodist about my feet? She says I'm lucky to be standing up. All your fault.'

Phil ignored all this and rubbed his hands. 'Well, I've started autogenics,' he said. 'I'm already sleeping better, and even when I don't sleep well I can get the equivalent of two hours' sleep with fifteen minutes of autogenics exercises. And I'm doing the *Times* crossword and memory exercises. I look at a list, try and memorise it, then test myself. I'm doing all right. So if you're wondering why I'm so cheerful that's the reason.' He stared at our blank faces. 'Well? You wouldn't want a depressed navigator for tomorrow, would you?'

Freddy raised his glass. 'You know what you're in danger of?'

'What?'

'Confusing a clear conscience with a bad memory.'

Phil cackled. 'Good one, Freddy, very good. I like that. Clever. Now what about my pint?'

Treat day dawned, another cold and sunlit day, ideal for hiking. Phil took us on the start of a mystery tour, leaving the green at Alstonefield. Within the hour we were striding along the ridge of Shining Tor, the scene of Phil's 'personal best' attempt last January. We walked briskly in the sharp keen air.

Freddy kept glancing suspiciously at Phil. 'Just tell me one thing,' he said. 'Does this hike lead to the treat? Or are we going back to the car and then driving to it? What's it going to be?'

Phil just grinned and increased his pace, to Freddy's frustration.

Down below, in his garden, Harold Barker stood, easing his back after clearing out the remaining dead leaves from around the borders. He glanced upwards and, squinting against the bright sky, caught a glimpse of three figures on the ridge top. He went back inside the house and came out again with his binoculars. What he saw confirmed his suspicions. This time his quarry would find no escape.

'Now then, let's be having you!' We had reached the bottom to find Harold beaming at us from his garden. 'Come on, let's toast the season.'

Freddy and I caught Phil looking at his watch. But Freddy was eager to get inside and down some whisky on the assumption that every minute spent in pleasure here might mean a minute less of pain later.

We sat around the fire, sipping Famous Grouse and listening to Harold tell the story of Lovers' Leap, a craggy outcrop above the Dove a mile or so downriver. In Victorian times, a jilted woman had thrown herself into the gorge at this point. She had been saved from serious injury by landing in soft bushes part way down the cliff. Phil fidgeted and looked impatiently out of the window, yearning to be off.

As Harold concluded his story Phil judged the moment opportune to rise. 'Harold, thank you for the drink but –' He broke off as Harold's wife came in with a dish of warm mince pies. 'Oh, lovely,' said Freddy and shot a grin at an exasperated Phil. It took two or three more false starts after the mince pies were eaten, but eventually our conscientious leader managed to extricate us from the fireside and whisky. We wished Harold and his wife, albeit a little early, a happy Christmas.

The tang of wood smoke signalled, once again, the hamlet of Milldale ahead. As we walked over the little bridge I could hear a choir singing 'Adeste Fideles' on a radio in one of the cottages.

Phil declared lunch. We sat by the riverside and watched a flotilla of mallard ducks bobbing and diving, always facing the current. Wreaths of smoke curled upwards in the calm air from the cottage chimneys. A tiny old lady with stooped shoulders crossed the packhorse bridge, leading two miniature Schnauzers on a split lead. She walked carefully towards us with a happy smile, giving a little trill of a laugh and a genteel greeting as she passed by. She knew us and we knew her. You could set a clock by her doggy walks.

After lunch we set off down Dove Dale until we reached the wooden bridge, then crossed it to climb the bank on the far side, digging our feet in against the loose rock. As we neared the top a rumble could be heard, followed by a roar which grew quickly into an ear-splitting shriek. A jet fighter passed not more than three hundred feet over our heads, the racket trailing in its wake. The rumble faded. We gathered our breath. 'That was a Tornado F3,' Phil announced.

'That was frightening,' said Freddy.

We arrived at the green at Alstonefield at two o'clock, but any hopes that the treat was to be a drink in the George vanished as Phil walked towards his parked car. A couple of geese watched us from under the tree. Two hikers, a man and a woman both wearing brand new hiking gear, were peering at an Ordnance Survey map and waved a greeting as we passed by. A mouth-watering smell of hot stew came from the pub kitchen.

Freddy luxuriated in it all. 'This is what it's all about, Gruppen-führer,' he said. 'Not the blood, sweat and toil you put us through, but these little things: geese on the green, that delicious smell, the people, familiar places that warm the heart.'

Phil listened to him with patient scepticism. 'You're an old romantic, Freddy,' he said.

'Maybe, Gruppenführer, but have you considered what you are? When it's all over, when you have done your worst, do you know what will be remembered? Not your painful hikes but all those wonderful skies, streams, characters and flowers and everything that nature has produced. And when the hike is over – we know you think it will never end but it will, even for you – as age and infirmity take their toll, how good to take out the emotions and, like Wordsworth, remember them in tranquillity. Now, where the hell are you taking us?'

Freddy laughed at his own humour, but sobered up when he got in the car. Matters were serious. 'The stress is killing me. Put me out of my misery, Stevens! What is this treat going to be!'

Phil chuckled. 'Tee hee. Tee hee.' Freddy looked at him blankly. 'It's a clue, Freddy!'

The mystery tour took us to the Ashbourne–Buxton road, at which Phil turned northwards. After nine miles of the curving, hump-backed road he braked at the bottom of a long descent and turned right towards Bakewell. The prospect of the treat being in that pleasant market town raised Freddy's hopes. 'Gruppenführer, if it's Bakewell tart with custard you shall be canonised.'

But Phil passed through Bakewell, heading south. Freddy exhaled and slumped in his seat. 'There's the Druid's Inn at Birchover,' he said with a hopeful glance at Phil, who remained impassive. Or did the glint in his eye sharpen? And then Phil arrived at Rowsley and turned off the road into a drive by the riverside. He pulled up outside a stone building, got out of the car and walked quickly towards the locked door. A printed notice, covered in waterproof plastic, was pinned to it. Phil read it, gestured and turned away in dismay. We joined him.

'What's wrong?' we asked.

'Read it,' said Phil.

Freddy read the notice aloud: 'We are sorry that "The Wind in the Willows Experience" has now moved to Henley-on-Thames. We announced the move six months ago.'

'So Toad's escaped into the Wide World with Ratty and Mole,' I said.

Phil gave the matter intense thought. 'I know, get in,' he said.

We piled back into the car and drove off towards a junction, where we turned left towards Chatsworth.

'Chatsworth,' Freddy said. 'There's nothing else up here.' He settled back in his seat. 'Tell us it's Chatsworth and I'll be happy.'

We passed by the car park we use for hiking and drove up to the House. The low sun, against a crimson backdrop, was reflected from the great golden building. Drawing nearer, we could see the outside decorations and lights. Phil parked the car and got out, to return a few minutes later. He walked with a deliberate pace towards Freddy, who was pretending to cringe in the front seat. Phil opened the door and handed him a ticket. Freddy dared himself to look at it, then sagged in mock relief. The ticket allowed entry to the gardens, stables and farmyard.

'Gruppenführer,' breathed Freddy, 'you could have told me.'

We were about to set off when a party of children arrived in several coaches, a school trip, it appeared. As they walked towards the House one of the adults with them stared up at the parapet and pointed an arm. The children looked up. Father Christmas, wearing traditional costume and white beard, stood behind the parapet waving at the children below. Then his reindeer came into view – well, a pair of antlers – and Santa patted its back, which was out of sight. Then the antlers and Santa disappeared.

The adults shouted: 'He's coming down the chimney! Hurry up, kids! Come on, or you'll miss him!' Pandemonium. In great excitement the children raced towards the entrance, yelling and cheering. They did not know that a second Santa was waiting to walk out of the huge chimney bottom.

Later we discovered that the children had come from local villages and the Duke had invited them, as was traditional, to a Christmas party. And Father Christmas? Well, the late Duke used to play the role, we heard from the staff, but in his later years was a wee bit too old to clamber down a chimney.

Without a guide, Freddy's newly acquired knowledge of botany proved helpful. He told us the fascinating story of the giant water lily, Victoria Regia. Joseph Paxton, head gardener at Chatsworth and designer of the Crystal Palace in 1850, had based the design of the Palace on the water lily's leaf structure, which he first used as the principle for the design of the lily-house at Chatsworth.

As we drove home, Freddy said he was grateful for the treat not involving any form of physical suffering, but why had Phil not told him that beforehand? 'Why didn't you tell me it wouldn't be painful? I know, let me guess, the pain came beforehand, in the waiting. Yes, you had to put me through the wringer – and you enjoyed it, didn't you!'

Phil gave his familiar cackle, but said nothing.

'Sadist,' said Freddy.

*

In an uncharacteristic show of generosity, Phil declared that Freddy and I had shown such unstinting loyalty over the past twelve months that we should each be rewarded by being given the leadership of a hike. Freddy, he suggested, should navigate the last hike of the year before the seasonal imprisonment with our families.

Freddy jumped at the chance, and chose the Tissington Trail via Parwich hike. Immediately Phil raised an objection: it was too short, and we'd walked it recently. He was certain, he insisted, to suffer from claustrophobia locked for a week in the bosom of his family. He would need a long hike beforehand to get enough air into his lungs to stop them from collapsing.

'But at least it's a flat hike,' said Freddy. 'I know you like running up and down hills but I don't and I'm navigator. Okay, I shall now do what you do, ask Don.' He turned to me. 'Don, you okay for Tissington?'

I shrugged my shoulders. 'Suppose so.'

'The vote is two to one, Stevens. I seem to have heard that somewhere before.'

Shortly after we stepped out on the Tissington Trail three young men, wearing anoraks and carrying rucksacks, passed us heading south. They had not a hiking boot between them. Instead, they wore trainers – blue and white with a touch of sparkling silver.

Phil was speechless for a moment. Then he gave vent. 'I don't *believe* it! Did you see them? Those things! Why do we hike? To get away from all that stuff. Okay, sometimes we see it differently – you, Freddy say it restores your soul, you talk about Wordsworth. I see it as a challenge. Fine, but the boot is a symbol – like that water lily was for the lily-house or Crystal Palace. In any case, what if it rains? Or you stub your foot in a rock? People who wear trainers should be … should be …' He searched for a word.

'Boiled in their own pudding?' asked Freddy. 'With a stake of holly through their heart?' As Phil frowned, he explained. '*A Christmas Carol* – it's what Scrooge said. Scrooge, who you are beginning to sound more and more like.'

Phil said, 'You've got to have standards. And you've got to be practical.' He muttered to himself for the next five minutes, then breathed in deeply and blew out his cheeks. The hike, thereafter, proceeded peacefully and Phil's grumbles petered out. But fate had selected him this day for worse torment.

Just before Alsop-en-le-Dale, where we were due to leave the trail, a woman and child rode their cycles towards us. The woman seemed to be in distress, shaking her head. 'There's a man back there –' She shouted something else but was now too far behind for us to make out what she said. A minute later the man came into view. He wore a hat and carried a large rucksack on his back. And nothing else. He was naked apart from his booted feet. He strode forward quickly, his tackle flapping as he walked. We stopped, gawked and waited for him to pass. He gave us a super-cilious smile: 'Morning.'

Phil growled in reply. We turned to watch the nudist walk away, his bare buttocks paler than the rest of his body, like jiggling moons.

We talked of nothing else all the way to Parwich. We agreed that he would be the nude hiker who had been arrested numer-ous times on his walk from Land's End to John o' Groats. Or had he finished the walk? In which case, was this chap an imitator? 'He's got a sixty-pound load in his rucksack,' Freddy said. 'But what is it in his rucksack that weighs sixty pounds if he doesn't wear anything?'

I grinned at Phil. 'Thank God he'd not worn trainers. Then he'd have been for it.' Freddy laughed heartily at this, but Phil was not amused. His sacred hike had been defiled – twice in one morning.

He was still muttering about this double dose of infamy as we headed across the fields towards Parwich. We crossed a stile by the side of the junior school playground. The girls were clustered in small groups, some skipping. Others congregated around the duty teacher, who clutched a cup of tea for warmth. The boys chased each other or kicked a ball. It could have been a scene from my own school playground all those years ago.

We walked towards the bus shelter. Once again, there was someone inside – a tramp this time, his belongings (backpack, walking stick, a rag bundle) spread out around him. He saw our hesitation. 'Oh, sorry,' he said, gathered his things and went to sit at the end of the seat. We looked at each other. Evidently we were thinking the same thing: the probability was that he would smell. However, it was too late to retreat to the seat on the green – that would have been an insult. And the tramp's apology, the fact that he had spoken in an educated tone, was reassuring.

We sat down. Phil was quick to bag the far end of the seat. I sat next to him and Freddy had no choice but to sit next to the tramp, who had a salt-and-pepper beard cut square in nautical fashion. He looked a tough character, with a partially bent nose, broad shoulders and a thick neck. He wore a brown Crombie overcoat which, when new, would have cost a minimum of £500. It had two dirty-looking suede lapels, deep cavernous pockets and was covered in stains. A length of rope wrapped around his middle and knotted in a bow at the front acted as a belt. A blue silk scarf, which had also seen better days, hung round his neck. He wore a tan-coloured velour Homburg hat with a silk band around it which, like the other items, would have been expensive when new. It was spotted with oily marks. His boots also looked as though they had originally come out of Bond Street and the uppers were made of the best quality leather. But they too were badly stained, as well as muddy. His square hands sported two gold rings, one on the wedding finger.

Somehow he had procured – or made himself – a mug of tea. The brown mug had the lettering 'Queen's Silver Jubilee, 1952-1977' printed on it. A kettle hung from the enormous backpack, which had a green quilted bedding roll piled on top and a cane-handled umbrella strapped to it by a leather belt. He glanced at me with a smile on his face, disturbing because it was a *knowing* smile.

As we sorted out our lunch things I was relieved to find no unpleasant odour coming my way.

'Going far?' the tramp asked, opening a flap on his rucksack.

'Back to Tissington over the fields.'

He smiled once more as he withdrew a folded pink newspaper from his backpack, opened it up, found the page he wanted, dug into one of his pockets and dragged out a small grubby notebook and the stub of a pencil.

He started to take down the price of individual shares on the London Stock Market. I could make out the date of the paper. It was two days old. Then he looked at us, three faces in a line and grinned. 'Never seen a tramp with the *Financial Times*?'

A clearing of throats and a few mumbles: 'Well, no, but we don't see many ... er ... tramps. Do we?' We looked at each other, shaking our heads vigorously.

'Well, there you are. There's always a first time.' He unzipped a large square waterproof pocket at the side of the backpack and slid out a Dell laptop computer, which he switched on. He tapped some buttons and shot another glance across our bows, chuckling once more. 'You've never seen a tramp with a laptop before?' Before we could say anything he stuck out his grubby hand. ' My name's Bruce.' We shook his hand in turn and gave him our names. Being of a queasy disposition, I decided to hold my food in the napkin Liz always pops inside my lunch box.

As he was clearly at ease with himself it was natural to ask the obvious question: how did a tramp come to use a laptop and have investments?

'Why not? You assume all tramps are down-and-outs. They're not. Some do it because they enjoy it.' Was that why he did it? The story unfolded. He had been a successful owner of a plastics company. When his wife, who was also his business partner, died he had allowed himself to be bought out. With his newfound wealth he had bought a house near Lyons, a Cessna 182 light aeroplane and another house in Chichester, with Goodwood airfield close by for easy travel. A small private airfield near Lyons – Brindas – officially only accepted members' aircraft but had turned a friendly blind eye to his arrivals and departures in that true Gallic tradition of happily breaking rules when it suited them. He had been delighted with the *aménagement*, and a base in central France was ideal for touring.

But, we asked, having set up that idyllic lifestyle why not pursue it?

'Oh, I will do. I've only been doing this for six months. I finish at Christmas. I'm going up to my son's in Scotland for the New Year. I'm actually writing a book. This is research.' We were silent as we digested the information. He finished his arithmetic and carefully packed away the laptop in its waterproof cover.

'What is the book about?' asked Freddy. 'Is it going to be like W.H. Davies's book, *Autobiography of a Super Tramp?*'

'No, it's meant to be funny. I go for people's reactions – like your amazement when I brought out the *FT* and the laptop. I also get invited to functions as Bruce the businessman and then turn up as a tramp. Now, that does raise a few eyebrows. Mind you, I can't get into the Ritz or the Savoy or any clubs dressed like this but I can pay for a first-class rail ticket and –'

'Hah!' Freddy said, mouth gaping wide. 'You go first class! Fantastic!' He was breathless with excitement. 'What happens?'

'I talk to anybody I recognise – MPs, TV people. I start by offering to buy them something from the bar. They're usually flabbergasted.'

'I can't believe this!' Freddy stared at me. 'This is onedownmanship!' Bruce's capers were an extension of his own larks. But was Bruce a genuine tramp or did he go home at the end of the day and take his clothes off and have a shower?

'Oh no. I live rough. Only if the weather gets really bad do I cheat. Then I pay for somewhere cheap for the night. What is wonderful is that all the things you take for granted in normal life you don't as a tramp. Take a cup of tea, as I do, on a cold day.

Boiled on a wood fire. Do you know how long it takes? When that tea's in the mug I breathe it in. It's heaven, I tell you.' He held the mug to his nose and breathed in its warmth and aroma.

'Buddhists recommend smelling the tea,' said Freddy reflectively. 'Feeling the warmth. I suppose it's all about basic pleasures, getting back to nature.'

Phil shook his head. It was grossly unfair. Ruth would never permit him to be a tramp, he said. But it would be doing what he loved most – hiking! And the time-stretching it would accomplish! He could hike around Britain. He would make sure his boots were of the best quality – that was the important thing. He stared at nothing, lost in his newfound dream world.

As we left to restart the hike Freddy marvelled at the coincidence of Phil meeting an exponent of autogenics in the same bus shelter that had produced Bruce, the perfect onedownman.

A few days later, Phil punched his chest with both fists, stretched, breathed in and exhaled slowly, allowing his arms to descend. He was awake, out of his 'AT', as he now called autogenics, completely refreshed. He remembered to replace the phone on the hook. He had found that a ringing phone during the AT exercise caused genuine shock, a measure of how potent the self-hypnosis was.

It was almost Christmas and already, Phil claimed, the rot had set in – that idle, self-indulgent eating and drinking session that stretched until the New Year, corroding the will and weakening the body. The previous night he and Ruth had attended a party at which several females had bestowed kisses on him. He said that one at least must have had a cold. He thought it appalling.

He picked up the phone and dialled Freddy's number. He had deliberately timed his call for the moment that Freddy's misery was about to begin – Jean's relatives were due the following day, Christmas Eve. 'Freddy, how are you doing?' He tried to sound cheerful.

'All right, what about you?' Freddy did not have to be psychic to know that Phil wanted something. He never called without begging, pleading, ordering or bribing. Phil's phone calls had to be treated with caution.

'Look,' Phil said. 'I can't breathe. I'm already dying from lack of air. All I want is to get out into the hills. We must go for a hike before the New Year. Could you manage one?'

'No. They've got me fixed. Every day. No escape.'

Phil paused, 'Okay. I'll try Don. See you tonight.' He referred to our annual get-together that evening with our wives. It would celebrate another year of hikes completed without a broken leg or any other disablement. Fainting, hypothermia and frostbite were not counted as serious derailments.

Phil called me and received much the same answer. I was doubtful that I could pull in another hike before New Year, but I would let him know after Christmas. Phil sat in contemplation for an hour while his brain scanner revolved slowly around the various aspects of Freddy's life. Could he find a weakness to exploit as he had in the past?

He switched the television on and watched a clip that featured steam trains of the first half of the twentieth century. Trains! That was it, of course! He remembered that somewhere in his attic was a series of cigarette cards, which he'd collected as a child. He pulled down the concertina ladder and climbed up into the loft, switching on the solitary light bulb to crawl around the partially boarded floor.

Amidst the suitcases and fold-up garden chairs were a Second World War gas mask, a pair of bomber pilots' flying boots – which he'd worn in his Lambretta scooter days – a disabled pistol and loads of school memorabilia including old photos, presentation certificates and school magazines. He picked up the 1953 edition of *Bemrosia*, his school magazine, and as he flicked through it found – under the caption 'School Sports Day' – these words: 'Philip Stevens won acclaim for his performance in the sprinting event as well as the long jump. His house, Newton, has risen to the top of the house league, mainly as a result of his determination and talent.'

Phil continued his search. He came across an old Fulview camera which he had bought in 1949 with money saved up by working on a farm in his school holidays, a forty-hour week for which he had been paid one pound in total. Finally he found what he was looking for. The cards were contained in an old tobacco tin, sandwiched between a set of golf clubs and an Amstrad computer monitor with a green screen, a relic of the stone age.

He had a shower to get rid of the dust before he rang Freddy to give him the good news. 'Want to see them?'

Phil was round within ten minutes to show Freddy his treasures. He knew he'd scored a hit when Freddy's tone became perceptively lighter and more measured, as he pretended not to be influenced by a pack of fifty cards at the bottom of the tin. These were 'Wills Locomotives and Rolling Stock', printed in 1901. This was a rare find and Freddy tried not to betray his excitement. He hummed and haahed, apparently undecided. 'How much do you want for these old ones?' he casually enquired.

'Five hours of your time. Day after Boxing Day.'

Freddy paused. This set, he knew, was valuable. He felt tempted to accept the deal there and then, but then he reminded himself that an early display of enthusiasm might result in a higher price. 'Yes,' he said. 'These are not bad. But look, I'll have to see how the land lies with Her Majesty and retinue. I'll let you know.'

'No. I need to know now. Come on, those cards are worth it.'

'Stevens, you do not realise what a delicate balancing act I have to perform with Jean's tribe. But I'll do my best.'

That night we sat in the Mount Pleasant, Freddy and I tucking into steak and kidney pies, and Phil into a plate of Irish hot-pot, while our wives struggled to remove pieces of pellet from locally shot pheasants.

The pub was crowded, the normal hubbub of conversation increased by the beery conviviality from a successful local football team around the bar. The background noise suited us because Ruth and Liz, with a liberal drop of Bordeaux inside them, would be sure to react noisily to Freddy's tales of Phil's antics. It was in a mellow state, and bathed in the glow from the firelight, that Freddy, a pint of Marston's Pedigree to the good, kicked off with the one about Phil and the trainers.

Predictably, it was met by a screech from Ruth and laughter from Liz. Ruth poked Freddy. 'Come on Freddy, more stories. You always have loads!'

Freddy shook his head. 'Oh, I can't tell you – ladies present.'

'Oh gawd,' said Liz. 'It isn't, it can't be – not –' she grimaced in mock horror. 'Not a man riding a bike without a bell?'

'No,' Freddy said. 'He was, well ...' He put on an expression of pious rectitude. 'He wasn't dressed properly.'

Phil, anaesthetised by a couple of single malts chasing Pedigree, and insensitive to Freddy's attempt to build suspense, broke in: 'He was starkers.'

Gasps of incredulity all round. Ruth, mouth agape, turned to stare at Phil, a smile of delight on her face. 'You're joking.'

'Except for his boots,' Phil added.

'So there I was,' Freddy said, with a shake of his head at Phil for stealing his thunder, 'wondering if I could enter the guy in the Naked Boys' Race.'

'But he disqualified himself!' shrieked Ruth. 'He was wearing boots!'

'That was the only thing that saved him.' Freddy had to raise his voice to be heard. 'If he'd worn trainers Phil would have had him arrested.'

Ruth screeched again. Jean beamed at Phil and picked up her fourth glass of wine. Her face now matched the colour of her hair. She looked more like a ginger pudding than ever.

Freddy brought out a palm-sized tape-recorder. 'Now, picture the scene. We're walking along and it starts to rain. What do you do? You put up an umbrella if you've got one – and I happened to have one.'

'Wait a minute ... wait a minute ...' Phil held up his hand, staring at the tape-recorder. Then he levelled a finger at Freddy. 'That umbrella, that pink umbrella – you didn't ...' The finger was now accusatory. 'You did.' Phil shook his head, mortified by his own gullibility.

Freddy nodded with an air of deep gravity. 'It had to be done, Gruppenführer, to expose your sadistic behaviour, to show what Don and I have to put up with.' Anticipatory gurgles of laughter spilt out from Ruth and Liz. Freddy put his finger over the 'play' switch. 'The umbrella's was Jean's. It was pink,' he said, and flipped the switch.

Phil: *'What are you doing? Freddy, for God's sake!'* His voice was crystal clear.

Ruth shrieked and I spluttered over my beer. Liz made little fluttering waves with her hands for us to keep quiet and listen.

Freddy: *'Sorry, Gruppenführer, could you speak up?'*

Phil: *'What do you think you're doing?'*

Freddy: *'Oh, the umbrella? It does the job. You have to admit. Is that better?'*

Phil: *'Okay, Freddy, very funny. But hikers do not carry umbrellas –'* The rest of the delivery was lost in laughter pierced by another shriek from Ruth.

Liz continued to shake her hand for silence, craning her head towards the recorder. We heard Freddy's voice: *'... heavy rain gets down my neck. A gypsy told my mother I'd be all right if I kept dry!'*

Phil's next words – *'Are you setting me up?'* – had Ruth sobbing with laughter, clutching her chest, eyes watering.

Phil: *'Not on the hike, Freddy. Do your mad things at home, not on the hike. Please, not on the hike?'*

Ruth's face crumpled and, keeping her mouth clamped shut, she sank her head to the table top, tapping it gently with her forehead. Liz found it difficult to laugh, it was so painful. Even Phil was reduced to a smiling nod, nod, nod of his head – he was the fall guy – he should have known.

After that presents were exchanged. Freddy received a bum-warmer from Phil. In return Freddy handed him a small home-made book, on the cover of which was a colourfully drawn picture of a conservatory with a hippopotamus inside and the title 'Phil's Hippo'. Inside were a series of black ink sketches of the hippo reading, eating and relaxing. The last one had a balloon above his head with the caption: 'No, Phil, I won't go in sun, rain, snow or fog. I only go when it's glorious mud.'

Freddy produced a silvery whistle for me. 'That's for when we get lost. When the Gruppenführer goes off with a Rhine maiden.' Freddy kept his mouth puckered up to stop himself from laughing at Phil's glare.

'What Rhine maiden?' asked Ruth, with a hard look at Phil.

'It's a long story,' Phil said. 'And not what you think.'

'Well, it happened like this,' said Freddy, settling himself comfortably. 'Phil hauled us up Kinder Scout.'

'I did not haul you, you came of your own volition,' Phil intervened.

'Did you hear that, everybody? We came of our *own volition*. We never do anything on our own volition – that'll be the day. I want my book back.'

It was nearly midnight. We stood outside the pub, the wives some distance away chatting, as we waited for the taxi to arrive.

'Another year gone,' said Phil.

'But a good one – on the whole,' I replied.

'Freddy,' Phil said, with a glance towards the wives. 'You've got to get away the day after Boxing Day.'

'I've told you,' insisted Freddy. 'I can't.'

'Don and I'll go then.' He turned to me. 'Fancy it?'

'No good,' I said. 'I'd like to, but it's not going to be possible.'

Phil looked at Freddy. 'Do you realise you won't be hiking for almost a fortnight!'

'Yes.' Freddy put his head back, closing his eyes, breathing in deep pleasure. 'Bliss, pure bliss.'

'You can have those cigarette cards.'

Freddy hesitated and then shook his head. 'No good. Incarcerated.'

'You know what we should do,' I said. 'We should video all our hikes, all the way round, each of them. Then, when we're past it, we can meet on hike days, sit by the fire and watch a hike. Virtual reality.'

'What a *brilliant* idea!' enthused Freddy. 'We should have been doing that all along. Coffee break in your own kitchen. Lunch on the patio. You two go round and video them and I'll watch. I'll go round every one with you. I will never complain. That's a promise, Gruppenführer.'

Phil copied Freddy, putting his head back and closing his eyes. 'Bliss,' he said and then opened them quickly. 'Look,' he said in an urgent tone. 'Next year we've got to really go for it, big time. There's lots to do. New hikes and new projects.' Phil grinned. 'And steeper hills, Freddy. We've got to get you started on personal bests. We'll start with Thorpe Cloud – you'll be up it in no time.'

'Pain,' groaned Freddy.

'But with a purpose. Come on, the taxi's here.'

ACKNOWLEDGEMENTS

This book owes a great debt to the people of the Peak District, and especially David Allard and Peter Scragg, who provided me with colour, material and inspiration. I must also thank the characters who appear in the book, in particular Graham Goodall, Harold Barker, Donald and Maureen, Bernard the bodger, Lab Sum and Rui.

I am much indebted to Mary Tomlinson in London for her encouragement and help in the early stages. A special thanks to Sir Ranulph Fiennes for his support and endorsement. I owe much to Sue Rann for her vigorous criticism and Alex Bulford for copy-editing with such care and concern. Deep-felt thanks to Maxwell Craven, historian of Derbyshire, for his close scrutiny of historical references and detailed comments.

I also want to thank Derek Penrose of the Chatsworth estate, Graham Rudd in his role as High Sheriff of Derbyshire, Sir Richard Fitzherbert of Tissington Hall, John and Sandra Lemmon of Etwall and Jane Inglefield (ex-mayor of Buxton), all of whom have helped, encouraged or assisted me in some way.

A sincere thank you to my son Andy, whose idea for the front cover won acceptance, and to my daughter Jane, for her literary criticism and encouragement.

I am also indebted to Derby Heritage Development Trust and Ron McKeown, for his advice and enthusiastic assistance.

Above all, my greatest debt of gratitude is to Susanne McDadd of Publishing Services, whose hard work, expertise and enthusiasm brought this book to fruition.

Also available in Ebury Press paperback

To order, please tick the box.

SCENES FROM A SMALLHOLDING – Chas Griffin
A hilarious and touching warts-and-all tale of one family's journey from leafy Nottingham suburbia to the dung-sodden joys of lambing, ploughing, milking and marketing on a small West Wales smallholding.
'A Bill Bryson "down on the farm"...' Alan Gear, HDRA
(ISBN 0091905079 – 9780091905071)   £7.99 ❑

A COUNTRY WIFE – Lucy Pinney
A young London girl arrives in the Dorset countryside as a bemused bride, spending her honeymoon harvesting. What happens next is a fast and frantic rural education, raising a family in the farmyard, divorce, and a new relationship with the hills and valleys she has grown to love. A bewitching, bucolic romp from the popular *Times* columnist.
(ISBN 0091891868 – 9780091891862)   £7.99 ❑

BRITISH AS A SECOND LANGUAGE – David Bennun
Born in Swindon but raised in South Africa, David discovers on his return to Britain aged 18 that the country he has read about and the real one he finds are vastly different. 'I could not have been less prepared had I spent my life up to that point listening to 30-year-old broadcasts of the *Light Programme*.' A brilliantly witty and irreverent view of Britain through alien eyes.
'Laugh-out-loud look at British life... one of the country's funniest writers' *Guardian*
(ISBN 0091900352 – 9780091900359)   £7.99 ❑

FREE POST AND PACKING
Overseas customers should allow £2.00 per paperback

BY PHONE: 01624 677237
BY POST: Random House Books
c/o Bookpost, PO Box 29, Douglas, Isle of Man IM99 1BQ
BY FAX: 01624 670923
BY EMAIL: bookshop@enterprise.net

Cheques (payable to Bookpost) and credit cards accepted.
Prices and availability subject to change without notice.
Allow 28 days for delivery.
When placing your order, please mention if you do not wish
to receive any additional information.

Copies are available at special rates for bulk orders. Contact the sales development team
on 020 7840 8487 or visit www.booksforpromotions.co.uk for more information.

www.randomhouse.co.uk